Matters
of
Life
and
Death

Today's healthcare dilemmas
in the light of Christian faith

**The London Lectures
in Contemporary Christianity**

John Wyatt

inter-varsity press

INTER-VARSITY PRESS
38 De Montfort Street, Leicester LE1 7GP, England

First published 1998
Reprinted 1999, 2000

British Library Cataloguing in Publication Data
A catalogue record for this book is available from the British Library.

ISBN 0–85111–588–8

Set in Garamond Three

Typeset in Great Britain by Parker Typesetting Service, Leicester
Printed in Great Britain by Creative Print and Design (Wales), Ebbw Vale

Inter-Varsity Press is the book-publishing division of the Universities and Colleges Christian Fellowship (formerly the Inter-Varsity Fellowship), a student movement linking Christian Unions in universities and colleges throughout Great Britain, and a member movement of the International Fellowship of Evangelical Students. For information about local and national activities write to UCCF, 38 De Montfort Street, Leicester LE1 7GP.

Matters
of
Life
and
Death

Contents

Foreword by John Stott 9

Acknowledgments 11

Introduction 13

1. What's going on? Fundamental themes
in medicine and society 22

2. Biblical perspectives on humanness 48

3. Reproductive technology and the start of life 74

4. Fetal screening and the quest for a healthy baby 94

5. Brave new world: the new genetics 108

6. Abortion and infanticide:
a historical perspective 119

7. When is a person? Christian
perspectives on the beginning of life 141

8. The dying baby: dilemmas of neonatal care 159

9. A good death? Euthanasia and assisted suicide 169

10. A better way to die 192

11. Old values for a new century:
the Hippocratic tradition and modern medicine 213

References 241

Useful addresses 246

Index 249

To Celia – wife, mother and research assistant

Foreword

This book began as the 1997 London Lectures in Contemporary Christianity, which drew a large, varied and responsive audience. Now that the lectures have grown into a book, I prophesy that they will attract an equally appreciative readership.

What is so impressive about Professor Wyatt is that he combines within himself three persons. First, he is a trained and well-informed scientist, with an extensive knowledge of biology, genetics, paediatrics and reproductive technology. He also takes his readers into his confidence, shares his expertise with them, and expects them to make up their own minds on each issue only after having been inducted into the relevant facts.

Secondly, he is a Christian, who stands firmly in the tradition of historic Christianity. His well-grounded Christian faith informs all his thinking, as he seeks to relate his biblical worldview to the complexities of the modern world.

Thirdly, he is a human being, with all the personal vulnerability which this entails. He sees in the incarnation the perfect model of empathy, of entering deeply into other people's experience of pain. As a neonatologist, he regularly has the grievous responsibility of telling parents that their baby has died. Then he weeps with those who weep.

John Wyatt's personal integrity shines through his book from beginning to end. He makes no attempt to conceal disturbing facts, or to hide his own struggles and uncertainties. He ducks no questions, and offers no glib solutions to complex contemporary problems.

Nor does he underestimate the seriousness of the current liberal assault on traditional Christian doctrine and ethics, not least on the sanctity of human beings because made in the image of God. He has read the principal professional assailants. The names of Richard Dawkins, Peter Singer, Ronald Dworkin, Max Charlesworth and John Harris keep recurring. Their works are summarized and quoted, and John Wyatt begins to formulate a reasoned response to them.

I find him at his most fresh and imaginative when he develops his analogy of God as the artist and of the human being as his 'flawed masterpiece'. Each person is a masterpiece of divine creation, reflecting the divine image, and so possessing incalculable value. Yet evil has spoiled God's creation. A quotation will give readers a flavour of John Wyatt's skill:

> The original masterpiece, created with such love and embodying such artistry, has become flawed, defaced, contaminated . . . The reflection of God's character is distorted and partially obscured. But through the imperfections, we can still see the outlines of the original masterpiece. It still inspires a sense of wonder at the underlying design.

'The task of health professionals', he continues, 'is to protect and restore the masterpieces entrusted to our care, in line with the original creator's intentions.'

John Stott
Rector Emeritus of All Souls Church, Langham Place, London,
and President of the Institute of Contemporary Christianity

Acknowledgments

This book is based on the 1997 London Lectures in Contemporary Christianity, and I gratefully acknowledge the support, encouragement and wisdom of the committee of the London Lectures Trust, especially John Stott, Elaine Storkey and Betty Baker. Many other friends contributed to the lectures, including Nick Page, Richard Bewes, Diane Baird, Sue Radford, Tony McCutcheon, Charlie Colchester, and the staff of the Institute for Contemporary Christianity. I am grateful to Christopher's parents Alan and Verity, and to Stuart's parents Eve and Harry, for permission to tell their stories. I am most grateful for the stimulating discussion and encouragement provided by members of the Medical Study Group of the Christian Medical Fellowship, especially Andrew Fergusson, Caroline Berry, Graham McFarlane, Catherine Myers, Trevor Stammers, David Stone, Duncan Vere and Anthony Wing. I am indebted to many other friends who have shared their wisdom and insights over the years, including Steve Beck, Roy Clements, David Cook, Rob George, Janet Goodall, Pete Moore, Oliver O'Donovan, Vinoth Ramachandra, Peter Saunders and David Turner. My parents-in-law Malcolm and Ann Richard provided much-appreciated hospitality and seclusion while I wrote most of the manuscript. I am extremely grateful for the advice and help of Jo Bramwell, Stephanie Heald and Frank Entwistle of Inter-Varsity Press, who have patiently guided and encouraged me through the process of writing my first book. Several people have read earlier versions of the manuscript and provided invaluable advice, including Caroline Berry, John Stott, Duncan Vere and Vinoth Ramachandra;

and John Stott very kindly contributed a foreword. I, however, retain full responsibility for all inaccuracies and errors which remain. I am grateful to my children JJ, Timmy and Andrew, who have put up with my absence in front of a computer. Above all, I acknowledge the loving support of my wife Celia, who has acted as research assistant and has patiently coped with the extra burden of a preoccupied, stressed and frequently absent husband.

Introduction

When I was a medical student in London in the 1970s, I received just one lecture on medical ethics in my six years of undergraduate professional training. I was taught that all the practising doctor needed to know about the subject could be summarized under five 'A's – Abortion, Adultery, Alcoholism, Association (with non-medically qualified physicians or 'quacks') and Advertising. Of these evils, which the General Medical Council was dedicated to stamping out, it was widely held that the most objectionable was Advertising.

But the world has changed. Medical ethics has been transformed from an obscure and unimportant branch of professional practice into a high-profile media activity. 'Shock horror' tabloid journalism and highbrow television documentaries have brought the issues to a world audience. A single medical case can now achieve the same media prominence as the latest disclosure about the British Royals or a soap-opera scandal. On a trip to Australia in 1996 I discovered that the top story of Australian television news was the latest development in the case of Mandy Allwood, the British woman pregnant with eight fetuses following fertility treatment. Perhaps the most bizarre feature of that tragic case was the million-dollar exclusive publicity deal negotiated for Ms Allwood by a prominent public-relations agent. In the battle of the media ratings if seems that, handled professionally, a good juicy medical dilemma can make the patient rich as well as famous.

What are the underlying forces behind the modern transformation in medical ethics? And how can people who wish to be faithful to the historic Christian faith respond to the challenges and the opportunities of recent and dramatic medical progress?

This book attempts to formulate a Christian perspective on a number of central ethical dilemmas raised by modern medical practice. While writing from my individual perspective as a practising clinician and Anglican layperson, I have tried to reflect a broad theological position of historic or 'foundational' trinitarian Christianity – a theological position which takes a high view of Scripture and of the doctrines of the ancient creeds and councils of the early church. I am not a professional ethicist, philosopher or theologian. I am a practising paediatrician and a Christian believer who has to face some of these agonizing dilemmas as part of my daily medical practice. What I have to offer is a view from the coal face. It is a view which has been created in the personal struggle to understand what is going on in the world of modern medicine and the attempt to develop an authentic Christian response.

These questions are not just matters for an interesting academic debate, of the sort that philosophers, ethicists and students love to engage in. These dilemmas touch us at the most intimate, painful and vulnerable part of our lives. Many of the people who read this book will be carrying secret sorrows which they cannot share with others. The statistics show that up to one couple in seven will suffer from infertility, and will never be able to bear children naturally. Some parents who pick up this book will have watched their child die, or will have given birth to a stillborn baby. Some will have had an abortion, although even their closest friends and relatives may not know. Some will have watched a close relative die in pain or emotional distress. A few will know that they suffer from a major genetic disorder which is likely to curtail their life, and they are wondering how they and their families will cope with the future. Many more of us are unknowingly carrying genes which may result in major illness, disability and death later in life: diseases such as Alzheimer's, stroke or breast cancer. Virtually all of us are carrying the genes for devastating illnesses which we might pass on to our children. Many people who pick up this book, for instance, will be carrying the gene for cystic fibrosis, though they are completely unaware of it.

So these are not just ethical issues 'out there'; they touch us at the core of our being. Nobody is immune; we all share in a common humanity, a physical nature which is painfully vulnerable and deeply flawed. As you read the following case histories, you may well find them disturbing and painful, as indeed I have. A French philosopher of the Enlightenment once said that 'death, like the sun, should not be stared at'. Yet that is precisely what we shall be doing in this book: staring at death and at the questions and fears that it raises.

The vision behind the London Lectures in Contemporary Christianity is the Christian task which John Stott has termed 'double listening' (Stott 1992).

First, our task is to listen to the modern world in order to try to understand the real issues. Next, our task is to listen to the unchanging historic Christian faith in order to develop an authentic Christian perspective. Finally, our task is to build a bridge which spans these two foundations, the modern world and the authentic biblical Christian faith. The task of biblical Christians is to understand the modern world in the light of the Bible, and to understand the Bible in the light of the modern world. Unless our bridge is securely rooted in both foundations it will be unable to bear the weight which is demanded of it.

Of course, bridge-building is a perilous art. My father was a structural engineer and I have a vivid memory of watching with him as a child while a concrete bridge he had designed was being tested by huge weighted lorries driving across it. I embark on my process of bridge construction with due trepidation. I have made no attempt to be exhaustive, as I lack the expertise and the experience to span the vast range of ethical issues raised by modern medical practice. Instead, I have concentrated on the ethical dilemmas surrounding the twin 'edges of life,' the start of life and its end.

These are not easy matters. I have no simple answers – indeed, there are no simple answers. Yet I do have a deep conviction that the historic Christian faith, the faith of the Bible and of the church fathers, gives us a way forward as we approach these agonizing dilemmas. It is a way forward that is intellectually coherent and satisfying, and also immensely practical and down to earth. The historic Christian faith does have something vital to say to the world of the Human Genome Project, the intensive-care unit and the hospice for the dying. As I have researched and written this book, my sense of optimism, hope and confidence in the answers which the Christian faith provides has grown. I hope that I manage to convey a little of that optimism.

To set the scene, I will outline a number of important and influential medical cases which have hit the headlines over the last decade. My purpose is to illustrate some of the technical possibilities and human dilemmas which modern medical technology has created, before we attempt to analyse the fundamental trends and social forces which underlie them.

Lillian Boyes: a case of mercy killing

In August 1991 Lillian Boyes was admitted as an in-patient to the Royal Hampshire County Hospital in Winchester. She had suffered from severe rheumatoid arthritis for many years, and now, at the age of seventy, the progressive and disabling disease had reached a terminal stage. She had chronic painful ulceration on her arms and legs, swollen, tender joints, vertebral fractures and severe limb deformity. The pain appeared to be uncontrollable. Simply to be touched and nursed caused her distress. Dr Nigel Cox, the consultant rheumatologist responsible for her care, had known her for thirteen years and was a trusted family friend. As Mrs Boyes' condition had deteriorated, she had repeatedly told Dr Cox that she wished to die. He was sympathetic to her plight but said he was not able to give her a lethal injection. At her request, however, he agreed to stop all further life-prolonging treatment. Despite increasingly large doses of diamorphine the pain worsened. According to an eye-witness, she was in such distress that 'she howled and screamed like a dog'.

By 16 August the situation had reached crisis point. Mrs Boyes again told Dr Cox that she wanted to die. Her family also pleaded with him to put her out of her agony. He gave her a further injection of diamorphine (100mg – twenty times the normal dose) but with no apparent effect. Then, while she was crying out in pain, Dr Cox injected intravenously a large dose of potassium chloride, a lethal chemical. As the solution entered the bloodstream, cardiac arrest occurred and death came instantaneously. Dr Cox recorded in the casenotes the details of what he had done. It was only some days later that a nurse reported his action to the hospital management. The police were called, and Dr Cox was arrested and charged with attempted murder. (The charge of murder could not be substantiated as the body had been cremated.) He was convicted and given a suspended prison sentence. The judge told him that he had 'betrayed his unequivocal duty as a physician'.

Subsequent events showed there was a great deal of sympathy towards Dr Cox, and the case focused national and international attention on the debate about the legalization of euthanasia. Although strongly criticized by the General Medical Council, Dr Cox was allowed to continue his practice as a consultant in the National Health Service (*British Medical Journal* 1992: 305:1311).

Was Dr Cox an unwitting victim of outdated concepts about the sanctity of human life? Should mercy killing, with proper legal and professional controls, be accepted as a part of a compassionate medical response to the suffering of patients like Lillian Boyes?

Tony Bland and the persistent vegetative state

On 15 April 1989 Tony Bland, a seventeen-year-old football fan, went to Sheffield to see his team, Liverpool, play Nottingham Forest. He was caught in the tragic Hillsborough Stadium disaster as thousands of fans pushed to get into the ground. Like many others, his body was crushed against the metal perimeter fences, leading to severe oxygen starvation. Over ninety fans died on that afternoon, but Tony Bland survived. At least, his body survived. Tragically, his brain had been severely damaged, leading to the profound coma known as the persistent vegetative state (PVS). He was alive and the basic bodily functions remained intact. He could breathe, and digest food. His eyes were open at times, and the lowest part of the brain, the brain stem, was functioning at a rudimentary level; but there was absolutely no evidence of conscious awareness or of responsiveness to his environment. The cerebral cortex, the brain region essential to normal conscious activity, was irretrievably damaged. His life was maintained by an artificial pump which passed liquid food via a tube into his stomach. For more than three years, Tony Bland existed in this twilight state, as his devoted parents waited and hoped against hope for any flickering sign of improvement. Eventually Tony's family and his doctor, Dr J. G. Howe, applied to the High Court for permission to stop the feeding. There was worldwide media interest. 'Let poor Tony die', proclaimed one newspaper headline (*British Medical Journal* 1992: 305:1312).

The case went ultimately to the House of Lords. The legal debate turned on the question, 'What course of action is in the best interests of the patient?' (Airedale Trust *v.* Bland 1993: 374). In a landmark decision, the Law Lords agreed that, as Tony Bland was not consciously aware of his surroundings and as there was no realistic chance of an improvement in his medical condition, the treatment that was sustaining his life brought him no 'therapeutical, medical or other benefit' (1993: 331). They agreed that artificial feeding should be withdrawn. Tony Bland died some days later.

Many have argued that this was a commonsense development of medical practice in response to an intolerable problem. But others have suggested that the Bland case marks the point at which the British courts ceased to respect the traditional principle of the sanctity of human life (Singer 1995: 68). For the first time, the courts accepted as lawful a course of action whose sole purpose and intention was the death of an innocent human being.

It is not only painful dilemmas about the ending of life which have challenged the traditional presuppositions of medical ethics. At the start of human existence, the questions raised by technical advances are troubling and wide-ranging.

Reece O'Sullivan: a 'wrongful life'

The *Daily Mail* of 11 June 1996 reported that Christina O'Sullivan and her boyfriend were pursuing a legal action against Northwick Park Hospital, near London, because its staff had failed to perform an abortion on their unborn son. Reece, who by then was three years old, suffered from the crippling condition of spina bifida. Ms O'Sullivan claimed that the hospital should have made the diagnosis by ultrasound during the fourth month of pregnancy, so that an abortion could have been performed. 'He is a beautiful, bright, little boy and I love him dearly, but he will never be able to walk or lead a normal life . . . I would not have put my boyfriend and me through this, and I would not have chosen this life for Reece.' The front-page headline was stark. It read, 'My son should have been aborted'.

This is an example of a so-called 'wrongful life' legal action. Although, in the UK, the child whose very existence is a result of medical negligence may not undertake a legal action on its own behalf, parents are able to sue the health authorities for the cost of raising the child. But what will be the effects of these legal cases on social attitudes to disabled children and adults? And what are the practical consequences of 'wrongful life' suits? Legal experts commenting on the case of Reece O'Sullivan warned that a flood of similar cases might lead to massive compensation bills for the NHS.

Since 1990, when the Abortion Act was amended by Parliament, in the event of a risk of serious fetal abnormality legal abortions can be performed at any stage of pregnancy up to full term. Although only small numbers of relatively mature fetuses are aborted each year, this practice can cause the most tragic dilemmas.

Jacqueline James: a late abortion gone wrong

Jacqueline James, aged twenty-six, had two children aged nine and five. In the winter of 1993, she became pregnant again, and was referred for antenatal care to the obstetric department at Wordsley Hospital in the West Midlands. In May 1994, when the pregnancy was in the twenty-seventh week (over six months), a routine ultrasound scan showed that the fetus had severe abnormalities. Ms James was referred to the Birmingham Maternity Hospital, where a second scan was performed by an expert who confirmed the original diagnosis. The doctors were adamant that there was a severe problem, and Ms James and her partner decided on a late abortion. Drugs were given to induce labour. When the fetus was delivered, the doctors became aware of two facts. First, the baby was delivered alive instead of being killed during the abortion procedure, and secondly, there was no evidence of any abnormality: she appeared to be normally formed. Tragically, however, the infant had suffered damage because of shortage of oxygen due to the drugs used in the abortion process. No attempt was made to resuscitate the baby, who was named Natasha by her parents, and she died forty-five minutes later. The Medical Director of the hospital, Dr Blunt, said that the decision was taken not to resuscitate, despite the baby appearing healthy, because Ms James was undergoing a termination. The coroner at the subsequent inquest concluded that none of the usual verdicts was appropriate in the circumstances, and recorded a verdict of 'death due to legal termination' (*The Independent*, 10 May 1996).

One of the ironies of the current medical scene in the UK is that while it is legal to perform an abortion where there is fetal abnormality at any stage up to term, technical advances in my own field of neonatal paediatrics mean that many babies can survive from twenty-three or twenty-four weeks of gestation. Yet the ability to keep babies and infants alive with intensive-care techniques may also lead to terrible dilemmas, as the next case shows.

Samuel Linares: an act of desperation

In 1989 Samuel Linares was a happy, healthy infant living with his parents in a Chicago suburb. Then disaster struck. At seven months old, Samuel choked on a toy balloon, which stuck in his trachea, leading to severe oxygen starvation. He was rushed into the paediatric intensive-care unit in a Chicago hospital, where he was attached to life-support machinery.

Sadly, it became apparent that there was profound and overwhelming brain injury. Although his parents maintained a vigil at his bedside in the intensive-care unit, Samuel remained unresponsive and in a deep coma. His biological functioning could be sustained only by complex life-support equipment. The doctors told Samuel's parents that there was no prospect of recovery. Samuel would remain in a deep coma however long the life support was maintained. According to newspaper reports, his parents had repeatedly asked that the machinery should be stopped and that Samuel should be allowed to die. The doctors had refused, saying that it was against the law. There was no option but to carry on.

Eight long months passed by, while Samuel remained on the intensive-care unit attached to a battery of equipment. Then, one day, Samuel's father appeared on the unit, carrying a gun. Holding the nurses at bay, he disconnected the respirator, and, with tears in his eyes, he cradled his son in his arms. 'I'm not here to hurt anyone. I'll only hurt you if you try to plug my baby back in,' he told the hospital staff. When he was sure that the child was dead, he broke down weeping, threw the gun down and surrendered to the police, who had been called. They took him away and charged him with first-degree murder (*Evening Standard*, 27 April 1989).

Who was right in this tragic and bizarre set of circumstances? The doctors, who felt it their duty to preserve some form of biological life whatever the cost, or the father, who wished his son to be released from an interminable and futile existence, and was driven to desperation out of concern for his child? One bioethicist, commenting on this case, said, 'Samuel's father acted against both the law and the traditional ethic that upholds the sanctity of life: but his impulses were in accordance with an emerging ethical attitude that is more defensible than the old one, and will replace it' (Singer 1995: 3).

The Davises: frozen embryos

The long-standing questions raised by abortion have been supplemented by new and complex issues arising from mind-boggling advances in so-called 'reproductive technology'.

In 1978, the birth of Louise Brown, the world's first 'test-tube' baby, showed that human fertilization could be successfully controlled and monitored in the laboratory. Once the resulting embryo has been implanted into a womb, the pregnancy can continue normally, leading to the birth of a healthy child. The ease with which surplus embryos can be created in the laboratory means that there is a ready supply of embryos for medical research, and the discovery that living human embryos can be stored indefinitely in a frozen state in liquid nitrogen opened up other strange possibilities. The first pregnancy from the transfer of a frozen-thawed embryo was reported in Australia in 1983, and the first live birth took place in the same year in the Netherlands.

Mary Sue and Junior Lewis Davis from Maryville, Tennessee, USA, wanted desperately to have a child. They suffered from prolonged infertility, however, and despite six separate attempts at *in vitro* fertilization (IVF), the embryos had failed to implant in the womb and no pregnancy had resulted. Then, in December 1988, on the seventh attempt, nine embryos were created. Two were reinserted into Mary Sue's womb, and the remaining seven were frozen in liquid nitrogen. Once again the two inserted embryos failed to implant.

Two months later, in February 1989, the Davises separated, and Junior Lewis filed for divorce. Mary Sue wanted to use the frozen embryos in another attempt to get pregnant, but Junior Lewis said he did not want a child to be created now that the marriage was over. At the divorce trial, Junior Lewis testified that he would feel 'raped of his reproductive rights' if the embryos were 'inserted in Mary or any other donor'. But Mary Sue violently disagreed. 'It's not just his child, it's my child too. They've already been conceived. I feel it is my right to have my child.'

The trial judge concluded that in such a case, the best interests of the children must be paramount. In this case the interests of the embryos were best served by allowing them to develop to maturity within Mary Sue's body. Junior Lewis appealed against the decision and it was eventually reversed by a higher court. But in another strange twist, by this time Mary Sue had remarried, and it appears she was no longer concerned to have the embryos implanted in her own womb. She suggested that they be donated to another infertile couple (Silver 1997: 84–85).

Mandy Allwood: multiple pregnancy

The final case history is that of Mandy Allwood from Knowle in the British Midlands. Mandy had one child from her first marriage, but after she was divorced she developed an unusual relationship with a business contact, Paul. They did not live together, and Paul was still sleeping with another partner, Maria, with whom he had had two children. But Mandy was clear what she wanted. 'For the past two years my life has revolved around my battle to have a child with Paul. He wanted a child too, but for me it became more than a want. After I had three miscarriages it became more and more of an obsession.' In the summer of 1996 Mandy was referred to a private fertility clinic, and started taking injections of a hormone to stimulate her ovaries to produce eggs. 'I hadn't told Paul I'd been to the clinic, and after starting the injections I felt guilty and stopped.' A few weeks later an ultrasound scan showed that she was pregnant with eight fetuses. Most experts advised the procedure of 'selective fetal reduction', in which some fetuses are killed by injection under ultrasound guidance, in order to reduce the number of fetuses to two or three to improve their chances of viability. But Mandy refused, and the pregnancy continued under the supervision of specialists at Kings' College Hospital. Mandy hired the well-known publicity agent Max Clifford, and her story was sold to the *News of the World* and other publications for sums reputed to be over £1 million.

Paul made the headlines again when it was revealed that he had developed a new relationship with an estate agent, Louise. The story ended in tragedy when Mandy went into premature labour at twenty-one weeks at King's, and all eight babies died (*The Times*, 3 October 1996).

As we look at these cases which have caused controversy and national debate, it is important to recognize that each one represents not just a medical and ethical dilemma, but also a deeply painful personal tragedy. Lillian Boyes demonstrates the frightening possibility of unbearable pain which seems to be uncontrollable by medical means. Tony Bland's case highlighted the tragic destruction of a young life at a football match and the agony of loving parents who waited in vain for recovery. Christina O'Sullivan watched her son struggle with profound disability. Jacqueline James faced the guilt and pain of a tragically unnecessary abortion. Samuel Linares was trapped in a high-tech medical system that could not allow him release, until the trap was sprung by the despairing courage of his father. The Davises were locked in painful conflict following a broken relationship. Mandy Allwood suffered the disastrous results of an obsession to have a child.

As Christians we must never reduce medical ethics to cold theology and unfeeling moral principles. We must never forget the human pain that lies behind every ethical dilemma. Before everything else, our first duty is to empathize, to enter into the experience of human pain, despair and perplexity. We must wrestle with these ethical dilemmas not with anger, hatred or judgment in our voices, but with tears in our eyes. For empathy is the way of Christ.

We shall return to each of these case histories in the course of this book. But before we can attempt to formulate an authentic Christian response, we need to reflect on the fundamental trends and developments which have brought us to the current position. How on earth did we get here? What are the underlying forces in science, in technology and in society which have brought us to this point?

1. What's going on? Fundamental themes in medicine and society

In this chapter I shall highlight five fundamental themes, or trends, which seem to lie behind the controversies and developments of the last few years. Although the list is not exhaustive, these seem to me to be some of the most significant forces which have brought us to our current position.

Theme 1: Progress in human biology and the triumph of scientific reductionism

The period from the 1980s onwards has seen the spectacular and unparalleled success of a scientific reductionist methodology applied to human biology. 'Reductionism' is a term which is frequently bandied around, often as a term of abuse. But what does it actually mean?

As a scientific method, reductionism can be seen as a way of investigating and understanding processes from the bottom up. As I type this sentence on my computer I am watching words appear on the monitor screen in front of me. I can analyse the sentence in terms of language, vocabulary and grammar. But those images, which appear to be words that I can recognize, are in fact constructed from a screen display which is generated and regenerated 100 times per second. The screen display is produced by small collections of phosphorescent material which are being bombarded by electrons generated by a cathode ray tube. And the refraction of electrons is described by fundamental physical laws of electromagnetism. The images on my screen can be analysed at a number of different levels, each more fundamental than the previous one. There is what is sometimes described as a hierarchy of levels at which explanations can be sought. Reductionism attempts to analyse processes at the most fundamental level possible, in order to provide the most detailed and comprehensive understanding of which we are capable.

This analogy may be helpful because it illustrates that the appropriate level of analysis depends on the question being asked. If I ask, 'Why are the words at the edge of my screen fuzzy and distorted?', the answer may well depend upon understanding the processes of electron refraction and electromagnetism. But if I ask, 'Why is this sentence written in English and not in Chinese?', an answer in terms of electrons is unlikely to be helpful. The level of explanation required is completely different.

Much of modern biological science is reductionist in the sense that it depends on the progressive breakdown of awesome complexity into relatively simple fundamental cellular and molecular mechanisms. As a way of tackling scientific and medical problems, reductionism applied to biology has been awesomely successful.

The area of molecular genetics is just one example of the success of reductionist biology and the resultant growth in scientific knowledge about ourselves. The Human Genome Project, a massive research enterprise which co-ordinates genetic research in laboratories around the world, has an audacious but totally realistic goal. It aims to identify the nature and function of every one of the 100,000-odd genes, the design programmes spread across the twenty-three pairs of human chromosomes in each cell, which together make up the human genome, the design blueprint for the human body. It is these 100,000 packages of genetic code, imprinted in DNA molecules, which programme every aspect of our physical structure, from eye colour to brain characteristics, as well as determining our hidden susceptibilities to future diseases.

By understanding the genetic machinery which programmes our bodily structure, we can also identify the genetic malfunctions which lie behind a wide range of human diseases. Employing automated laboratory techniques and massive computer power, research groups around the world are racing furiously to pinpoint the genetic defects which underlie both common and exotic diseases. Every month or so the list of genes that have been identified, and the diseases that have been accounted for, grows longer. The pace of discovery is mind-boggling. We have learnt more about the genetic make-up of *Homo sapiens* since the early 1990s than in the whole of the preceding thousands of years of human life.

By comparing their genetic codes, it is possible to identify the degree of physical relatedness between two individuals. And by taking DNA samples from different geographical and racial groups, geneticists have a new and powerful tool to investigate our human history and the racial migrations which have taken place since *Homo sapiens* first appeared on the planet. This is because our DNA has been passed down to us from our ancestors, accumulating mutations on the way. Modern techniques for DNA analysis have led to an upsurge of scientific interest in human diversity and evolution.

Terrible, crippling conditions such as thalassaemia, sickle-cell disease and Huntington's disease all stem from 'point mutations', minute abnormalities in our genetic code – a single misprint in an encyclopedia of millions of words. Many more common diseases, such as insulin-dependent diabetes and many forms of cancer, result from a combination of abnormal genes which lead to an increased susceptibility to environmental factors. Disturbingly, serious abnormalities are surprisingly common in our genetic code. In fact, all of us harbour within our cells abnormal genes which carry the possibility of serious diseases for ourselves and for our children. 'For his birthday Daddy gave him a time bomb' reads the slogan of a recent poster campaign about hereditary heart disease. By detailed analysis of an individual's genetic code, it is already possible to calculate the risk of developing a range of medical diseases; and in the near future it may be possible to generate predictive tests for any one of hundreds of conditions, from coronary artery blockage to Alzheimer's disease.

Of course, it is not only human genetics that has seen an explosive rate of scientific advance. In virtually all areas of human biology – embryology, neurosciences and immunology, for example – the reductionist scientific methodology has been spectacularly successful since the late 1980s, leading to an explosive growth in the basic medical sciences. The importance of this development for the future of medicine is hard to overestimate.

What is our reaction to this explosion of scientific information about our bodies, about the stuff of our humanity, the microscopic mechanisms of which our physical being is constructed? How have these scientific advances affected our view of ourselves and our place on the planet? What does in mean to be a human being in the light of modern biology?

As a number of Christian writers have pointed out, a successful scientific approach, splitting down complex systems into more basic constituents, tends to become a philosophical view which assumes that any system can be explained wholly by the properties of its component parts. To put it more technically, a reductionist methodology tends to merge imperceptibly into a reductionist ontology. Professor Donald MacKay, a distinguished Christian neuroscientist, christened this attitude 'nothing buttery'. Nothing buttery is the belief that because we are composed of chemicals, we are 'nothing but' chemicals (MacKay 1974: 40–45).

Certainly nothing buttery seems to be alive and well in modern biology. The well-known zoologist Professor Richard Dawkins, of Oxford University, writes in his influential book *The Selfish Gene*: 'We are survival machines – robot vehicles blindly programmed to preserve the selfish molecules known as genes. This is a truth which still fills me with astonishment' (Dawkins 1976: ix).

Dawkins describes his striking vision of human evolution from the first living, replicating cell:

> Replicators began not merely to exist, but to construct for themselves containers, vehicles for their continued existence. The replicators which survived were the ones which built survival machines for themselves to live in . . . Survival machines got bigger and more elaborate, and the process was cumulative and progressive . . . Four thousand million years on, what was to be the fate of the ancient replicators? They did not die out, for they are past masters of the survival arts. But do not look for them floating loose in the sea; they gave up that cavalier freedom long ago. Now they swarm in huge colonies, safe inside gigantic lumbering robots, sealed off from the outside world, communicating with it by tortuous indirect routes, manipulating it

by remote control. They are in you and in me; they created us, body and mind; and their preservation is the ultimate rationale for our existence. They have come a long way, those replicators. Now they go by the name of genes, and we are their survival machines (1976: 21).

Dawkins once asked a little girl what she thought flowers were for. She thought for a moment and said: 'Two things; to make the world pretty and to help bees make honey for us.'

'Well, I thought that was a very nice answer,' said Dawkins, 'and I was very sorry to tell her it wasn't true.'

What then is Dawkin's answer? What are flowers and human beings and everything else for?

'We are all machines built by DNA whose purpose is to make more copies of the same DNA. Flowers are for the same thing as everything else in the living kingdoms, for spreading "copy me" programmes about. That is exactly what we are for. We are machines for propagating DNA . . . It is every living object's sole reason for living' (Dawkins, quoted by Poole 1994: 57–58).

To the consistent reductionist, our bodies are ultimately *just* survival machines; our brains are in reality computers constructed out of flesh and blood rather than silicon and wires, dedicated to ensuring our ability to survive and replicate. Even our most erudite thoughts or passionate emotions are merely the by-products of our neural-computer circuitry. When challenged about the nature of human love in an interview in *Third Way* magazine, Dawkins replied: 'Brains being what they are, they have a capacity to invent spurious purposes of the universe . . . [love] is an emotion which is a manifestation of brain stuff' (*Third Way*, April 1995).

Of course, there are problems with thorough-going reductionism as a philosophy. If all our thoughts and beliefs are mere by-products of neural-computer circuitry, there may be reason to doubt whether our beliefs should match with reality, with the way the world is. It could be that my beliefs have survival value but are ultimately faulty, including my beliefs about reductionism. If the reason my brain has evolved as it has is to ensure my survival, it is not obvious why its beliefs should be reliable. Dawkins has claimed that religious belief represents an aberrant way of thinking which replicates from mind to mind. But the argument is two-edged. A belief in ontological reductionism may also be aberrant and faulty. Thorough-going reductionism raises the question whether it is possible to generate rational beliefs through a process of discovery and discussion. Yet Dawkins clearly believes most passionately, not only that his view of the world has survival value for his own self-replicators, but also that it is *true* – that it matches with reality.

Despite its philosophical problems, biological reductionism is part of popular culture today. It has penetrated into the foundations of modern people's thought-forms. It is the unchallenged perspective of the scientific and educated élite. How has this perspective affected our view of ourselves as human beings? I want to spell out four consequences.

Scientific reductionism leads to a 'machine' view of humanity

In the history of biology, we have always created ways of understanding the human body from the most potent forces we observe in the world around us. The ancient physicians conceived of the body as operating according to the four basic substances: fire, water, air and earth. The Victorians, in an age when ideas of the power of hydraulics were common, conceived of the body as composed of incompressible fluids which generated powerful pressures and forced their way through microscopic tubes.

Now, as modern society has been transformed by machines of all types, it is perhaps not surprising that the commonest perception of our bodies is as merely another sort of machine. We understand machines; we operate and control them. They are part of the furniture of modern life. So the idea that the human being is merely another form of machine makes sense to modern people. It is a frequent theme in scientific documentaries and high-school and undergraduate courses in biology. We explain the working of the human body by analogy with machines.

An undergraduate textbook of cell biology shows a photomicrograph of a neuron growing on top of a Motorola 68000 microprocessor. The text states: 'The neuron is the fundamental information-processing unit of the brain, which might be compared to the transistor as the fundamental processing unit in the computer. However, the brain has 15 billion neurons, whereas microprocessors may have up to a few million transistors' (Becker, Reece & Poenie 1996: 716).

There is a paradox here. All the machines we know were designed by humans in order to achieve a particular purpose. That is what a machine is – a way for a human designer to achieve a purpose. The Motorola 68000 microprocessor was laboriously created by teams of human designers in order to accomplish a series of complex design objectives set by other humans. Yet in the human body we have a machine which is apparently designed by no-one for no purpose! The analogy begs more questions than it answers. In the words of theologian Helmut Thielicke: 'Instead of man being the measure of things, the things he has made . . . come to determine the lines along which man himself is to be structured' (Thielicke, quoted by D. G. Jones 1984: 16).

This 'machine' thinking leads inexorably to a sense of alienation from our own bodies. In some sense, the real me is trapped in a frighteningly complex and ultimately alien machine which has its own agenda, its own programme, its own laws, and its own capacity for breakdown. The human 'I' is a passive observer, trapped like an abandoned astronaut in a bewilderingly complex but ultimately doomed space station. Each person's future is determined by the mysterious and ultimately incomprehensible laws of science which are controlling the machinery.

This sense of alienation from our own physical structure, and from the lives of other people, strikes deep in our modern society. It contributes to the modern philosophical concept of the isolated autonomous individual, to which we will return later in this chapter.

Scientific reductionism offers a way to self-mastery or self-transcendence

It may not be very comfortable to discover that we are only survival machines, but it has an advantage for modern people. By understanding how the machine works, we can satisfy a deep drive we all have to understand and hence control ourselves. I think this explains the particular fascination of modern neuroscience, the observation of the living, functioning, thinking, feeling human brain. By observing our own brain function we can learn to conquer it. By making ourselves an object of study we assert our own self-mastery; in philosophical terms, we attempt to transcend ourselves.

The managing director of a high-technology Japanese company which is currently devoting large amounts of research money to the design of a new form of brain scanning told me that his ultimate aim was the prevention of war. 'What causes wars and conflicts between people is the malfunctioning of the human brain. By understanding how the brain works we can bring world peace.'

In a scientific culture it is by making things the object of scientific study that we assert our mastery over them. By making our own human functioning an object of scientific study – by objectifying ourselves – we hope to control ourselves, to achieve self-mastery.

Scientific reductionism leads to a belief in pure chance – the lottery of life

Ever since the triumph of Darwinism as the dominant theory of modern biology, the ruling intellectual orthodoxy is the idea that all organisms, including the human organism, are products of blind chance. Any hint that organisms have an underlying purpose or design, apart from replication, is derided by most modern biologists. Jacques Monod, the eminent biologist, summed it up in this eulogy to chance: 'Chance alone is at the source of every innovation, of all creation in the biosphere. Pure chance, absolutely free but blind, is at the very root of the stupendous edifice of evolution. The universe was not pregnant with life . . . . Our number came up in the Monte Carlo game' (Monod 1971, quoted by Ramachandra 1996a: 83).

The eighteenth-century clergyman William Paley used the analogy of a watch to defend the divine creation of human beings. If, when you were crossing the heath, you stumbled upon a watch on the ground, you may not know where the watch came from, but you must conclude that *somewhere* there was a watchmaker, someone who planned, designed and constructed the mechanism. Richard Dawkins demolishes Paley's argument:

> The analogy . . . between watch and living organism is false. All appearances to the contrary, the only watchmakers in nature are the blind forces of physics . . . A true watchmaker has foresight: he designs his cogs and springs, and plans their interconnections, with a future purpose in his mind's eye. Natural selection, the blind, unconscious, automatic process which Darwin discovered . . . has no purpose in mind. It has no mind and no mind's eye. It does not plan for the future. It has no vision, no foresight, no sight at all. If it can be said to play the role of the watchmaker in nature, it is the *blind* watchmaker (Dawkins 1988: 5).

Each individual evolutionary step that led to the production of *Homo sapiens* was pure accident, 'chance caught on the wing' in the evocative words of Jacques Monod. Any appearance of design is purely illusory – the effect of billions of random genetic mutations and varying environmental pressures.

Reductionism leads to pessimistic fatalism

As reductionism penetrates our modern worldview it goes hand in hand with a resurgence of pessimistic fatalism. Our future is totally determined by the chance alignment of genes which occurred at our conception. Our belief that we can alter the future by our choices is purely a comforting illusion. In reality we are trapped by the hidden but inexorable blind forces of genetics and biology. As medical knowledge advances, it reveals more of the stupefying complexity of the machine and more about its understandable tendency to malfunction. With increasing knowledge we can predict when malfunction will strike, but what are the psychological effects of living with this godlike knowledge? How can we live knowing which diseases will strike us in the future, and the likely date and manner of our death?

Clinical geneticists thought that most people, when offered genetic testing for an incurable condition like Huntington's disease, would want testing so that they could plan their lives. In fact, when given the choice, most people would rather not know their future fate or that of their children. A recent study of pregnant women at risk of Huntington's disease found that only 30% requested prenatal testing, some of them withdrew before performing the test, and only 18% actually underwent testing (Adams *et al.* 1993).

The ability to foretell our biological future can be a curse as well as a blessing. One of the paradoxical effects of modern biology is that it tends to lead to a fatalistic worldview similar to that of the ancient Greeks: human beings are seen as the playthings of inexorable and possibly malevolent forces – the Fates.

If blind chance is our ultimate creator, this has profound implications for the ethics of medical interventions. If our human structure is ultimately the product of random forces, then it is hard to understand why it should have any intrinsic value, any more than the design produced by the random etchings of waves and wind on a shoreline. It is nonsensical to believe that our bodily design is in any way sacrosanct. Therefore, it is argued, we do not have to surrender to a pessimistic fatalism. We are free to improve on our design. We can do better than the blind watchmaker, for, thanks to the workings of blind chance, we have eyes and minds. Medical technology can be used to improve and enhance the fundamental structures and capacities of our bodies. For the first time in human history we can improve on the physical structure of our humanity. At last we can wrest our humanity from the forces of blind chance and become our own creators. If the biological structure of our bodies, with all their quaint idiosyncrasies, is a product of blind chance, there is absolutely no reason why we should not attempt to improve on our own design.

Dawkins ends his book *The Selfish Gene* with this triumphant flourish: 'We are built as gene machines . . . but we have the power to turn against our creators. We, alone on earth, can rebel against the tyranny of the selfish replicators' (Dawkins 1976: 215). This is where technology, our second theme, comes in.

Theme 2: Advances in biotechnology – unparalleled technological inventiveness

Along with growing scientific knowledge goes the technical ability to manipulate our bodies and the potential to alter the stuff of our humanity. As Gareth Jones, a professor of anatomy and ethics, put it, 'Science aims not merely to describe the world, but also to control it.' (D. G. Jones 1984: 33).

The idea of using genetic technology to enhance the capacities of the human body is a potent dream for many biological scientists. In a remarkable book entitled *Remaking Eden*, Lee Silver, a molecular biologist from Princeton University, USA, anticipates what the combination of genetic and reproductive technology (for which he coins the neologism 'reprogenetics') will lead to over the next fifty years (Silver 1997). The mechanisms for implanting modified or completely artificial genes into mammalian cells are advancing rapidly in laboratories across the world. Genetically modified animals are being produced in large numbers. If we are prepared to accept genetic enhancement of plants and animals, on what rational basis can we possibly forbid parents to seek to enhance the capabilities of their own children?

> While selfish genes control all other forms of life, master and slave have switched positions in human beings, who now have the power not only to control but to create new genes for themselves. Why not seize this power? Why not control what has been left to chance in the past? Indeed we control

all other aspects of our children's lives and identities through powerful social and environmental influences . . . On what basis can we reject positive genetic influences on a person's essence when we accept the right of parents to benefit their children in every other way? (Silver 1997: 236).

This is how Silver sees the future unfolding:

Genetic engineering will eventually be used by future reprogeneticists. It will begin in a way that is most ethically acceptable to the largest portion of society, with the treatment of only those childhood diseases – like sickle cell anaemia or cystic fibrosis – that have a severe impact on quality of life. The number of parents who will desire this service will be tiny, but their experience will help to ease society's trepidation . . .

As the fear begins to subside, reprogeneticists will expand their services to nullify mutations that have a less severe impact on a child, or an impact delayed until adulthood. Predispositions to obesity, diabetes, heart disease, asthma and various forms of cancer all fall into this category. And as the technology spreads, its range will be extended to the addition of new genes that serve as genetic inoculations against various infectious agents, including the HIV virus that causes AIDS . . . The final frontier will be the mind and the senses. Alcohol addiction will be eliminated, along with tendencies toward mental disease and antisocial behaviour like extreme aggression. Visual and auditory acuity will be enhanced in some to improve artistic potential. And when our understanding of the genetic input into brain development has advanced, reprogeneticists will provide parents with the option of enhancing various cognitive attributes as well (Silver 1997: 237).

Of course, these rather sensationalist speculations remain in the realm of science fiction. What is striking is that they come not from an ill-informed futurologist but from a practising molecular biologist.

What are the effects of medical technology on our view of the world and of our own humanness? These explosive developments carry with them a number of subliminal messages.

Biotechnology changes our view of what is 'natural'

In the past, the world was divided into things which were natural (given in nature) and things which were artificial (made by human craft). But technology changes this understanding. As Professor Oliver O'Donovan of Oxford University expressed it: 'When every activity is understood as making, then every situation is seen as a raw material, waiting to have something made out of it' (O'Donovan 1984: 3).

In his 1983 London Lectures in Contemporary Christianity, published under the title *Begotten or Made?*, Professor O'Donovan argued that the relation of human beings to their own bodies is in some ways the last frontier of nature. However much we modify the natural environment in our modern cities and our homes, and surround ourselves with the products of our invention, we cannot get away from the 'givenness' of our own bodies. 'When we take off our clothes to have a bath, we confront something as natural, as given, as completely non-artefactual, as anything in this universe; we confront our own bodily existence' (1984: 5).

But now this last frontier of the natural is being broken. We do not have to accept our bodies as they have been given to us. The Mark I human model is not the only one in town. We can improve things; we have the technology. I shall call this the 'Lego kit' view of the human body. There is nothing 'natural' about a Lego kit. There is no right or wrong way to put the pieces together. There is no masterplan from the designers. There is no ethical basis of Lego construction. You can do what you like. In fact, as it says in the adverts, 'the only limitation is in your own imagination'.

In the area of reproduction we can see most clearly that the way that we make babies has changed for many people, due to the advent of reproductive technology. The case of the Davis family and their conflict over frozen embryos, mentioned in the Introduction, illustrates how technology has brought new and mind-boggling choices for parents. Technology is changing the very nature of parenthood, and the boundary between what is natural and what is unnatural becomes blurred. Is a frozen embryo in a tank of liquid nitrogen a being of nature, or is it a product of human planning, ingenuity and forethought, an *artefact* of human creation? Does reproductive technology mean that the process of making babies has changed from being a 'natural' activity to being an 'artificial' activity? Or is the distinction no longer meaningful?

Biotechnology allows us to conquer our fears

The growth in health technology demonstrates how greatly modern people and societies value health and long life. It shows the extreme measures we are prepared to undergo in order to improve the chances of survival for ourselves or our children – to buy an extra year or two of life. These are the words of Stanley Hauerwas, a distinguished theologian from Duke University, North Carolina:

> I sometimes point out to my students that people now go to Europe to see the great cathedrals, wondering what kind of people would build such things . . . Some day I think that people may well come to see major medical centres like the one we have at Duke University, and ask what kind of people would build such things. If they are astute they will think the builders certainly must have been afraid of death (Hauerwas 1996: 64).

In medieval society it was the church building which dominated the local community, as an illustration of the social and economic power of religion in that society. Now the billions of pounds spent every year on healthcare and on medical research tell their own story. Why do the public pour money into medical research? Is it a desire to help humankind, or is the public support for research at least partly motivated by fear – fear of death, fear of disease, fear of disability? The way we spend our money is very revealing. In the words of Jesus, 'where your treasure is, there your heart will be also' (Mt. 6:21; Lk. 12:34).

Biotechnology gives us new responsibilities for 'quality control'

Technology always brings new responsibilities. When we make choices, we must carry responsibility for the consequences. This process can be seen especially in the area of reproductive technology. When we change the nature of parenthood, imperceptibly our attitude to our children changes. Most people in our society still see their newborn baby as a gift: a mysterious present from a higher power, a gift from God, or, if they do not believe in a God, then from Nature with a capital N. But when a child is created by the wonderful technology of embryo donation and *in vitro* fertilization, the child may be seen no longer as a mysterious and wonderful gift, but more as the product of human ingenuity and meticulous planning. Unfortunately, no form of human construction is perfect, and an essential part of all technology is 'quality control'. If technology has gone wrong, if the product of our planning is less than perfect, then we must take responsibility to prevent the consequences. If we make a baby by technology, we must use technology to make sure that the baby is all right. That is the essence of quality control. The concept of a 'wrongful life', that we saw in the case of Reece O'Sullivan, stems directly from the drive for quality control in a medical approach to pregnancy. If technology provides the knowledge that a fetus is abnormal, many feel that we have a responsibility, even a duty, to end that life and prevent the birth of a handicapped child. So godlike knowledge has given rise to godlike responsibility.

The history of the twentieth century has taught us that technology is a mixed blessing. The sad stories of Tony Bland, Samuel Linares, Jacqueline James and Mandy Allwood are all examples of the mess in which medical technology can land us.

Theme 3: Consumer expectations

Medical technology has led to new expectations. To many people it seems that doctors really can perform miracles. They can allow us to fulfil our dreams and overcome our limitations. Every problem, every malfunction, can be overcome by a technological fix. After all, that is what doctors are there for.

The story of Mandy Allwood reflects this assumption: 'For the past two years my life has revolved around my battle to have a child with Paul. He wanted a child too, but for me it became more than a want. After I had three miscarriages it became more and more of an obsession . . .' The implication is that medical technology is there to allow people to fulfil their deepest desires. And it seems that many of our deepest desires are centred on having children. For some people, embarking on a pregnancy with medical supervision is akin to entering a contractual arrangement. My part of the deal is to be a compliant, well-informed and responsible patient. But the professional's part of the deal is to provide me with a perfect baby. Having a baby is a lifestyle choice. I want the perfect baby to match my perfect lifestyle. If the baby is less than perfect, the response may be not only grief but also a degree of outrage, as revealed in the words of Christina O'Sullivan: 'I would not have put my boyfriend and me through this, and I would not have chosen this life for Reece.'

Spina bifida may have occurred in the bad old days when medicine was still primitive, but some would argue that handicapped children should not still be being born on the threshold of the twenty-first century. Technology should make sure that such fetuses are identified and aborted before they come to term.

Moreover, if I can use technology to abort an imperfect child, why can I not use technology to determine the sex of my child? If I can choose where to live, what my work is, how to spend my money, whom to marry, and when to have a child, then why can I not choose whether I have a boy or a girl?

In a book called *The Perfect Baby: A Pragmatic Approach to Genetics*, Glen McGee argues that there is no difference between spending money on eduction and spending it on genetic enhancement of our children. Both are ways of improving our children's chances in the lottery of life. Although we should proceed cautiously and gradually, there is no reason why we should not use genetics to improve human nature a little at a time (McGee 1997). In fact, some biologists are claiming that the improvement of the genetic make-up of each individual is an essential goal of the human community. Biologist Bentley Glass said: 'The right of individuals to procreate must give place to a new paramount right: the right of every child to enter life with an adequate physical and mental endowment' (Glass 1971).

In the not-too-distant future, as the results of the Human Genome Project become available, it may be possible to test embryos to determine a wide range of characteristics, including aspects of intelligence, physical strength and size, as well as susceptibility to a large number of diseases. For the first time in history couples will be genuinely able to select the child of their choice. Perhaps, before too long, selecting the best embryo will be seen as an essential part of responsible parenthood. 'I owe it to myself and to my future child to give him or her the best possible genetic start in life.' Under the guise of middle-class responsibility, the stranglehold of the god of consumerism will have finally extended to parenthood. (We shall explore further the difficult issues of genetic screening and enhancement in chapters 4 and 5.)

Just as we have rising expectations at the beginning of life, so we have them at the end of life. Modern people expect to maintain health, mobility and independence right through to their eighties and beyond. Why should we accept a gradual decline into senescence and disability? Along with the rest of society, the elderly are becoming better informed about the range of available treatments and more assertive about their needs and demands. And when we reach the stage where curative medicine has no more to offer, we are no longer prepared to be passive observers as we approach death. We want the right to be in control at the end of life. We want to decide when it is time to die and how it should happen. We want to procure the death which will fit with our lifestyle choices. (We shall look in more detail at dying, euthanasia and physician-assisted suicide in chapter 9.)

Theme 4: Health economics and resource limitations

At the inception of the UK National Health Service in 1948, it was widely predicted that the provision of free nationwide medical care would lead to a *fall* in the total amount of money spent on healthcare by the country. It seemed obvious to the early health planners that improved medical care would lead to a healthier population and this in turn would lead to less demand for medical care. The subsequent experience of the NHS and of every other developed nation has demonstrated the naïveté of this prediction. The combination of new technology and new consumer expectations has had an inevitable consequence – a dramatic and steady rise year on year in the cost of providing healthcare. This has been exacerbated by demographic changes in developed countries. Rising numbers of elderly people in the population are now major and expensive consumers of healthcare resources. When death approaches, health expenditure in many cases rockets as the patient is admitted to hospital and expensive surgery or intensive care is undertaken in a desperate attempt to ward off the inevitable.

Every year expensive new treatments become available for previously untreatable conditions. In 1996 Aricept, the first drug to delay the onset of symptoms in Alzheimer's disease, was released in the UK. The approximate cost of a year's treatment with the drug is £1,000, and it is estimated that in the UK there are around 200,000 patients with mild to moderate Alzheimer's disease who might benefit.

But it is not just at the end of life that healthcare seems exorbitantly expensive. In my own field of intensive care for newborn babies, the 1997 cost of intensive care in the UK was approximately £1,000 per baby per day. The total cost of ensuring the survival of an extremely premature baby may involve several *months* of intensive care, with a total cost of £100,000 or even more.

In 1995 the case of Jaymee Bowen, a ten-year-old girl suffering from acute myeloid leukaemia, hit the headlines. After a bone-marrow transplant at Addenbrooke's Hospital in Cambridge, the disease seem cured; but then the leukaemia returned and specialists told Jaymee's father that she had only weeks to live. He embarked on a desperate search to find a specialist who was prepared to treat Jaymee. Dr Gravett, a private practitioner, was willing to treat Jaymee with an experimental new treatment, donor lymphocyte infusion, but the medical costs would be £75,000. The Cambridge and Huntingdon NHS Health Authority refused to fund this treatment, or to provide a second bone-marrow transplant, as expert medical opinion was that the chances of success were extremely slim. A high-profile legal battle ensued, and eventually the Court of Appeal backed the Health Authority. Mr Stephen Thornton, the Chief Executive of the Authority, was subjected to sustained criticism and even abuse from sections of the media. An anonymous benefactor provided the money for Jaymee to receive the new treatment privately in London, and Jaymee survived for another year before a further relapse led to her death. Her tragic story led to a national debate on the rising costs of medical care and the agonizing decisions which health administrators and doctors must take about rationing healthcare resources.

In a liberal society which values the right of individuals to choose, basic health is seen as one of the indispensable conditions for the exercise of personal choice or autonomy. The 1976 declaration of the World Health Organisation stated: 'The enjoyment of the highest attainable standard of health is one of the fundamental rights of every human being without distinction of race, religion, political belief, economic or social condition.'

The high view of health in a modern society means that the ever-increasing resource requirements of healthcare have the potential to trump all other economic demands in the modern state. In Britain, the total annual health expenditure rose from £17 per head in 1960 to £717 per head in 1994. Even when inflation is taken into account, this represents more than a fivefold increase. In the USA the total health bill in 1960 was £9.8 billion, rising to £617 billion in 1994. As a percentage of total economic wealth, health spending in the USA rose from 5.2% in 1960 to 14.3% in 1994 (OECD Health Database, 1997). The demand within modern societies for expensive healthcare seems inexhaustible.

Faced with the spectacle of inexorably rising costs, the aim of central-government health planners has been to attempt to maximize the economic efficiency of the provision of healthcare. If costs are to be controlled, it is essential to maximize the benefits of healthcare while minimizing the expenditure. In the crude language of big business, planners want to buy 'the maximum number of bangs for each buck spent'. This has led to a strong drive to assess in quantitative terms both the exact costs and the 'benefits' of each intervention. The aim is to provide a ranking system to guide spending priorities. What has happened is that the old paternalism, in which the medical profession controlled the allocation and distribution of healthcare resources, has been replaced by a new paternalism, where health economists, policy planners and bureaucrats are increasingly controlling healthcare in the name of 'rational' cost-effective planning.

An army of accountants, economists and managers has descended on the health services. Although it has added significantly to the cost, at one level their work has been remarkably successful. Using computerized accounting and complex financial models, modern medical managers have attempted to quantify the economic costs of each form of health provision, ranging from a visit to the general practitioner to a cardiac transplant operation. But, in the common phrase, economics teaches us about the cost of everything, but the value of nothing.

What have been the results of all this economic analysis? Some of the findings are hardly surprising. One of the main findings is what I have christened the 'first law of health economics'. It states that 'the cheapest patient is a dead patient'. In financial terms, death is always a 'cost-effective' solution. The patients planners need to worry about are the living ones, the long-term sick or the chronically disabled. They are the really expensive ones.

One of the main arguments put forward for making antenatal screening universally available is the cost saving to the country that follows abortion of affected fetuses. One study in the *British Medical Journal* concluded that the total estimated cost of providing antenatal screening to 'avoid' the birth of a baby with Down's syndrome was £38,000 (Wald *et al.* 1992). The report concluded: 'This is substantially less than the costs of lifetime care, which were estimated in 1987 at £120,000.' The authors found that antenatal screening is 'cost effective', and argued that the NHS should ensure that antenatal screening for Down's syndrome is available throughout Britain.

Similarly, an argument frequently used in cases such as Tony Bland's is the so-called 'waste' of resources in keeping severely brain-damaged patients alive. One newspaper article put it this way: 'More than 1,000 people in England and Wales are like Tony Bland. The cost of caring for these "living dead" could be in excess of £100 million per year. At the same time thousands languish on waiting lists. An awful lot of hip replacements, coronary bypasses and kidney dialysis treatments could be carried out for £100 million.' (We shall return to these complex financial issues later in the book.)

These trends are set to continue. There is little doubt that economic pressures and the reality of resource limitations will play an increasing role in the ethical debates which modern medicine faces in the years to come.

Finally we turn to the fifth and possibly the most important theme of all.

Theme 5: Bioethics – an adventure playground for philosophers

The academic discipline of bioethics has been one of the most remarkable growth industries since the late 1970s. Ethical reflection on medical practice has become a major branch of academic moral philosophy, and seems increasingly divorced from the experience of practising clinicians and their patients.

Contemporary bioethicists start from the recognition that modern western societies are unique in the history of civilization in the breadth and depth of their diversity. They are multicultural, multi-religious and ethically pluralist. There is wide disparity between individuals in religious and moral beliefs and practices. The traditional sources of moral teaching, the religious and political authorities, no longer receive universal or even majority support in our society. How then can we resolve the intractable ethical problems raised by biological and medical advances? Where can modern people find the 'core values' for morality on which we can base our bioethical discussion and debate?

The 'four principles' approach to medical ethics: Beauchamp and Childress

The most influential approach to this fundamental problem has been that of two American ethicists, Tom Beauchamp and James Childress. Their major textbook, *Principles of Biomedical Ethics* (now in its fourth edition), has had a remarkable influence in the field, being regarded by many as the Bible of modern bioethics. Beauchamp and Childress conclude that the only hope for consensus in modern societies is to find the lowest common denominator on which we can all agree. They base their approach on a rather strange animal which they call the 'common morality'. This, as its name implies, is a set of moral rules shared by all the members of a society. It is 'unphilosophical common sense and tradition – ordinary shared moral beliefs' (Beauchamp & Childress 1994: 100). According to their view, this is the morality that serves as a common denominator of all our beliefs, and it is therefore a source (and possibly the only source) of consensus in a pluralistic society. Beauchamp and Childress have reduced this commonsense morality to four fundamental principles or rules of medical ethics:

1. Respect every person's desire for *autonomy*, for self-determination, for a 'personal rule of the self that is free from both controlling interferences by others and from personal limitations that prevent meaningful choice' (1994: 121).

2. Inflict no harm or evil on others (the principle of *nonmaleficence*).

3. Act in the best interests of others (the principle of *beneficence*).

4. Ensure that healthcare is distributed in society in a way which is fair and equitable (the principle of *justice*).

The 'four principles' approach has been widely adopted and popularized. It has the great merit of being simple to remember, providing an *aide-mémoire*, even a modern-day ethical mantra, which can be chanted by medical students and busy doctors. Yet anyone who has tried to use these four principles as a means to finding a practical solution to the problems of medical ethics is immediately made aware of the limitations of this approach.

Take the case of a mother who is carrying a fetus with a genetic abnormality, such as Down's syndrome. Should she be offered an abortion? First, we have the principle of respect for autonomy. But whose autonomy should we respect? The mother's, the father's, the doctor's or the fetus's? Does the idea of respect for the autonomy of a fetus have any meaning? Conversely, can we simply ignore the fetus's *future* right to self-determination?

Secondly, we should do no harm to others. This principle immediately seems to rule out abortion, which clearly harms the fetus. But some ethicists argue that in reality the life of a severely disabled child can be a greater evil than no life at all. To 'inflict' life on a disabled fetus is to inflict harm on it. Thus, to end a disabled life is not to cause harm; in fact, an abortion may be carried out in order to respect the third principle, that of beneficence. We may be acting in the fetus's best interests by ending its life cleanly and painlessly. Of course, others would violently disagree with this interpretation, claiming that life is always a 'good' in itself. Although we can agree on the principles of beneficence and nonmaleficence in name, then, it seems that we cannot agree on what they actually mean – on the substantive content of the principles – when applied to particular cases.

Finally, how does the principle of justice apply to the case of a fetus with Down's syndrome? If we must respect fairness, does this mean we must offer abortions to *all* mothers carrying Down's syndrome fetuses? But what about the thousands of people in our society who have Down's syndrome? Is it unjust to them to discriminate against fetuses with the same syndrome? What is justice? Who says?

Liberal individualism: Ronald Dworkin

The difficulty of finding a moral consensus in modern societies has led some ethicists in a more radical direction. Rather than pretending that there is a mysterious common morality, a common ethical denominator, we should recognize the truth. We shall never agree on these fundamental issues. The only way that we will live together in peace is to *agree to disagree.*

This is the concept of radical liberal individualism which has been eloquently expounded by the eminent legal philosopher Professor Ronald Dworkin in his important book *Life's Dominion.* 'The most important feature of [western political culture] is a belief in individual human dignity: that people have the moral right and the moral responsibility to confront the most fundamental questions about the meaning and value of their own lives for themselves' (Dworkin 1995: 166). 'At the heart of liberty is the right to define one's own concept of existence, of meaning, of the universe, and of the mystery of human life.' Only if we are free can we respect ourselves. 'Freedom is the cardinal, absolute requirement of self-respect: no-one treats his life as having any intrinsic objective importance unless he insists on leading that life himself, not being ushered along it by others' (1995: 239).

As a constitutional lawyer, Dworkin appeals to two fundamental constitutional principles of liberal societies. First is the right to *religious toleration.* He states that, even for atheists, ethical decisions about life and death are at heart religious questions. Even for atheists, convictions about the meaning of human life are in effect religious beliefs. He quotes a US Supreme Court judgment which concluded that an atheist's system of beliefs may have 'a place in the life of its possessor parallel to that filled by the orthodox belief in God' (1995: 155). As such, these beliefs are matters of individual conscience, not public legislation. Therefore we must tolerate our religious differences. 'We must insist on religious tolerance in this area as in all others . . . Tolerance is a cost we must pay for our adventure in liberty. We are committed by our love of liberty and dignity to live in communities in which no group is thought clever or spiritual or numerous enough to decide essentially religious matters for everyone else' (1995: 167).

Secondly, Dworkin appeals to the constitutional right of *privacy*. Like many other liberal philosophers, he draws a strong distinction between the public and the private arena. The public arena is the place in which laws must govern human behaviour. But in the private arena of personal morality, the law must withdraw. In the words of the US Supreme Court, 'If the right of privacy means anything it is the right of the individual . . . to be free from governmental intrusion into matters so fundamentally affecting a person as the decision whether to bear or beget a child' (quoted by Dworkin 1995: 157). In other words, the state must withdraw to allow individuals to exercise their own individual autonomy. In the field of reproduction, Dworkin calls this 'the right of procreative autonomy'.

Dworkin accepts that the state has an interest in protecting the sanctity or inviolability of life, but says there are two ways in which this can be achieved. The state may have the goal of conformity (to enforce people to obey moral rules), or the goal of responsibility (to encourage people to act from individual moral responsibility). 'If we aim at responsibility we must leave citizens free, in the end, to decide as they think right, because that is what moral responsibility entails' (1995: 150). We shall see how Dworkin applies these principles to issues at the beginning and end of life in later chapters, but his overall thrust is clear. We must agree to disagree. 'Whatever view we take about abortion or euthanasia, we want the right to decide for ourselves' (1995: 239).

Radical libertarianism: Max Charlesworth

Another eminent bioethicist, the Australian Professor Max Charlesworth, argues for an even more radical concept in his book *Bioethics in a Liberal Society* (Charlesworth 1993). His ideas develop those first put forward by the Enlightenment philosopher John Stuart Mill. A liberal society is one in which personal liberty and moral autonomy are paramount. To the greatest degree possible, people should be free to make their own life choices. Like Dworkin, he draws a strong distinction between the public arena, in which the law can exercise authority, and the private arena, in which the individual is in control. The coercive role of law is strictly limited. It is not the purpose of the state or the law to make us virtuous or to establish a common morality. In John Stuart Mill's words, 'the only purpose for which power can be rightfully exercised over any member of a civilized community against his will, is to prevent harm to others . . . Over himself, over his body and mind, the individual is sovereign' (quoted by Charlesworth 1993: 16). The wording is significant. There are other sovereigns in the public or political realm, but in private life and morality, the individual is sovereign; there is no-one who can exercise authority over him or her. As Charlesworth puts it, the area of private morality is 'out of bounds' for state intervention and the criminal law. As a society develops, the sphere of personal liberty should be progressively maximized, and the sphere of paternalistic action by the state should steadily dwindle (1993: 17, 18).

Charlesworth draws a distinction between two types of society. On the one hand, there is the traditional, religiously based or authoritarian society. In this form of social organization there is agreement on a set of 'core values', to which all members of the society are supposed to give assent and allegiance. On the other hand, there is the genuinely liberal society in which there is no consensus on core moral or religious values, *except for an agreement that personal liberty or autonomy is the supreme value*. In such a society, social and moral diversity or pluralism is not seen as a threat to the ethical 'consensus'. Rather, they are positively welcomed and seen as an index of social vitality. In traditional western ethical thinking, autonomy was seen as an essential condition for people to exercise moral choice. But in a liberal society, autonomy is a good in itself – in fact, it is the supreme good. Each person within a liberal society has his or her own moral style of life or vocation. Each person is engaged on an individual 'experiment in living' (1993: 15–27).

As Charlesworth recognizes, the logical foundation of this view of individual autonomy is that the conscious subject, the self, the person, has no predetermined nature. There is no such thing as human nature derived from the way we are made. Instead, individuals make themselves, constructing an identity through making autonomous choices. Little by little, we construct the meaning and the value of our own lives. In Dworkin's striking words, 'Value cannot be poured into a life from the outside, it must be generated by the person whose life it is' (Dworkin 1995: 230).

Charlesworth recognizes that 'the liberal society's emphasis on the value of personal autonomy and liberty, with all its consequences, is bought at a certain price. The autonomous agents of a liberal society cannot seek the communal warmth and comfort of traditional societies and are bereft of the paternalistic guidance available in religiously based and authoritarian societies'. Individuals cannot escape the full burden of ethical responsibility for their own actions, performing their own 'experiment in living'; 'The liberal ideal, with its focus on individual liberty, social diversity and cultural pluralism . . . goes against the grain of our human tendency to escape the burdens of autonomous behaviour and to seek conformity and refuge in the crowd. Thus we tend to invoke nostalgically the idea of a moral consensus on a set of core values that are supposed to be at the basis of our society' (Charlesworth 1993: 26). But this is pure illusion. There can be no values on which we agree, except the agreement to disagree.

In effect, both Dworkin and Charlesworth have reduced the four 'common morality' principles of Beauchamp and Childress to one overriding principle: respect for autonomy, with all its implications. 'No life goes better by being led from the outside, according to values the person doesn't endorse. My life only goes better if I am leading it "from the inside",' says Charlesworth. In Dworkin's words, 'No life is a good one if lived against the grain of conviction.' Against the complaint that he puts too much emphasis on autonomy, Charlesworth states trenchantly that 'autonomy is not something that one can have too much of' (1993: 34). There is, however, a major task of public education. 'We must enable others to awaken to the meaning of their autonomy and the realization that they are masters of their fate and captains of their own souls' (1993: 121).

Here are the philosophical roots of the deep sense of aching loneliness, isolation, alienation and estrangement which is the experience of so many in our society. It is a bleak vision of humanity in which a collection of ultimately egocentric selves are making autonomous choices, continually reconstructing themselves in isolation from other unknowable selves, and striving for autonomous independence. Dependence is seen as threatening and dehumanizing precisely because it threatens one's sense of identity, one's sense of personal worth.

In this vision of society, justice is merely an aspect of respect for autonomous individuals. 'We treat people with equal respect precisely because they are autonomous moral agents or "persons". To discriminate against people because of their race, colour, gender or age is unjust, because these characteristics have nothing directly to do with a person's status as a self-determining moral agent.' Charlesworth continues in a rather ominous vein: 'If it could be shown that a person's race, colour, gender, age or social class in some way makes them less of a moral agent in the full sense, then discrimination would not be unjust' (1993: 115).

He points out that there is a paradoxical character in the nature of a liberal society in that the 'core values' of the society are precisely that it has no core values, except for autonomy. 'An agreement on the supreme value of autonomy is precisely an agreement to disagree about substantive and partisan moral positions' (1993: 24). He complains that although modern western societies claim to be liberal, they are in fact riddled by traditional authoritarian and paternalistic attitudes. These need to be overthrown if the ideal of the liberal society is to become a reality. 'We claim that we are living in a liberal society and yet we very often adopt quite illiberal attitudes in many areas of bioethics'

(1993: 161). This is, at least in part, because of the influence of religious groups and communities within a multicultural society. 'The very fact of religious pluralism and multiculturalism presupposes that religious groups give up any absolutist or exclusivist claims and are prepared not merely to tolerate other religious and non-religious groups, but to positively respect and welcome them.' This, however, is not an optional standpoint for religious groups. 'Multiculturalism *requires* that the constitutive subgroups recognize some form of the liberal ideal and subscribe to the liberal "act of faith" that it is possible to have a society without moral, religious and social values, save for consensus upon the values of personal autonomy and liberty' (1993: 166, my emphasis). So belief in the possibility of a liberal society is an act of faith. But faith in whom or what? Presumably in the liberal philosophers who are our benevolent mentors.

Charlesworth argues that in a multicultural society the mainstream or majority culture must not abuse its position. 'The mainstream culture must tolerate and be sensitive to a minority culture's views as well as recognizing that its own views are embedded within a complex network of cultural beliefs and attitudes, and that they have a certain degree of cultural relativity. *This does not however involve any kind of culturalism which would see the values of liberalism as being culturally determined*' (1993: 42, my emphasis).

As has often been pointed out, modern liberalism is remarkably illiberal when it encounters a challenge to its own 'core values', and here is a classic example. Charlesworth argues that we must realize that all our moral beliefs are culturally determined, embedded within our own belief systems, and therefore relative, except for the 'values of liberalism' themselves, which are apparently culture-free and objectively true for everyone. Yet, as a number of philosophers have observed, the 'values of liberalism' are very clearly a product of a particular culture and historical period – the Enlightenment of the eighteenth century. To claim that those liberal values are unique among all other beliefs by being culture-free and objective is the most blatant form of special pleading.

Finally, the emphasis on individual autonomy leads Charlesworth to a startling conclusion. 'If we contrast two acts, (a) one that is freely chosen but objectively wrong and (b) one that is coerced and not freely chosen but objectively good, the liberal will say that the first act is more morally valuable than the second' (1993: 13).

This seems both outrageous and illogical. First, it implies that provided Hitler freely chose to exterminate the Jews of Poland, that act was more morally valuable than would have been the cessation of that policy due to Allied military might. Secondly, to say that an act is *objectively* wrong can have no meaning in a genuinely liberal society, because the only 'objective' ethical value is autonomy itself. All else is a matter of culturally embedded beliefs and personal opinion.

The five new commandments of bioethics: Peter Singer

As we have seen, the new discipline of bioethics offers the opportunity for radical voices to challenge the medical and religious establishment and its prevailing orthodoxy. One such voice is that of Professor Peter Singer, of Monash University in Australia. In his important book *Rethinking Life and Death* (Singer 1995), he proclaims (not without a certain glee) the end of the era in which Christian views of the sanctity of human life have dominated. 'After ruling our thoughts and our decisions about life and death for two thousand years, the traditional Western ethic of the sanctity of human life has collapsed' (Singer 1995: 1). He points to the tragic examples of Lillian Boyes, Tony Bland and Samuel Linares. 'The traditional religious view that all human life is sacrosanct is simply not able to cope with the array of modern medical dilemmas' (1995: 189).

Singer cannot be accused of excessive modesty. To replace the old worn-out Judaeo-Christian ethic based on the biblical revelation, he puts forward five new commandments from his own Mount Sinai.

First, in place of the command to treat all human life as of equal worth, he offers: *Recognize that the worth of human life varies.* For Singer, it is self-evident that the lives of people such as Boyes, Bland and Linares are of no value to themselves or to anyone else. We should cease our 'pious pretence' that their lives have any special significance. He points to the Law Lords' judgment in the case of Tony Bland, saying that they 'have taken the brave step of recognizing that, at a minimum, consciousness is essential if life is to be worth having' (1995: 80). If you are permanently unconscious, therefore, the value of your life is reduced to nil. Similarly, he argues that the widespread acceptance of prenatal diagnosis and abortion for fetal abnormality implies that we do accept that the life of a handicapped child is not as worthwhile as that of a healthy child. Hence 'we should treat human beings in accordance with their *ethically relevant characteristics*'. These include consciousness, the capacity for physical, social and mental interaction with other beings, having conscious preferences for continued life and having enjoyable experiences. Other relevant character-istics depend on relationship to others – having relatives, for instance, who will grieve over your death. These characteristics are the proof of a worthwhile life, and the ultimate value of a life varies according to how much they are present.

Singer concludes, in effect, that a worthwhile life depends upon the adequate functioning of the cerebral cortex, the part of the brain which governs the highest cerebral functions such as consciousness. Human beings who do not have a fully functioning cortex, including fetuses and even newborn infants, as well as brain-damaged individuals or those with conditions such as Alzheimer's disease, cannot be regarded as having a right to life. They are human beings, but they are not 'persons' in the full sense of the word. We should cease our hypocritical pretence that their lives are as valuable as that of a healthy and normally functioning adult, a real 'person'. Instead, we should recognize the obvious truth that some lives are more valuable than others; some human beings are 'persons' (or, as it is sometimes expressed, they have 'personhood'), and some are not (1995: 190–192). Society consists of a hierarchy: at the top are the prize specimens of humanity – the Olympic athlete, the Nobel Prize winner – then ordinary, healthy, adult human beings; then the less healthy, with enough brain activity to recognize their own existence; and then the non-persons – babies, the brain-damaged, the mentally disabled, the sufferers with Alzheimer's disease, those whose lives are of little value. All of us fit somewhere in the pecking order, and the value of our life goes up or down according to the passage of events.

Secondly, Singer argues that the traditional prohibition of the taking of innocent life should be replaced by an acceptance of mercy killing: *Take responsibility for the consequences of your decisions.* This means in practice that if we have decided that a life is not worth living, on the grounds of 'ethically relevant characteristics', then we as a society should take the responsibility to end that life in a humane way. It is immoral to allow a human individual to linger on in a condition that is 'not worth living'. Singer recognizes that this new approach to worthless life may lead to 'a colder, less cohesive society', but he thinks this is a small price to pay (1995: 192–196).

Thirdly, the traditional prohibition of suicide should be replaced by the new commandment, *Respect a person's desire to live or die.* If autonomous individuals want to carry on living, then we should respect their wishes. Of course, only a 'person' can want to go on living. Hence killing a 'person' against his or her will is a much more serious wrong than killing a human being who is not a 'person'. In other words, only a 'person' has a right to life. Conversely, if an autonomous individual, a 'person', concludes after due reflection that his or her own life is valueless, it is a medical duty to end that life cleanly and painlessly (1995: 196–198).

The old biblical command to be fruitful and multiply should be replaced by a fourth new commandment: *Bring children into the world only if wanted.* There are already as many people on this planet as it can reasonably be expected to support. This, together with the fact that the human embryo and fetus are not 'persons' and hence have no intrinsic value or rights, means that there can be no harm in killing an embryo or fetus. Hence contraception and abortion on demand are a matter of individual choice. But Singer goes further. He argues that, in addition, we should be prepared to accept the medical infanticide of unwanted or deformed newborns. 'Human babies are not born self-aware or capable of grasping that they exist over time. They are not persons. Hence their lives seem to be no more worthy of protection than the life of a fetus' (1995: 210). Why on earth should we use expensive technology and scarce medical resources to ensure the survival of a handicapped or unwanted baby, when the world already has too many mouths to feed (1995: 198–200)?

In his earlier book *Should the Baby Live?*, Singer and his colleague Helga Kuhse suggested that a period of twenty-eight days after birth might be allowed before an infant is accepted as having the same right to life as others. This would give time for a couple to decide whether it is better 'not to continue with a life that has begun very badly' (Kuhse & Singer 1985: 155–161).

Finally, in place of the old commandment, 'Treat all human life as more precious than non-human life', Singer offers his modern replacement: *Do not discriminate on the basis of species.* Modern western liberalism recognizes that we should not discriminate on the basis of attributes that lack moral significance. Racism, sexism and ageism are wrong because these attributes lack moral significance. But why, the argument goes, should an individual's species be of any greater ethical importance than his or her race, gender or age? To value a human life as of more importance than that of another sentient being is to be guilty of *speciesism.*

'If we compare a severely defective human infant with a non-human animal, a dog or pig for example, we will often find the non-human to have superior capacities, both actual and potential, for rationality, self-consciousness, communication, and anything else that might be morally significant' (1995: 201). Even rats and fish 'are indisputably more aware of their surroundings and more able to respond in purposeful and complex ways to things they like or dislike, than a human fetus'. With unimpeachable logic but questionable wisdom, Singer follows the train of his argument. 'There is no reason to think that a fish suffers less when dying in a net than a fetus suffers during an abortion, hence the argument for not eating fish is much stronger than the argument against abortion . . .' (1995: 209).

In summary, on the basis of 'ethically relevant characteristics' not all members of the species *Homo sapiens* are persons, and not all persons are members of the species *Homo sapiens.* Singer suggests that we are on the brink of a new Copernican revolution in human self-understanding. Four hundred years ago Copernicus braved the wrath of the religious establishment by showing that human beings were not at the centre of the physical universe. Now we are coming to realize that we are not at the centre of the moral universe either. We must abandon the old religious prejudices about human superiority. *Homo sapiens* is just one among many sentient species on this planet, each with its own moral rights and privileges.

Of course, one could point out, in passing, that Singer has merely replaced one kind of discrimination with another. He wants to discriminate between individuals, not on whether they are members of the human race or not, but on whether their cortex is working properly. One could call him a 'corticalist'. Is there any logical basis to the assertion that corticalism is morally preferable to speciesism?

The maximum happiness for the maximum number: John Harris

The final philosopher we shall look at is John Harris, Professor of Applied Philosophy in the University of Manchester. He takes a similar position to Singer's in his widely read book *The Value of Life: An Introduction to Medical Ethics* (Harris 1985). Harris's definition of a person, however, is subtly different. A person is 'any being who is capable of valuing his or her own life' (1985: 18). This leads to a similar division of human beings into persons and 'non-persons'. Non-persons have no right to have their lives protected. 'To kill a person not only frustrates their wishes for their own future, but frustrates every wish a person has. Creatures that cannot value their own existence cannot be wronged in this way, for their death deprives them of nothing that they can value' (1985: 19). In his view, embryos and fetuses are clearly non-persons, and Harris argues that abortion should be allowed on demand.

Unlike Singer, however, Harris believes that ethical choices should be made so as to maximize the welfare or happiness of all the people in the world, the philosophy usually called *utilitarianism*. This means that fetuses who are aborted should be used for experiments or transplants, rather than just 'killed wastefully', so as to maximize the benefits for other people (1985: 123). Research on non-persons which will enable persons to benefit is clearly worthwhile, and any restriction on such research is illogical. Similarly, newborn babies cannot be regarded as persons. 'Nine months' development leaves the human embryo far short of the emergence of anything that could be called a person, far short of an individual capable of valuing its own life or possessing any of the capacities that would be required for such valuing' (1985: 129). Harris, like Singer, regards autonomy, the right to choose, as the central value of life. 'Since it is my life, its value to me consists precisely in doing with it what I choose' (1985: 80). If I choose to die, then euthanasia should be available on request. 'If death is a benefit, how can those who confer it fail to be benefactors?' Euthanasia should also be provided to severely handicapped babies 'which face a painful and short life'. Harris argues that there is nothing wrong in adults choosing to sell their reproductive capacities for profit, as in commercial surrogacy arrangements, and that it is inconsistent to prevent homosexual couples or single women or men to use reproductive technology to have children if they so wish (1985: 136–146).

Following the logic of his utilitarian position, he concludes that new genetic technology provides many opportunities for maximizing happiness in the world. For instance, individuals should be allowed to use genetic technology to create one or more clones of themselves for medical purposes. This would ensure that there was a secure supply of genetically identical organs for transplant. In order to prevent the unwelcome prospect of the clone demanding its own rights, its brain could be destroyed at an early stage to prevent the development of consciousness and hence any right to its own life (1985: 124–126).

Many people are tempted to dismiss this kind of ethical argument as the sort of ivory-castle self-evident nonsense that academics are paid to produce. I have a certain amount of sympathy with the cynic who remarked that 'medical ethics has become an adventure playground for philosophers'. But Singer, Harris and other radical bioethicists are not other-worldly eggheads. They are highly sought-after and popular speakers at conferences and public debates on ethical issues. They give the impression of being engaged in a 'charm offensive' designed to disseminate and popularize their views. Their writings, elegantly written and popular in style, have become basic reading material for undergraduate courses in ethics. It seems they regard themselves as the storm-troopers of the 'big push', a major assault on traditional medical ethics, designed, according to its proponents, to rid medicine of its roots in 'religious prejudice' and usher in a new dawn of rational, benevolent and enlightened ethical practice.

These, then, are five important influences on the development of bioethical thinking today: biological reductionism, technology, consumerism, limited resources and ethical diversity. Of course, many more issues could be brought out, but I believe these are five of the most important influences in the public debates about medicine and biology in which we are currently engaged.

In the next chapter I attempt a brief panoramic view of the historic biblical worldview as it relates to humanness and health. As we shall see, this biblical perspective reveals an understanding of the nature of persons that is very much at odds with the presuppositions of the ethicists discussed above. Later, in chapter 3, I will endeavour to highlight two fundamental and contradictory ways of looking at human beings.

2. Biblical perspectives on humanness

When we turn from recent advances in biology and medical technology to the Bible, we are immediately struck by the gulf between the biblical world and our own.

The world of the Bible is pre-scientific, technologically primitive, predominantly rural and dominated by the realities of an agricultural existence. It reflects a society in which knowledge about the universe scarcely changed from one generation to the next. It is a world in which no-one questioned that unseen and powerful spiritual forces controlled all aspects of human life, from the weather to the mysteries of human reproduction and infertility. How can the Bible possibly have anything relevant to say in the complexities of medical ethics in our radically different society?

But historic, trinitarian Christianity can retain its authenticity only if it remains faithful to the biblical revelation. We are not at liberty to conclude that the Bible has little or nothing to say of relevance to contemporary ethical debates. Nor are we free to manipulate or distort the biblical message to make it more acceptable to modern ears and prejudices. If Christians are to be faithful to our calling to live in the modern world as disciples of the historic Christ revealed in Scripture, we must learn to apply with integrity the unchanging principles of the Bible to the world in which we live. My profound conviction is that if we are prepared to enter into the historic biblical worldview, we can find insights and principles which connect directly with the debate about medical ethics. There are no simplistic or slick answers, but I believe there is a way forward, a way of thinking about these issues which is at the same time authentically Christian, relevant and practical.

We cannot minimize the difficulty of the task that we face. There is no hope of finding simplistic proof-texts which will genuinely apply to the dilemmas of embryo research, genetic enhancement or the persistent vegetative state. God has not given us a selection of isolated epigrams, like a dictionary of quotations. Instead, he has given a comprehensive revelation which covers the sweep of world history. It is our task to saturate ourselves in the fullness of the scriptural revelation.

I have found it extraordinarily helpful to use the four-fold scheme of biblical history developed by a number of theologians over the centuries and used by John Stott in his important book *Issues Facing Christians Today* (Stott 1990: 34–36). The Bible divides human history into four epochs: creation, the fall, redemption and the future consummation. As we view any issue from each of these four perspectives, we appreciate a different aspect, so that as we integrate the four perspectives into one whole we develop a full-orbed and detailed image.

I have become convinced that we frequently obtain distorted and partial ideas of Christian truth because we fail to use this four-fold perspective. In particular, modern evangelical Christians frequently concentrate on the middle two perspectives to the exclusion of the first and the last. To caricature this view: 'all human beings are fallen, but Jesus can save us through the cross'. But we cannot understand what it means to be fallen unless we grasp the full meaning of the creation, what we have fallen *from*. Similarly, we cannot understand what it means to be 'saved' unless we understand the end in store, the purpose, the goal that God has saved us *for*.

As we attempt to develop a biblical understanding of medical ethics, we need to work at a full-orbed understanding of creation, and in particular of creation design and creation order, the moral principles that God has embedded into the structure of the universe. This is a theme to which we shall return on several occasions as we approach different ethical dilemmas. So it is to creation that we must turn first.

Creation

Biblical teaching about creation is present in many places in Scripture (see, for example, Pss. 8; 104; 139) but the majestic first two chapters of Genesis are where we must start. Henri Blocher, in his book *In the Beginning* (Blocher 1984), provides a wonderfully helpful overview of these chapters and I am indebted to him for much of what follows.

The seven days of creation

The first chapter of Genesis is not just a list of God's creative activities, but a marvellously skilful literary composition, an artistic construction. In days 1–3 we have the creation of the sky, the waters and the land, and in days 4–6 we have the creation of their corresponding inhabitants: heavenly bodies, sea creatures and birds, and land dwellers. The careful, symmetrical structure of Genesis 1 allows the author to express his theological purpose. As Blocher puts it, the narrative has two peaks: humankind and the Sabbath. The creation of human beings crowns the work, but the Sabbath is its supreme goal. The existence of the Sabbath keeps human beings from total absorption in the task of subduing the earth. It reminds them that they will fulfil their humanity not finally in their work of transforming the earth, but in the delight and *recreation* of relationship with God himself.

Throughout the creation narrative of Genesis runs the important concept that God imbues his creation with *order*. His creative work brings order into the world of living creatures. Everything is assigned a place and a function. In biblical imagery, the sea is often used as an image of disorder, of chaos. In creation, however, God imposes limits on the sea itself. As he said to Job:

> 'Who shut up the sea behind doors
>   when it burst forth from the womb . . .
> when I fixed limits for it
>   and set its doors and bars in place,
>   when I said, "This far you may come and no farther . . ."?'
>
> (Jb. 38:8–11)

God creates the limits beyond which his creation cannot transgress. There is no part of creation, however chaotic, however autonomous, which is not subject to intrinsic limits set by the Creator.

Within the order of creation, although each element has its own dignity and receives the commendation of its Creator, human beings are pictured as the crowning work of God. 'What is the work of the six days', asked Gregory of Nyssa, 'other than the building of the palace, until the entry into the place prepared of the prince beloved by the Father?' (quoted by Blocher 1984: 77).

At the centre of the biblical worldview is the concept of God as designer. God is the one who imposes order, meaning and purpose on the whole creation. In the biblical narrative both the origin of the human species (Gn. 1 – 2) and the development of the individual fetus within the womb (Ps. 139:13–16) are pictured in terms of meticulous and loving design. This is the creation order imposed by the Creator's will. If we lose the concept that human beings are designed by God, we strike at the heart of the biblical understanding of what it means to be human.

Of course, the questions of *how* God's creative activity was expressed in the development of humans is a matter of continuing controversy and debate among Christians. Some see God's creative design in terms of the providential ordering of environmental contingencies in Darwinian evolution from hominid life forms (for example, Berry 1996: 29–57), whereas others have doubted whether Darwinian thinking can be compatible with Christian thought (for example, Johnson 1993). This is not the place to enter into that debate. But whichever view we take of the origin of human beings, we cannot escape the biblical teaching that God's loving and meticulous design, enshrining the Creator's purpose for each of our lives, lies at the heart.

The image of God

Then God said, 'Let us make man in our image, in our likeness, and let them rule over the fish of the sea and the birds of the air, over the livestock, over all the earth, and over all the creatures that move along the ground.'

> So God created man
> in his own image,
> in the image of God
> he created him;
> male and female
> he created them.
>
> (Gn. 1:26–27)

Human beings are unique in all the vast array of creation because they alone of all the creatures are made in God's image, or, as an alternative translation puts it, they are made *as* God's image. Human beings are Godlike beings. God has chosen no other image-bearer, animate or inanimate, on planet Earth. In the ancient world it was apparently common for a king to set up a stone or metal image of himself as a physical symbol of his sovereignty over a particular territory. It represented him to his subject peoples. A recently discovered statue of an ancient Assyrian governor carried this inscription written in Aramaic, a language closely related to biblical Hebrew: 'This statue is the image and likeness of Hadad-yis'i the Governor of Gosan.' The words used for 'image and likeness' are virtually identical to those of Genesis 1:26 (Millard & Bordreuil 1982).

It is human beings, then, who are called to rule over the rest of creation in the place of God, as his authorized representatives. Adam and Eve are instructed to subdue the earth and to rule over the rest of the biological kingdom in God's name. We bear God's image so that we can truly be God's representative, so that we can reveal God's character to the rest of creation. Sadly, this concept has frequently been abused and distorted to imply that we can dominate and misuse the rest of creation as we wish. The biblical narrative reveals God's rule as one of ordering, life-generating, life-preserving servant-hood and as a celebration of his kingdom. These, then, should characterize human rule over the physical creation. It should not be abusive or exploitative, but enabling, so that each part of the created order is able to express its full potential. '[Man's] rule is the rule which liberates other beings to be, to be in themselves, to be for others, and to be for God' (O'Donovan 1994: 38). In the words of theologian Vinoth Ramachandra, 'We are neither owners of the planet – to do with it as we please, nor mere guests – to observe its development passively. We are stewards' (Ramachandra 1996a: 70).

But what does it mean to be made 'in God's image'? Since the writings of the early church fathers, theologians have laboured to explore the significance of this tantalizing phrase. It has frequently been suggested that its meaning lies in the *capacities* or attributes that human beings possess which are Godlike – their rationality, creativity and spirituality, for instance. In particular, the rationality of human beings, in distinction from animals, has been emphasized by theologians from Augustine onwards. In ancient Greek philosophical thought, humanity was defined by individuation (separateness from others) and by rationality. But although rationality is part of the biblical understanding of humanity, as distinct from the animal kingdom, Greek influences may have led to an overemphasis. As we face the challenges of advances in biology and biotechnology, it is vital for Christians to rediscover an authentically biblical view of what it means to be a human being – a biblical *anthropology*. As we shall see, the Bible tends to emphasize that God's image is seen not only in our capacities or attributes, in what we can *do*, and in the duties which God gives us, but also in what we *are* by creation, in the stuff of our humanity.

God's image implies dependence

Human beings are not self-explanatory. They derive their meaning from outside themselves – from God, in whose image they are made. We are not autonomous individuals, constantly creating ourselves by the decisions and choices we make. No; we are images, we are reflections. The dignity of our humanity is derivative; it comes from him whose image we bear. As Blocher says, being made in God's image 'stresses the radical nature of [our] dependence' (Blocher 1984: 82).

The ethicist Paul Ramsey, speaking of the unborn child, put it in these words: 'The dignity of a human being is an overflow from God's dealing with him or her and not primarily an anticipation of anything they will ever be by themselves. The Lord did not put his love upon you because you were intrinsically more than a blob of tissue in the uterus.' The theologian Helmut Thielicke expressed it like this: 'The divine likeness rests on the fact that God remembers us . . .' The divine image is like a mirror reflecting God's glory. Like a mirror, it goes dark if the source of light is withdrawn. In Thielicke's words, 'it possesses only borrowed light' (Thielicke 1966: 177).

As we saw in the previous chapter, Ronald Dworkin said that 'Value cannot be poured into a life from the outside, it must be generated by the person whose life it is.' I beg to differ; the biblical worldview claims that the dignity of our humanity comes precisely from outside ourselves; it comes from God, whose image we bear. The 'radical nature of our dependence' has inescapable consequences for medical ethics. Within the story of my life, I have a degree of independence, the dignity of genuine choice, the relative freedom of a creature. But it is not simply 'my' life to do with as I please. My life can have meaning only in relation to God

For a society penetrated by liberal individualism as ours is, this concept is peculiar, nonsensical, even outrageous. Yet the biblical revelation stresses our creaturely dependence. Job expresses this poetically:

> 'Your hands shaped me and made me.
>   . . . you moulded me like clay . . .
> Did you not pour me out like milk
>   and curdle me like cheese,
> clothe me with skin and flesh
>   and knit me together with bones and sinews?
> You gave me life and showed me kindness,
>   and in your providence watched over my spirit.'
>
> (Jb. 10:8–12)

Similarly, Elihu in the book of Job reflects on the dependence of the entire human race on God's continual sustenance:

> 'If it were his intention
>   and he withdrew his spirit and breath,
> all mankind would perish together
>   and man would return to the dust.'
>
> (Jb. 34:14–15)

The same concept is found in the words of Jeremiah: 'a man's life is not his own; it is not for man to direct his steps' (Je. 10:23).

We have to recognize that current secular views of autonomy are a modern fantasy; they are out of touch with reality, with the way we and the rest of the universe are made. The Christian revelation reminds us that 'we are most ourselves not when we seek to direct and control our destiny, but when we recognize and admit that our life is grounded in and sustained by God' (Meilander 1997: 2).

God's image implies relationship

In the mystery of the Trinity, historic Christianity teaches that God is in loving relationship or communion from eternity to eternity. In Bernard of Clairvaux's evocative phrase, 'the Spirit is the kiss between Father and Son'. God the Father loves God the Son, God the Son loves God the Father, God the Father loves God the Spirit, and so on. This is the ultimate meaning behind the biblical statement, 'God is love', a continual self-giving of the persons of the Trinity. It seems that the persons of the Godhead do not, even cannot, exist in isolation. God's being is defined as being *in relationship*. To be a person is not to be an isolated individual, nor is it to be lost in a collection of identical beings. To be a person is both to be a unique 'other' and to be in relationship with others (Carson 1996: 229).

Thus, when the text of Genesis says, 'Let *us* make man in our image', the 'us' is the Godhead-in-community. And because the Godhead consists of persons-in-community, to be made in God's image is to be made a person-in-community, in relationship. An isolated person, an 'autonomous individual' in the language of Dworkin or Singer, is a contradiction in terms. The meaning of personhood is derived from the Godhead; it is in relationship, in self-giving, in community. Hence, in biblical thought, humanity is defined not so much by *rationality* as by *relationality*. The apostle John states that 'No-one has ever seen God; but if we love one another, God lives in us and his love is made complete in us' (1 Jn. 4:12). John implies that the invisible God is made visible when human beings are in loving relationship. We reflect God's character to the world by love *for one another*.

Of course, rationality is an extremely important part of our created nature as human beings. But it seems to me that, biblically speaking, the defining characteristic of humanity is not so much our ability to think as the web of relationships into which we are created, as persons-in-community. God's creation of humans in his image is also a call to relationship with him. God creates us as relational beings and calls us to enter into communion with him. To speak of God's image is to speak of God's love for us. God creates each one of us out of love, calls us out of love and redeems us out of love. Even though the image is distorted by sin, God 'remembers' us and calls us back to himself.

Finally, the Genesis text may suggest that the creation of human beings as sexual beings, male and female, reflects the nature of the Godhead. The image of God is seen in our sexuality. Because we are made as male and female, we image God fully only when we are together, in a 'face-to-face' relationship, as God himself exists in face-to-face relationship. But the relationship of male and female implied in the Genesis narrative cannot refer only to the marriage relationship, but rather to all male–female partnerships. It is when man and woman are united in a partnership of co-operation that we are at our most Godlike.

God's image implies that we are his children

In the thought-forms of the ancient Middle East, the image of the father was passed on to the next generation when a child was begotten. In the fifth chapter of Genesis, we read the same statement as previously – that God created human beings in his own likeness – and then: 'When Adam had lived 130 years, he had a son in his own likeness, in his own image; and he named him Seth' (5:3).

Adam's image is passed to his own child in procreation. In the genealogy of Jesus found in Luke's gospel, the line is tracked back to Adam, 'the son of God' (3:37). The divine image is passed on as we beget children.

We must not, however, fall into the pagan belief that human beings are intrinsically divine. Although all of us carry God's image, it is only in a limited and incomplete sense. According to the New Testament, there is only one human being who rightfully bears the title of God's perfect image and God's Son: Jesus, the Second Adam, the perfect human being, who is both the Son and the supreme and unique image of the invisible God (Col. 1:15). As the apostle Paul puts it, we who are called by God are called 'to be conformed to the likeness of his Son, that he might be firstborn among many brothers' (Rom. 8:29). So the image of God is both a description of our created nature and a promise of what we may become by God's grace. It is what God has in store for us, what he has called us for – to be re-formed in Christ's image, to rediscover our status as God's children, to enter into a face-to-face relationship with our Maker and Father.

God's image implies the dignity of each human life

In biblical thought, as each human life has a unique dignity because of the divine image, therefore each life has an incalculable and incommensurable value. In other words, it is not possible to calculate the value of a human life in material terms, and it is not possible to compare the ultimate value of one human life with another. Each human being is a unique masterpiece of God's creation. Each individual is, in the literal words of the eighth Psalm, 'lacking a very little of God' (Ps. 8:5). It is as though an economist asked, 'How much is the Mona Lisa worth, and is it worth more or less than the roof of the Sistine Chapel?' There can be no answer, because the value of a supreme masterpiece is incalculable and incommensurable. In place of the Lego-kit view of humanity, then, we have what I will call the *flawed masterpiece* view of humanity. Yes, the masterpiece may get defaced, it may decay from old age, the varnish may be cracked and yellowed, the frame may be riddled with woodworm. But through the imperfections we can still perceive a masterpiece – and therefore, as we shall see, medicine is more akin to art preservation and restoration than it is to Lego construction.

To Peter Singer and Ronald Dworkin, the dignity of personhood depends on your function: on what you can do, on how well your cortex functions, on whether you can choose, and exercise autonomy. If your level of functioning is critically reduced, because of Alzheimer's disease, say, or just because you happen to be a fetus, then you have less worth. But in Christian thought, the dignity of a human being resides not in what you can do, but in what you are, by creation. Human beings do not need to earn the right to be treated as Godlike beings. Our dignity is *intrinsic*, in the way we have been made, in how God remembers us and calls us. So biblical ethics, the way we are called to treat one another, is derived from biblical anthropology, the way we are made.

God's image implies the equality of human beings

Our creation in God's image implies not only a radical dependence, but also a radical equality. Each one of us bears the family likeness, yet each one is a unique masterpiece. We are all equal because we all bear the family likeness. The need for justice, equality and fairness in human society comes from our radical equality by creation. Whereas Peter Singer's view of human society tends towards a hierarchy, the Christian view of humanity is fundamentally egalitarian. Males are equal to females, adults are equal to children, the powerful are equal to the weak, the disabled are equal to the healthy, the so-called non-person is equal to the person. Why? Because we are equal in the stuff of our being. As the book of Proverbs says: 'Rich and poor have this in common: the LORD [Yahweh] is the Maker of them all' (Pr. 22.2).

In the human community, we are surrounded by other reflections of God who are different but fundamentally equal in dignity to ourselves. The making of representative images of God is prohibited by the law of Moses (Ex. 20:4) at least partly because there is no need for another representation of God on the planet. God himself has placed his image here, and he wishes us to respect and care for his image in the way we treat one another. This is why Jesus joins the two great commands, 'Love the Lord your God . . . Love your neighbour as yourself' (Mk. 12:29–31). The two commands are interrelated, because in loving and respecting our neighbour we are in fact showing honour to God. Similarly, the apostle John shows the organic connection between love of God and love for human beings: 'anyone who does not love his brother, whom he has seen, cannot love God, whom he has not seen' (1 Jn. 4:20).

Responding to God's image in others

How then should we treat human beings – these amazing Godlike beings? I would like to draw out four responses.

Wonder

The first response to another human being should be one of wonder at the miracle of our creaturely existence. Of all the marvels of the creation, it is the existence of human beings which should evoke the greatest awe. Hard as it may be at times, we must try never to lose a sense of wonder at the mystery and the existence of another human being. It is the wonder which a parent feels at the moment of birth. Before, there were only two people in the room – but now there are three. I am afraid that a loss of the sense of wonder is especially common among health professionals and carers. We become blasé and cynical. We've seen it all before. We are just doing our job, just going through the motions. But Christian thinking calls us to retain a sense of wonder at the mystery of each human being.

Respect

Along with a sense of wonder goes respect – respect for the mysterious, immutable dignity of the image of God. I am increasingly convinced that respect for others is one of the hallmarks of authentic Christian compassion. We are called to treat one another with the same respect and dignity with which God himself treats us. Some modern secular philosophers tend to view the weak, the demented, the disabled, with a degree of contempt; they are non-persons, they have no autonomy, they don't count, their biology is substandard, their cortex is malfunctioning. But the mark of genuine Christian love for the disabled, the sick and the dying is not pity but respect – 'respect-love', as Mother Theresa called it.

To abuse, manipulate or ill-treat a fellow human being is to show contempt for God. In the words of the biblical proverb, 'He who oppresses the poor shows contempt for their Maker, but whoever is kind to the needy honours God' (Pr. 14:31). To abuse or manipulate another human being is in fact a form of blasphemy against God. It is to spit in the face of the Creator, to treat the divine image with contempt. This is why biblical ethics does not draw a distinction between religious behaviour (what we do in a church or a temple) and secular behaviour (what we do in the marketplace or, for that matter, in the hospital). God's moral order, the order of creation, permeates the whole of life.

Empathy

Empathy means to enter into the experience of the other, to share the pain and the joy. Because we are all the same in the stuff of our humanity, we are able to enter into the other's experience. We are not isolated, autonomous individuals locked in our own separate universes. We are able to share one another's joys and pains. Secular philosophers tend to emphasize the gulf between the healthy and normally functioning, and the severely disabled or the critically unwell: I am a person, you are a non-person; I am the doctor, you are the patient. But Christianity says, 'We are both human beings; we are the same, you and I. We are in this together; we will share the pain.'

Protection

Finally, because each human life carries God's image, each life is sacrosanct. In the ninth chapter of Genesis is found the *lex talionis*, one of the oldest legal formulae in the world literature, which prescribes the death penalty for the crime of shedding human blood:

> Whoever sheds the blood of man,
>   by man shall his blood be shed;
> for in the image of God
>   has God made man.

(Gn. 9:6)

It is because of the awesome dignity of human life that, paradoxically, only capital punishment is sufficient retribution for murder. To destroy innocent human life is uniquely scandalous because it desecrates God's image, God's masterpiece. In John Harris's view of society, stronger persons can use brain-damaged non-persons for their own ends. For instance, we can take the organs from PVS sufferers or malformed babies and transplant them into somebody who is worth more. The strong can make use of the weak. But Christian thought turns this on its head. The weak are worthy of special protection precisely because they are vulnerable, and the strong have a duty to protect the weak from manipulation and abuse.

Wonder, respect, empathy, protection: these are the responses which we owe to one another, because of the way we are made; because we are all bearers of God's mysterious reflection.

Made from the dust of the earth

Although the creation accounts stress the lofty dignity of humankind, they also draw attention to our physical nature and to our solidarity with the animal kingdom. Human beings are made on the sixth day, like all the other living creatures on land. In case we forget our lowly origins, the name that is given by God, 'Adam', is closely similar to the Hebrew for 'ground', *ᵃdāma*. Adam is the 'groundling'. In English also, the word 'human' may be derived from Latin *humus*, the soil.

Like all the other living creatures, human beings are formed out of the dust of the ground (Gn. 2:7), and, as with the animals, the breath of life is breathed into our nostrils. Although, as image-bearers, we are different from the rest of the animal kingdom, we are created in such a way as to share their physical structure. Like them, we are dust, we are the groundlings. Genetic analysis demonstrates that about 50% of our genetic material is identical to that of an oak tree. Over 98% of our DNA is identical to that of a chimpanzee. That is why molecular biology and basic science research have been so successful for human medicine. We are made out of the same stuff as the rest of the biological world.

Psalm 104, the 'ecological' psalm, in particular, emphasizes the common dependence of all living beings on God, the provider and sustainer. 'These all look to you to give them their food at the proper time' (Ps. 104:27). Or, in Job's words, 'in his hand is the life of every creature and the breath of all mankind' (Jb. 12:10).

One of the commonest Christian heresies that has recurred over the history of the church is that of 'superspirituality', the attempt to deny the significance, value and dignity of the body and the material world. But the biblical faith affirms the physical stuff of our nature. This is the way we have been made. In the wonderful words of Psalm 103, the compassion and gentleness of the Creator are seen:

As a father has compassion on his children,
   so the LORD has compassion on those who fear him;
for he knows how we are formed,
   he remembers that we are dust.

(Ps. 103:13–14)

If God, our Creator, remembers the physical stuff from which we are formed, so should we. The awareness of our dust-like origins should give us a gentleness, a compassion – dare one say a *humanity*? – in the way we interact with one another.

We are not angels, a form of spiritual life unencumbered by physical constraints; neither are we merely animals, limited to a physical existence. We are a unique creation, 'a disgusting hybrid', in the words of C. S. Lewis's whimsical devil, Screwtape. The human person is the place where freedom and physical dependence are united. Because of the created, multifaceted, yet integrated nature of human beings – physical, emotional, spiritual, social – when we express care for our fellow human beings, we must respect each aspect of human nature. In the buzz words of the health professions, caring must be *integrated* and *holistic*.

Made into one human family

God has not made us as independent individuals sprouting up like mushrooms in a field. He has put us in families, locked together in mutual dependence. Not only are we designed to depend on God; we are also designed to depend on one another. We are born not as 'autonomous individuals' but as helpless infants, totally dependent on another's love and care. And we end our physical life in dependence. Dependence is not an alien, subhuman, undignified condition; it is part of the narrative of a person's life. In the words of theologian Gilbert Meilander, 'We are dependent beings, and to think otherwise – to make independence our project, however sincerely – is to live a lie, to fly in the face of reality' (Meilander 1997: 59).

One of the greatest fears expressed by elderly or disabled people is that they will be a burden to others. But in God's creation order we are meant to be a burden to one another! This is an essential part of what it means to belong to a family or to a community. Paul commanded the Galatians, as members of the Christian family, to 'carry each other's burdens, and in this way you will fulfil the law of Christ' (Gal. 6:2). To be called into a family is to be called to share the burdens of the life which God has given us, the burdens which come from our creation out of dust. The life of a family, including the Christian church family, should be one of 'mutual burdensomeness', to use Gilbert Meilander's phrase.

'The family of man' used to be a common phrase of left-wing politicians, but the basic sentiment is biblical. We are a human family because in biblical thought we are physically descended from one couple. Each of us can trace, in theory, a direct lineage to Adam and Eve. When I was a medical student, the concept that all of the several billion humans on the planet were descended from a single couple was greeted with cries of derision by scientists. The biblical account was touchingly naïve, if not laughable. It seemed obvious to students of evolution that the human race must have evolved at multiple times and in multiple places from a range of hominid ancestors. But the recent advent of detailed DNA analysis has allowed the genetic relationship between different human beings on the earth to be investigated much more precisely. As Professor Steve Jones puts it, 'To a geneticist, everyone is a living fossil . . . Genes recreate history, not just since humans appeared on earth, but since the origin of life itself' (S. Jones 1993: 127). By making assumptions about the rate of spontaneous mutations in DNA, geneticists have estimated that modern humans, *Homo sapiens sapiens*, are a relatively recent innovation, probably appearing on the planet less than 200,000 years ago.

The evidence is incontrovertible that genetic variation is much greater in African populations than elsewhere, strongly suggesting that *Homo sapiens* had been present longer in Africa than anywhere else. Most population geneticists now support the 'out of Africa' hypothesis, which holds that there was a single origin for modern humans in Africa less than 200,000 years ago. Current evidence suggests that modern humans migrated out of Africa some sixty to seventy thousand years ago and dispersed all over the globe. In fact, although still the subject of fierce controversy, the current evidence from population genetics is consistent with the biblical view that all human beings are descended from one male individual and one female individual. Interestingly, there is no definite genetic evidence that modern humans, *Homo sapiens sapiens*, interbred with pre-existing hominid populations such as the Neanderthals, although the fossil record strongly suggests that they must have coexisted in certain regions.

There are obvious difficulties in relating the modern genetic and anthropological evidence to the biblical account of the creation of Adam and Eve, and many unsolved questions remain. How does the African origin of humans fit with the biblical location of the Garden of Eden in Mesopotamia, for instance, and how does genetic dating fit with biblical chronology? I am not able to address these issues here. If our common human ancestors did exist less than 200,000 years ago, however, they would have looked virtually identical to modern humans. If we could meet them we would recognize the family likeness. We must treat the biblical narrative with due seriousness. Human beings are both theologically and, it seems, in genetic reality a single extended family. Not only do we carry the mysterious image of God; we also carry the image of our distant grandparents, Adam and Eve. This is the meaning of the biblical phrase 'in Adam'. 'As in Adam all die, so in Christ all will be made alive' (1 Cor. 15:22). Adam is the representative of the human race because he is our great-great-great-grandfather. We have an *organic solidarity* with him.

Not only that, but when I meet another human being, whether it is down the street or in the distant jungles of Borneo or the Amazon rainforest, I am meeting a distant relation. That is why I can recognize the family likeness. The rules that should govern human relationships, then, are family rules. We must treat even the stranger with care, with respect, with affection and with generosity. Why? Because *we are family*.

Creation mandates and creation order

In the Genesis creation narrative, having created human beings to be his representatives, God blesses them and then gives them their instructions, like a king providing a mandate for his governor (Gn. 1:28–30). First comes blessing, the wonderful, liberal giving of our Creator. In the old saying, 'the best things in life are free'. But why is this? Because the best things in life have been bountifully given, extravagantly poured out on us, by our Creator. In the created order, Adam and Eve are given an astonishing degree of freedom and liberty to enjoy the gifts of the creation. But after being blessed, they are given creation mandates. 'Be fruitful and increase in number; fill the earth and subdue it. Rule over the fish of the sea and the birds of the air and over every living creature that moves on the ground' (Gn. 1:28). In the parallel creation account in Genesis 2, Adam is placed in the Garden of Eden 'to work it and to take care of it' (2:15). Although the basic creation order has been established by God, then, the work of creation is not completed. It is up to God's authorized representatives to continues and fulfil what God has initiated.

Notice that the creation mandates are given *jointly* to male and female, as an illustration of the partnership for which they were created. There is no clear evidence of division of labour prior to the fall and the terrible curses of Genesis 3. Human beings are jointly instructed, first to procreate, to fill the vast emptiness of the earth; secondly to subdue the earth, to impose order on to its chaotic elements; and thirdly to cultivate, to bring out the potential that God has placed within the creation. God is the Creator; humans are the cultivators.

The creation narrative goes on to give a beautiful poetic description of the search for Adam's partner, because 'It is not good for the man to be alone' (Gn. 2:18). In all the animal kingdom no suitable partner is found, and so the woman is created out of the body of the man. (One of the ancient commentators wrote that Eve was taken, not out of Adam's head to rule over him, or out of his feet to be dominated, but out of his side to be his companion.) Then comes Adam's joyful cry of recognition: 'This is now bone of my bones and flesh of my flesh' (2:23). Immediately after this comes the most-quoted text on marriage: 'For this reason a man will leave his father and mother and be united [cleave] to his wife, and they will become one flesh' (2:24). This passage implies that the union of man and woman in marriage is in some poetic sense a *reunion*, the recreation of a mysterious unity that was severed at the beginning of time. In other words, man and woman were created or designed for each other; we are complementary; we fit together, not just in the obvious physical sense but in the very nature of our beings. When we come together in marriage and in any form of male–female partnership, there is therefore a sense of naturalness. This is how it was meant to be.

In the Genesis account the literal Hebrew for the act of sexual intercourse was the verb 'to know'. 'Adam knew Eve his wife' (Gn. 4:1, Authorized Version). Part of the creation order is that in the intimate knowing and self-giving of sexual intercourse lies our ability to pass on our created image to our children. In God's plan, making love and making babies are inextricably linked.

Finally, God respects the moral integrity of human beings by giving them freedom to enjoy the rich diversity of his creation. 'You are free to eat from any tree in the garden . . .' (Gn. 2:16). But there are limits to freedom: of all the riches of the garden, there is one fruit which is forbidden: '. . . but you must not eat from the tree of the knowledge of good and evil, for when you eat of it you will surely die' (2:17). Human freedom can operate only within the limits set by God. This is the difference between human freedom (freedom within the limits set by our physical design and by the moral order) and Godlike freedom (freedom without limits, except those set by God's own unchanging character).

The biblical concept that God has placed a hidden moral order within the design of the creation is of central importance for a Christian view of ethics. God has not only created the physical structures of creation, including the physical structure of our bodies. He has also created a hidden moral order which directs how those structures should be used; in other words, how we should behave. It is as though there is a hidden 'grain' within all creation. If we live our lives 'along' the grain, behaving in a way which is consonant with the created moral order, then our lives will work and we shall flourish. This is what the Bible calls the 'way of wisdom' (as in Pr. 4:10–13, for example: 'Listen my son, accept what I say, and the years of your life will be many. I guide you in the way of wisdom and lead you along straight paths. When you walk, your steps will not be hampered; when you run, you will not stumble'). So wisdom, wise living, is living in accordance with the hidden moral order of the universe. God imprints his moral order in the design of the creation and makes his image-bearers rational and morally responsible, capable of both understanding and responding freely to God's commands.

The concept of a created moral order is central to an authentically biblical worldview. To most secular philosophers, morality is imposed on reality by the human mind. Ethical values are a human invention, part of human storytelling. But in biblical thought, the moral order is a part of objective reality. It is an aspect of the way that the world is made. This is why what philosophers call the fact/value distinction (see chapter 11) does not fit with a biblical worldview.

God created the physical universe – the facts – and God created the hidden moral structure of the universe – the values. The two are intimately related within the mysterious design of the cosmos.

If human beings live their lives in a way that is inconsistent with the created moral order, against the hidden grain of creation, their lives will not 'work'; they will find disaster. And of course this is exactly what happened.

Fall

At the heart of the account of the fall in Genesis 3 is a rejection by human beings of the creation order that God has instituted for their enjoyment and well-being. Adam and Eve strike a blow for moral autonomy independent of God. By eating the fruit which had been forbidden, they discover the catastrophic consequences of disobedience. The stark words of Proverbs 14:12 summarize the consequences of human autonomy detached from creation order: 'There is a way that seems right to a man, but in the end it leads to death.'

Although God's image is defaced, the biblical revelation makes it plain that it is not destroyed (Gn. 9:6; Ja. 3:9). Human beings are still Godlike beings, but our humanity is fatally contaminated and distorted by evil. In Pascal's words, 'Man is the glory and the shame of the universe.' C. S. Lewis said through Aslan: 'You come of the Lord Adam and the Lady Eve, and that is both honour enough to erect the head of the poorest beggar and shame enough to bow the shoulders of the greatest emperor on earth' (Lewis 1962: 185).

Although the universe is fractured and broken, a crucial part of biblical understanding is that the universe still displays the moral order, the hidden grain. Its brokenness is the brokenness of order, and not chaos (O'Donovan 1994: 88). The terrible three-fold curse which God pronounces after the fall (Gn. 3:14–19) brings home the reality of the human condition contaminated by evil.

Death and decay

As God had warned them, the disobedience of Adam and Eve led directly to the entrance of death into the world: '. . . for when you eat of it you will surely die'. In the poetic imagery of the creation narratives, within the Garden of Eden Adam and Eve had access, not only to almost all the other fruit within the garden, but also to the tree of life. They could have chosen to eat the fruit of that tree and live for ever. Instead, they chose to disobey God and eat the fruit of the one tree that was forbidden. By giving access to the fruit of the tree of life, God showed that his original intention for human beings was everlasting life.

In biblical thought, the death of human beings, in all its horror and mystery, is not 'natural', it is not part of God's original design. In fact, death is seen as a punishment which is inflicted on humankind because of our moral disobedience (Rom. 5:12; see also Stott 1994: 162–166). The deep intuition which most of us share, that physical death (especially the death of a child or young person) is an outrage, an alien interruption in the nature of being, coupled with the inexpressible longing we have for eternity, reflects the original creation order. We were not intended to die; we were made to live for ever. That is why death is the 'last enemy' (1 Cor. 15:26). It seems futile to speculate on what would have happened if human beings had not disobeyed. What is clear is that, in biblical thought, human death is not part of God's creation order; it is a mysterious and terrible interruption in the nature of being. And because human beings are 'in Adam', we have an organic physical solidarity with him. We too are subject to death and decay.

C. S. Lewis once pointed out how strange it is that human beings are constantly surprised by the passage of time, despite the fact that we spend the whole of our lives within time. 'It is as strange as if a fish were repeatedly surprised by the wetness of water. And that would be strange indeed; unless of course the fish was destined to become, one day, a land animal' (Lewis 1961: 115).

We may detect an echo of this in the biological understanding of human ageing and death. It is interesting that death is not a biological necessity. Every living cell and organism is equipped with the essential machinery to ensure repair and renewal so that life can continue indefinitely. Surprising as it may seem, eternal life is not a biological impossibility! In one sense, although individual cells are destined to die, organisms seem to be designed to live for ever. The ageing process involves active biological mechanisms, as yet very poorly understood, which cause the repair and renewal processes to malfunction, leading ultimately to biological decay and death. Perhaps this is a physical counterpart of the biblical truth that through human evil, the creation is in 'bondage to decay' (Rom. 8:21).

The inevitable accompaniment of death is fear. The blessing of human life is transformed into a slavery of fear, especially fear of death. The terrible, all-pervading fear of death drives human beings to extraordinary and frequently pathetic lengths. Perhaps the most bizarre example is seen in those who arrange for their bodies to be deep-frozen in liquid nitrogen in the forlorn hope that a future generation will discover the elixir of eternal life. But, as we saw in chapter 1, in less obvious ways the fear of death drives both medical research and our desperate attempts to use technology to prolong life.

There is a better answer to the fear of death. As the writer to the Hebrews states, Christ came to 'free those who all their lives were held in slavery by their fear of death' (Heb. 2:15). For all its terror and mystery, in the biblical worldview death is not an entirely negative concept. It may be, in C. S. Lewis's wonderful phrase, ' a severe mercy'. At the end of the account of the fall, human beings are banished from the Garden of Eden, precisely to prevent their eating the fruit of the tree of life and living for ever. And to prevent their return and capture of the fruit by force of arms, cherubim and a flaming sword are set to guard the way to the tree of life (Gn. 3:21–24). In God's providential care of his creation, then, human beings are not meant to live for ever in their degraded fallen state. The human lifespan is limited, not just as a curse, but *out of God's grace*.

Later on in the book of Genesis, because of the escalating wickedness of the human race, human longevity is limited to 120 years (Gn. 6:3); and Psalm 90, attributed traditionally to Moses, teaches that because of human sinfulness, 'the length of our days is seventy years – or eighty, if we have the strength; yet their span is but trouble and sorrow, for they quickly pass, and we fly away' (verse 10). The psalmist expresses grief and regret at the evanescence of human existence and the need to take this into account. 'Teach us to number our days aright, that we may gain a heart of wisdom' (verse 12).

In God's providence, death may be a merciful release from an existence trapped in a fallen and decaying body. Christian attitudes to death should reflect a curious ambivalence. We need to retain, first, a sense of outrage at its alien destructive character; secondly, an acceptance that the end of physical life may be evidence of God's grace, a 'severe mercy'; and finally a sense of future hope in the knowledge that ultimately death will be destroyed (as we shall see below). Christian healthcare professionals are called to struggle against death while recognizing the ultimate futility of their struggle and seeking to discern when active life-sustaining treatment may become inappropriate, when the dying process becomes a severe mercy, even a strange form of healing.

Futility

The entrance of death into human life condemns our physical existence to an awful futility. Humans are condemned to return to the ground from which they are taken. 'Dust you are and to dust you will return' (Gn. 2:19). In the poetic yet bleak words of the Anglican funeral service, the futile cycle of human existence is exposed, 'ashes to ashes, dust to dust'. So the dust of the ground which is both the origin of our human bodies and the source of their food becomes a symbol of their eventual decay and death.

The futility of human existence is expressed most powerfully by the Preacher, the writer of the book of Ecclesiastes, whose bleak perspective on life is limited to the natural world – 'life under the sun', as he puts it. 'I have seen all the things that are done under the sun; all of them are meaningless, a chasing after the wind' (Ec. 1:14). 'This is the evil in everything that happens under the sun: The same destiny overtakes all. The hearts of men, moreover, are full of evil and there is madness in their hearts while they live, and afterwards they join the dead' (Ec. 9:3).

The reality of death traps humans beings in the same cycle of futility as the rest of the animal world. 'As for men, God tests them so that they may see that they are like the animals. Man's fate is like that of the animals; the same fate awaits them both: As one dies, so dies the other. All have the same breath; man has no advantage over the animal. Everything is meaningless. All go to the same place; all come from the dust, and to dust all return' (Ec. 3:18–20).

The futility and grief of physical ageing, its progressive decay and biological malfunction, are also graphically illustrated by the Preacher at the end of Ecclesiastes (12:1–8). They are 'days of trouble . . . when you will say "I find no pleasure in them."' To the Preacher ageing brings darkness, physical weakness, fear, disability, apathy and loss of libido ('desire no longer is stirred'), before death brings its inevitable release. The biblical revelation is unsparing in its bleak depiction of the cycle of human life from an earthly perspective. We have come a long way from the creation blessings of Genesis 1 – 2.

This perspective helps us to retain a sense of the limitations of medicine and healthcare. For all our wonderful knowledge and technology, we are unable to redeem our physical bodies from the cycle of death and decay. There can be no technological or biological fix for the ultimate mysteries of the human condition. We cannot, by medical technology, overcome ageing and eventual death. In God's providential mercy, that route to the tree of life remains blocked by a flashing sword.

Suffering

'I will greatly increase your pains in childbearing; with pain you will give birth to children' (Gn. 3:16). In the past, some biblical commentators took this verse to imply that the pain of childbirth should not be combated. As a result, the introduction of obstetric anaesthesia was vigorously opposed by some. (Predictably enough, they were nearly all men.) It was not until Queen Victoria herself was treated with chloroform during delivery that obstetric anaesthesia became widely accepted. But it seems clear that the pains of childbirth described in this verse are merely illustrative of the physical and mental anguish which has invaded not only the experience of human procreation but also every other aspect of our created human experience.

Yet, like death, suffering in biblical thought is not an entirely negative phenomenon. To the secular mind suffering is a futile, bewildering and purposeless reality. It is the negation of all that is good in life. It is the destroyer of autonomy – an evil to be feared and avoided at all cost. But in the biblical worldview, suffering can never be meaningless, even if it seems so. We must cling by faith to the belief that suffering comes from the hand of a loving God, even despite appearances. In the experience of Job, physical suffering was revealed both as the destructive activity of Satan the accuser, and as a divinely authorized plan, to test the reality of Job's commitment to God. The book of Job has a great deal to teach us about human suffering. I believe it is particularly relevant in an age which has lost a belief in any positive aspect of suffering. Christians too have been affected by this secular disease. One of the greatest needs of the church today is to rediscover a biblical theology of suffering.

As psychologists have frequently pointed out, at the heart of suffering is *loss*. Job loses his family, his wealth, his security, his social status. And the final blow is the loss of his own bodily integrity. He is covered in 'painful sores from the soles of his feet to the top of his head' (Jb. 2:7). For thirty long chapters of theological argument Job protests his outrage at God's apparently capricious dealings, while his so-called friends try to persuade him that the root of his suffering is some hidden sin in his life. To Job's friends there is a clear explanation for his experience. Their simplistic theology relates suffering to guilt. But Job begins not with theological principles but with his own experience – suffering bequeathed capriciously by a silent and unaccountable God, an experience of chaos and meaninglessness. Job calls upon God for the opportunity to question him face to face.

Eventually God's prolonged silence is ended. He answers Job 'out of the whirlwind' (38:1, Revised Standard Version). As commentators have pointed out, for the first time since the prologue, the author uses the covenant name, Yahweh (the LORD). God reveals himself not as a capricious and unaccountable deity, but as the gracious and faithful Lord of the covenant. He does not rebuke Job for his temerity; rather, he rebukes his friends for their trite and blasphemous theology. God, however, *provides no explanation* for Job's suffering. Instead, he points to his own creative freedom and concern for all creation. The world expresses the freedom and delight of God. In place of the human-centred perspective of Job and his comforters, God gives glimpses of a radically different viewpoint. The cosmos does not exist merely for human beings, and the meaning of human suffering cannot be fathomed within a limited, anthropocentric worldview. When confronted by human suffering, like Job's friends we frequently have an overwhelming desire to provide neat explanations. 'This happened because of that . . . God is teaching you to . . .' Instead, we should learn from the book of Job. There can be no human explanations for the mystery of suffering – only the presence of a loving and suffering God.

The corruption of technology: the Tower of Babel

As the Genesis narrative unfolds, we see the gradual escalation of human folly and wickedness. Cain's jealous hatred of his brother erupts into murder. Wickedness spreads across the earth and is destroyed in the flood. And then comes the tragi-comedy of the Tower of Babel (Gn. 11:1–9). As Vinoth Ramachandra points out, 'the story of Babel is the story of Eden all over again, but the difference is between the individual deed and the collective act' (Ramachandra 1996a: 131).

Prior to Babel, several characters in the Adamic family had initiated different aspects of human work. Jabal was the father of all those who live in tents and raise livestock. Jubal was the father of all who play the harp and flute. Tubal-Cain forged all kinds of tools out of bronze and iron (Gn. 4:19–22). To the author of the narrative, it is likely that these characters are living out the creation mandates, subduing the earth and bringing out the wonderfully diverse potential locked in the raw material of the earth. In pictorial form this is the earliest reference to human artifice, to primitive technology.

At Babel we see a darker side to technology. The builders are driven by a two-fold desire: to 'make a name for ourselves' and to avoid being 'scattered over the face of the whole earth' (11:4). Ramachandra suggests that Babel is the marriage of three human dreams: the technological (to build a city that would be the envy of gods and nations), the religious (to divinize humankind by reaching up into the heavens) and the political (to build a totalitarian society based on technology). Babel symbolizes the use of human artefacts, technology, to celebrate human autonomy. The words 'Come, let us build . . .' (11:4) echo the very words of God in making human beings: 'let us make man in our image . . .' (1:26).

Babel symbolizes the myth of technology which recognizes no limits to human technical possibilities – technology that is used to seize God's rightful place as creator, and to overturn creation order. It is a story of human collective action, a unity which ends in confusion and dispersion. But the confusion created by God is both an act of judgment and, again, an act of mercy. The unfinished tower stands as a monument to the folly of human arrogance, and a sign of the mercy of a God who intervenes to prevent a technological dream (or nightmare) coming to fruition.

Redemption

Even as God pronounces the terrible curses in the Garden, the first glimmering of the gospel hope of redemption is seen. God promises that the offspring of the woman will come to crush the serpent's head (Gn. 3:15). Later, God enters into a solemn covenant with Abraham, promising to bless him and, through his children, ultimately bless all the nations of the earth (Gn. 12:2–3; 17.3–8). The giving of the law at Mount Sinai symbolizes the justice and mercy which lie at the heart of God's gracious covenant with his people. The Old Testament laws are not the arbitrary commands of a desert god. They are the Maker's instructions, endorsing and protecting the hidden moral order of the creation. They reinforce the equality of all human beings before God, and uphold the sanctity or inviolability of all human life.

Defending the defenceless

A beautiful expression of God's grace and mercy is found in the Deuteronomic law. In Deuteronomy 10 the mighty Yahweh is revealed as the defender of the defenceless. 'For the LORD [Yahweh] your God is God of gods and Lord of lords, the great God, mighty and awesome, who shows no partiality and accepts no bribes. He defends the cause of the fatherless and the widow, and loves the alien, giving him food and clothing. And you are to love those who are aliens, for you yourselves were aliens in Egypt' (Dt. 10:17–18).

There is a striking contrast in this passage between the person of Yahweh in his absolute power, and his gracious concern to defend the nobodies of society. The significant triad of widows, orphans and aliens recurs many times throughout the Scriptures. They symbolize those who were most *vulnerable* in the social structures of ancient Israel. The widow had no husband to defend her from abuse and hardship; the orphan had no parent; the alien or immigrant had no community, no religious or family structures to fall back on. All three were uniquely open to all kinds of abuse within society: physical violence, psychological manipulation, economic sharp practice and the effects of corruption. To the triad of the widows, orphans and aliens, the Old Testament also added the poor (as in Pr. 22:22), because of their *economic* vulnerability.

Yahweh, then, declares himself the defender of the socially defenceless, and calls on his people to defend them in his name. A particular responsibility was laid on rulers to create social structures that protected the weak. Jeremiah referred to the righteous reign of King Josiah. 'He defended the cause of the poor and the needy, and so all went well. Is that not what it means to know me?' declares Yahweh (Je. 22:16). Here, the knowledge of God is defined as practical concern for the defenceless in society. In the New Testament, James carries on the same theme. 'Religion that God our Father accepts as pure and faultless is this: to look after orphans and widows in their distress . . .' (Jas. 1:27).

As we debate the appropriate use of medical technology, a special responsibility rests on us, the strong, to defend the vulnerable in our midst. Who are the modern counterparts of the widow, orphan and alien? The God revealed in Scripture is committed to be their defender and calls on us to protect them from abuse in his name. The fetus, the newborn infant, the disabled child, the brain-damaged adult, the elderly sufferer with Alzheimer's disease, and the psychiatric patient – we do not have to look far to find them. Will we receive the commendation that Josiah received: 'This is what it means to know me . . .'?

Christ, the Word made flesh
In Christ, God affirms and fulfils the original creation

When God breaks into human history to bring redemption to his fallen people, does he overturn the created order he has previously established to introduce a completely new kind of reality, a radically new creation? No. God reveals himself as *a human being*, a Mark I, original human model. Christians treat the human body with special respect. Why? Because this strange and idiosyncratic collection of 100,000 genes, 10 billion nerve cells, several miles of wiring, 8 metres of intestinal plumbing, 5 litres of blood, and assorted biochemical engineering – this is the form in which God became flesh!

In the incarnation, death and resurrection of Christ, the created order is both re-established and fulfilled. Before the resurrection it might have been possible for someone to wonder whether creation itself was a lost cause: perhaps the only possible ending for the tragic story of a fallen creation is God's final judgment and destruction of the created order. But when Christ is raised as a *physical human being*, God proclaims his vote of confidence in the created order (see O'Donovan 1994: 53–75).

Jesus shares in the stuff of creation. His body, like ours, is made from dust. The gospel writers go to great lengths to stress Christ's full humanity. He is tired, angry, hungry, distressed, in agony . . . And in the resurrection of Christ, the physical creation is not overturned but subsumed, or caught up, into a greater and richer reality. In Jesus, the Second Adam, we see both a perfect human being (what the original Adam was meant to be) and the pioneer, the blueprint for a new type of person, the one in whose likeness a new creation will spring, the firstfruits of those who are to come (1 Cor. 15:20). Our humanity is not something which comes between us and God. No, it is the means by which God is made known.

' "Destroy this temple [said Jesus], and I will raise it again in three days" . . .' But the temple he had spoken of was his body' (Jn. 2:19, 21). Here is an exalted view of the human body – a temple. If Christ's body was a temple, then I must treat all bodies with a new reverence.

Furthermore, Jesus comes not as a sovereign king, as Caesar or Herod, the symbol of human power and authority. He comes as a defenceless and utterly *dependent* baby. We can no longer view the state of dependence as being less than fully human, because Jesus has been dependent in the same way. Jesus shares the created stuff of our humanity, and the narrative of a human life. As Gilbert Meilander puts it, 'Jesus has been with us in darkness of the womb as he will be with us in the darkness of the tomb' (Meilander 1997: 30).

In Christ, God reveals a deeper and richer reality

Jesus both shows us the importance of the physical body and also points to something that is even more important: the life of the Spirit. He shows us that the physical is not the only or the most important part of reality. As Jesus interacted with hurting people, he not only made blind eyes see and lame legs walk. He healed their relationships, their fears – and on the cross he healed their spiritual alienation from God himself. So Christians affirm the importance of physical healing, while recognizing that behind the physical body lies a deeper, richer, even more wonderful reality.

This means that we cannot make the extension of physical life by intrusive technology the ultimate goal of medicine. Sometimes we have to say no to medical progress. Sometimes we shall need the trust and the courage that enable us to decline what medical technology makes possible. This physical body is not all there is; we need a deeper healing.

In Christ, we see a new way to love, the way of self-giving

Jesus was not just a preacher, a talker, a teller of parables. He did not just sit on the Mount of Olives and instruct people how to live. He entered into the experience of pain, suffering, loneliness, emptiness and despair. Together the incarnation and the cross are the ultimate expression of *empathy*. God himself entered fully into the experience of being a human being. He experienced humanity *from the inside*.

As John Stott writes, 'Christ laid aside his immunity to pain' (Stott 1986: 336). And in doing so, he showed the paradoxical nature of God's love. God's love is love that gives; it is self-sacrificial, costly love. It is a practical love, down to earth, washing feet. As Jesus entered into the mystery of human suffering, he gave us a model of how we can care for others who are suffering – not by providing neat answers to the questions raised by human pain, but by *being there*. In the words of an anonymous writer, 'Suffering is not a question that demands an answer; it is not a problem that demands a solution; it is a mystery which demands a *presence*.'

If we want to care for people as Jesus cared for people, we have to give ourselves, we have to pay a price. We have to show genuine empathy, to enter into and experience the pain of the other. There is an old Christian proverb: 'He who would be Christ must expect a cross.'

Consummation

Christian caring does not stop at the agony of the cross. It is shot through with hope, expectation and longing for the future. The resurrection of Christ points towards the future of humanity. The gospel writers go to great lengths to emphasize the physical reality of Christ's restored body. He eats and drinks. He breaks bread. He talks. He is touched. He is recognized by his friends. His body even bears physical scars. It is as though the man Jesus is given back to his circle of human friends. So in one sense the resurrection looks back to Jesus' human life on earth. But in the same resurrection we also see that the physical man has been subsumed by the spiritual. The man of dust has been subsumed by the heavenly man. 'The resurrection appearances are encounters with divine power and authority. Humanity is elevated to that which it has never enjoyed before, the seat at God's right hand which belongs to his Son' (O'Donovan 1994: 56–57).

Christ's resurrection, then, points backward to the creation of human beings and forward to the transformation of human beings at the same time. Our humanity is both vindicated and transformed. In God's mysterious purpose, this is what human beings were always intended to become. This is the ultimate goal of the created order. As Paul writes: 'just as we have borne the image of the earthly man, so we shall bear the likeness of the man from heaven' (1 Cor. 15:49). The image of God inherited from Adam will be fulfilled and transformed into a new and much more glorious image. Yes, we shall still be reflections. We shall not lose our creaturely dependence. But we shall discover the true likeness that we were always intended to bear.

Not only that, but, in the future, it seems that humanity will regain its rightful place of rule over the created order, so that the original plan of humanity's role in the blessing of all creation will be fulfilled. For 'the created order . . . cannot be itself while it lacks the authoritative and beneficent rule that man was to give it' (O'Donovan 1994: 55).

Perhaps this seems like abstruse and speculative theology. What possible relevance can it have to the practical medical dilemmas that we face? Let me suggest just two practical outworkings.

We can make sense of the present only in the light of the future

When the apostle Paul talks about the resurrection of the body, he uses the dramatic image of the seed and the flower. 'The body that is sown is perishable, it is raised imperishable; it is sown in dishonour, it is raised in glory; it is sown in weakness, it is raised in power; it is sown a natural body, it is raised a spiritual body' (1 Cor. 15:42–44). The image is familiar and we easily lose its power. But if we had never seen a tiny brown seed transform into a wonderful flower, we would never believe it was possible.

Yet the transformation is a commonplace of the natural creation. And modern molecular biology has revealed the power of that image. In the tiny and pathetic brown husk is packed all the DNA, all the information, that is required to make the miraculous flower.

In my job as a paediatrician, I have the privilege of caring for babies who are dying. It is part of my job; it is what I am there for. I have held the body of a dead baby in my arms and wept together with the parents at an overwhelming sense of helplessness, of emptiness, of outrage, at this cruel, untimely death. And nearly every time I have this experience, I take comfort from Isaiah's wonderful description of the new heaven and the new earth:

> . . . be glad and rejoice for ever
>   in what I will create,
> for I will create Jerusalem to be a delight . . .
> I will rejoice over Jerusalem
>   and take delight in my people;
> the sound of weeping and of crying
>   will be heard in it no more.
>
> Never again will there be in it
>   an infant who lives but a few days,
>   or an old man who does not live out his years.
>
> (Is. 65:18–20)

God himself recognizes the peculiar outrage of an infant death. That is the Christian hope; and it is what this particular paediatrician longs for. That day is coming: the day when never again will there be an infant who lives but a few days. Just a few weeks ago, I shared the loss of another baby's death, and as I sat in a rather weepy silence with the family (who shared a strong Christian faith), the passage in Revelation came into my mind: 'Now the dwelling of God is with men [humans] and he will live with them . . . He will wipe away every tear from their eyes. There will be no more death or mourning or crying or pain, for the old order of things has passed away' (Rev. 21:3–4).

God will wipe away every tear from their eyes. It suddenly struck me what a remarkable image this is. It is not a picture of the majestic, all-powerful, glorious God. No, this is a picture of a weeping child, of a mother's lap, and the gentle stroking of a loving hand across a tear-stained face. This is our God, the one we will meet; this is our hope. Only this future makes sense of the present.

We can dare to act only in the light of the future

A fellow paediatrician, with whom I worked closely over many years, once said to me: 'You know, it's easier for you than it is for me, John. When I'm looking after a dying baby I'm sending them into the ground, into oblivion. When you're looking after a dying baby, you're sending them to heaven.'

It was meant as a joke, but we both knew it was true. Maybe it is easier for the Christian doctor who can act in the light of the future. I can dare to act, to take the really hard and painful clinical decisions – about withdrawing intensive treatment in a dying baby, for example, or decisions concerned with recognizing the point at which medical treatment becomes futile and meddlesome, and when death may be a strange kind of healing. We can dare to act because of the Christian hope, because of the new day which is dawning – because death has been ultimately defeated.

To the secular philosopher, life starts from nothing. It rises to a peak, to a brief flowering of autonomy, of pleasure, of meaning in the middle of life. And then it gradually declines into decay, dissolution and finally death. It rises to a crescendo and then slowly fades away into nothingness. But the Christian view of a human life transformed by God's power is totally different. It is a slow and growing crescendo. It is a journey, a pilgrimage, which starts from nothing but grows and grows: 'The path of the righteous is like the first gleam of dawn, shining ever brighter till the full light of day' (Pr. 4:18).

I have tried to give a brief panoramic overview of the biblical teaching about humanness. These are the principles which must guide us as we attempt to tackle the complex and ever-changing dilemmas of modern healthcare. In the next chapter we look at advances in reproductive technology and ask how biblical principles can be applied to the creation of new human lives.

3. Reproductive technology and the start of life

The ethical dilemmas that both doctors and parents face at the start of life are particularly complex and troubling. They have led to a ferocious debate which continues to rage in public and in private. This is especially obvious when we look at the painful subject of legalized abortion. In the USA, doctors working at abortion clinics have been assaulted and even murdered, rival demonstrators have fought each other, and hospitals and clinics have been fire-bombed. Although there has not been the same level of violence in the UK, the debate has at times become unpleasant, polarized and even vitriolic. Even the language has become a battleground. Do we talk about the fetus or the unborn child? About terminating a pregnancy or murdering unborn babies?

Sometimes, in the attempt to win the public-relations battle, Christian people have resorted to harsh rhetoric, negative campaigning and questionable publicity tactics. I strongly believe there is a better way to tackle these issues. If we are aiming to put forward a Christian perspective on these disturbing questions, we have not only to explain Christian ideas, we have to present them in a Christian way. That means speaking the truth in an honest but also a gentle and respectful manner. If we are to act with Christian integrity, the way in which we speak on these issues is just as important as what we actually say.

Above everything else, the dilemmas at the beginning of life are matters of extreme personal pain. Whenever we discuss infertility or abortion or handicapped babies, we are treading on other people's secret sorrows. Here are three terrible and sad problems: first, the lack of a baby who is desperately wanted; secondly, the baby who is developing but is desperately *un*wanted; and finally the baby who is severely handicapped, and will never live a normal life. They are tragedies which go back to the dawn of time; they are recorded in the biblical narrative and in other ancient literature. They are part of the human condition. These are not issues 'out there', that affect other people, but issues that affect us all, including those reading this book.

In the UK it is estimated that approximately one in four of all women between eighteen and forty has had an abortion, up to one couple in seven is unable to have children without medical help, and about one child in twenty-five has a significant disability or congenital malformation. Many of us are carrying secret and painful sorrows from our past which we cannot share with others. Indeed, every one of us is carrying genetic flaws and misprints which are likely to affect any children we have. None of us is immune from tragedy. So before all else, our responsibility is to try to empathize, to enter into the experience of people in our midst who are hurting.

First we turn to the problem of infertility.

Infertility and reproductive technology
The pain of infertility

The development of reproductive technology has brought to light the depth and extent of the pain felt by infertile couples within our society. A 1997 report from the National Infertility Awareness Campaign gave the results from a survey of one thousand infertile people. One in five said they had contemplated suicide while waiting for fertility treatment. Depression, isolation and frustration were reported by more than nine out of ten of those surveyed. One in three said that the relationship with their partner had been adversely affected by the result of their failure to conceive. Adding to the pressure of trying to have a baby were the financial and psychological consequences of undergoing fertility treatments. The sense of despair and isolation felt by couples is revealed by their willingness to spend large amounts of money and undergo the prolonged stress of repeated and sometimes increasingly desperate attempts to have a child.

Infertility is a silent suffering, largely ignored by the rest of society and by the Christian community. Yet unless we understand the experience of infertility, at least in part, we cannot make sense of the extraordinary pressure on doctors and biological scientists to employ increasingly technological methods to make babies. In his book *Trying for a Baby* (1996), Pete Moore outlines some of the factors. There is the family-orientated nature of modern society, including family-orientated churches, and the isolation from peer groups which infertility brings; the subtle pressure from well-meaning friends and relatives; the desire to give love to a child and the sense of loss when that love is thwarted; a feeling of 'genetic death' as a result of making no contribution to the next generation; the tension between partners which spills over into needless arguments and disputes; the loss of self-esteem and a feeling of biological failure. One woman described her menstrual periods as her body's way of mocking her hopes of pregnancy.

It is not being over-dramatic to say that infertility can be a form of bereavement; a loss that is ongoing and repetitive. It is ironic that while the very existence of reproductive technology offers a possible solution to those experiencing this bereavement, it also prevents acceptance and healing. The desperate but thwarted desire for a pregnancy is kept alive for years by the hope that maybe, just maybe, the next cycle of treatment will work.

Human reproductive technology has thus developed not because doctors and scientists have been consumed by an overwhelming desire to 'play God', but because of pressure from ordinary people with a desperate wish for a child. Although the problem of childlessness is an intricate web of biological, psychological, human and social factors and pressures, technology, as so often, offers a 'quick fix' for complex human issues. It is a theme which recurs constantly in medical ethics. Technology offers apparently neat solutions to the fundamental problems of the human condition. Unfortunately the last hundred years have taught us that the solutions which technology offers may come with a higher price tag than we had imagined.

The development of in vitro fertilization

When I was a medical student in the 1970s, virtually the only form of technological assistance for infertile couples was the use of artificial insemination, either by husband (AIH) or by anonymous donor (AID, now usually called donor insemination, DI). But the work of embryologist Dr Robert Edwards showed that it was possible to fertilize mouse eggs in the laboratory and reimplant them into a mouse uterus. A few years later he showed that it was possible to fertilize human eggs with human sperm and grow the embryos in a laboratory dish for several days – *in vitro* fertilization (IVF). Edwards struck up a collaboration with Patrick Steptoe, a gynaecologist from Oldham in the north of England, who was looking for ways to help his infertile patients. Steptoe reimplanted the embryos created by Edwards into the wombs of a number of his patients. After numerous failures, their perseverance was met with spectacular success. On 25 July 1978, Louise Brown, the world's first 'test-tube baby', was born in Oldham District General Hospital. One commentator has described this birth as 'a singular moment in human evolution' (Silver 1997: 67). Steptoe and Edwards were the founding fathers of a new science of reproductive technology.

From a single birth in a British hospital, the use of IVF has rapidly expanded worldwide. In 1993 there were 267 clinics in the USA alone, providing IVF services. In the UK, the Human Fertilization and Embryology Authority reported that in the fifteen months from January 1995 to March 1996, there were some 37,000 attempts at IVF treatment in almost 27,000 mothers. These resulted in 6,800 pregnancies and 5,500 live births, at a total cost of about £75 million. Almost one third of the births were of twins or triplets (leading to a greatly increased risk of complications) (HFEA, Sixth Annual Report).

By 1994, more than thirty-eight countries had established IVF programmes, including Malaysia, Pakistan, Thailand, Egypt, Venezuela and Turkey. In the same year it was estimated that, worldwide, about 150,000 children had been born following IVF (see Silver 1997: 69–70). (Remarkably, most of those children are still under seven years old at the time of writing.) Lee Silver estimated that if IVF services continue to expand at a comparable rate, by 2005 there could be more than 500,000 IVF babies born annually in the USA alone, and millions more worldwide (1997: 69). It has been estimated that, at present, there are more than two million couples in the USA alone who want to have a child and yet remain infertile, so there is remarkable potential for growth in the use of IVF.

There are also substantial commercial profits to be made. In a typical IVF clinic in the USA, a couple may spend between $44,000 and $200,000 to achieve a single pregnancy, and surveys have shown that reproductive specialists are among the highest-earning doctors in the US.

IVF changes our view of ourselves

Not only has IVF provided a means of providing children for infertile couples, it has provided laboratory access to the human egg and the human embryo, enabling embryo testing, research and manipulation to be carried out. It is no exaggeration to say that the development of IVF has changed for ever our understanding of human reproduction and parenthood. It is a classic example of how a technological development can lead to a change in our way of thinking about ourselves.

Following the development of IVF, each child can now be regarded as the product of four components: (1) an egg source, (2) a sperm source, (3) a womb or uterus and (4) one or more caregivers after birth. Another way of looking at this is that any child may have three mothers: a *genetic mother*, the source of the egg; a *carrying mother*, the provider of the uterus; and a *social mother*, the one providing care after birth.

The possible permutations and combinations are remarkable. Sperm or egg donation means that one element of the genetic make-up of the embryo is provided by an anonymous donor; alternatively, there is embryo donation, where the genetic parents donate the embryo to a carrying mother who goes on to care for the child. Then there is surrogate pregnancy, where the genetic parents donate an embryo to a carrying mother with the intention that the child should be handed back to them after birth. Finally there is embryo 'adoption', in which an 'abandoned' embryo is donated to a carrying mother who then passes the child to adoptive parents for care after birth.

How is IVF performed?

In order to induce a woman to produce a suitable number of eggs, it is necessary to give hormones to induce superovulation. Instead of producing one egg at each monthly cycle, the ovaries are stimulated to produce up to ten, or even more. This process carries a degree of risk to the mother from inadvertent overstimulation, but with clinical skill this complication is unlikely. The eggs are 'harvested' using a laparoscope, a fine telescope which is inserted through the abdominal wall. They are then incubated in the laboratory and mixed with sperm obtained from the donor. Fertilization occurs in a few hours and can be detected by microscopic examination of the resultant embryos. After a period of forty-eight hours or more, during which the embryos continue to develop by cell division, several are selected for insertion into the carrying mother's womb. By increasing the numbers implanted at each attempt, the chances of a successful pregnancy are markedly increased. But for every additional embryo implanted there is an increasing chance of multiple pregnancies (twins, triplets or more), with all the associated risks of prematurity, severe handicap and death. A decade ago, I and my colleagues at University College Hospital were responsible for caring for a group of tiny quintuplets, born three months premature, after six embryos were implanted by IVF. The headlines the next day proclaimed, 'WORLD'S FIRST TEST-TUBE QUINS'. Remarkably, all five babies survived, following several months of intensive care. As a result of growing concern in the UK about the rise in the number of multiple pregnancies, national guidelines now recommend that no more than three embryos be implanted on any one occasion.

If only three embryos are reimplanted, the question immediately arises: what ought to be done with the remaining or 'spare' embryos? In essence there are only four possibilities: (1) freeze them for reinsertion into the genetic mother's uterus at a later date; (2) allow them to be inserted into the womb of another woman (embryo donation); (3) use them for research, with their ultimate fate being destruction; or (4) discard them immediately.

Embryos frozen in liquid nitrogen and stored under laboratory conditions seem to keep indefinitely. (Similarly, frozen sperm can be stored for long periods, although at present unfertilized eggs cannot be stored.) But what are the implications of the prolonged storage of embryos? Should it be allowed? Who owns the embryos? How long should they be allowed to be stored? What happens if there is a disagreement about what should happen to them? Should embryo research and manipulation be permitted?

The UK Human Fertilization and Embryology Act

In the early 1980s there was growing public concern in the UK about the implications of these advances in reproductive technology. At the same time, many responsible scientists and clinicians were calling for the creation of official guidelines so that the legal and ethical position could be clarified. In response, the British Government set up a Committee of Inquiry into Human Fertilization and Embryology under the chairmanship of Dame Mary Warnock, known universally as the Warnock Committee. The committee received over 250 oral and written submissions from interested bodies and individuals, including many from churches and Christian organizations. A consultation document was issued in 1986, and ultimately, following years of debate and discussion, the 1990 Human Fertilization and Embryology Act was passed by Parliament.

In brief, the legislation enshrined in the Act (which remains in force at the time of writing) is as follows:

1. All uses of human reproductive technology are supervised by the Human Fertilization and Embryology Authority (HFEA), which reports to Parliament. IVF is acceptable as a form of infertility treatment, but it may be performed only in licensed centres, which must provide details of all treatment procedures to the HFEA. In all cases, counselling must be provided to a woman and her partner prior to IVF, and their consent must be obtained for the specific use to which embryos will be put.

2. Embryo donation (ED) and donor insemination (DI) are deemed to be acceptable, subject to licensing arrangements. Both semen donors and egg donors should have no parental rights or duties. The Act does not specify that a woman wishing to be provided with treatment services must have a male partner. It does state, however, that 'account' must be taken of the welfare of any resulting child and that this should include the child's need of a father. Counselling must be given prior to treatment. In all cases the carrying mother rather than the genetic mother is to be regarded as the legal mother of the child. The Act states that the legal father of a child born following DI is the husband of the woman receiving treatment. If the woman is not married, but presents herself for treatment with a (male) partner, he is regarded as the legal father, unless he fails to give consent to the treatment. If the couple subsequently divorce, the husband at the time of fertilization remains the legal father of the child. The Act states that a full record of all donors, recipients and resulting children must be kept. All information about the genetic origins of a child must be kept strictly confidential and must not be divulged, even to medical carers or health professionals, without the explicit consent of the legal parents. At any stage after the age of eighteen years, the child may request information about his or her genetic origins, and whether any intended partner is genetically related. Where there are paternity disputes, or disputes about any legal responsibility for children with congenital disabilities, the identity of the genetic parent may be revealed to a court.

3. Both embryos and sperm can be frozen and stored for future use with the consent of the donors, but the initial Act stated that embryos could be stored for only five years. This was subsequently extended to ten years.

4. Surrogate pregnancy arrangements are allowed, but they must be non-commercial in nature and they are not enforceable in law. Thus the law provides protection for a carrying mother who enters into a surrogacy arrangement but then wishes to change her mind during the pregnancy or at the birth of the child. The Act provides for a legal arrangement whereby a couple can become the legal parents of a surrogate child. The child must have been created from an egg or sperm from one of the couple. The couple must apply for a legal order within six months of the birth of the child and the child must be living with them at the time. The consent of the carrying mother and her partner must be obtained. There must be no transfer of money between the parties, except for reasonable expenses.

5. Research on human embryos is lawful provided it is carried out in licensed centres and with the consent of the egg donors and sperm donors. Research may be carried out on 'spare' embryos following IVF, and also on embryos specially created for the purpose of research. It may continue only until the fourteenth day of life, and at that stage the embryo must be destroyed. Research can be undertaken only for specified purposes; namely: (1) promoting advances in the treatment of infertility; (2) increasing knowledge about the causes of congenital disease; (3) increasing knowledge about the causes of miscarriage; (4) developing more effective techniques of contraception; and (5) developing methods for detecting the presence of gene and chromosome abnormalities in embryos before implantation.

The Act prohibits cloning or the insertion of a human embryo into any animal. It does permit the mixing of human sperm with an animal egg, but only for the purposes of testing the fertility of the sperm as part of infertility treatment. Any resultant hybrid must not be allowed to proceed beyond the two-cell stage. It states that at present it is not lawful to modify the genetic structure of a human embryo, although it keeps open the possibility of specified forms of gene therapy on embryos in the future.

The legalization of embryo research, including the creation of embryos especially for the purpose, caused considerable controversy at the time. In the parliamentary debate, Baroness Warnock spoke strongly in its favour, arguing that the rejection of research would put the clock back to the seventeenth century, when scientific progress was regulated by religion: '. . . we must be allowed to take risks when we pursue knowledge, and regulate our lives in accordance with the knowledge we have. We cannot undo the Enlightenment and it would be morally wrong to place obstacles, derived from beliefs that are not widely shared, in the path of science and the practice of medicine' (reported in *British Medical Journal*, 16 December 1989).

The UK legislation represents the most detailed form of governmental supervision of reproductive technology, but while the Warnock Committee was meeting, many other developed countries were struggling with the ethical and legal implications of IVF and embryo research. The range of conclusions was wide. In a number of European countries, such as Norway and Denmark, embryo research was banned. In others, assisted-conception techniques were restricted to married couples or those in permanent relationships. In the USA no formal regulatory authority exists.

Egg donation

The growing demand for fertility treatments has meant that there is a marked shortage of suitable eggs for the creation of embryos. Many women are infertile because they are unable to produce eggs at all. Some fail to respond to the hormone treatment used in IVF. Other women may be carriers of inherited disorders, such as haemophilia, which are passed on through their eggs. At the same time, there is a growing demand from the scientific community for eggs to create embryos for medical research. At present, the only source of eggs is from adult women who are prepared to undergo hormonal and invasive treatment which carries a small but definite risk. Recently, several clinics have launched public campaigns to encourage women to become egg donors. As the HFEA has restricted the payments that can be made to individual donors to the sum of £15 plus 'reasonable expenses', the emphasis has been placed on altruistic reasons to become a donor; the primary reason should be to help a childless couple have a baby. Understandably, not many women appear to wish to undergo the invasive, complex and potentially dangerous process of donating eggs. In the USA, commercial arrangements for egg donation are common. In fact, the Center for Surrogate Parenting and Egg Donation Inc., of Los Angeles, reported in December 1995 that they had a list of 150 women who were waiting for recipient couples to choose them as egg donors (Silver 1997: 156).

Fetal egg donation

In 1994 the HFEA raised another startling possibility. Researchers in Edinburgh had shown that it was possible to take ovarian tissue from fetal mice and use this as a source of eggs to create mouse embryos. Similarly, eggs could be retrieved from ovaries removed shortly after death. Why not take tissue from the ovaries of dead aborted female fetuses and use them as a source of human eggs? After all, with the large number of medical abortions occurring each year in the UK, there was no shortage of available tissue. But would fertilization using fetal eggs lead to new problems? Eggs from an aborted fetus would not have been subjected to the biological forces which govern survival and normal development to adulthood. In effect a generation would be skipped. Perhaps there would be a greater risk of harmful genetic mutation and subsequent malformation. And what would be the medical and psychological effects on any child whose genetic mother was an aborted fetus? What about the vexed issue of consent to the donation of biological tissue? Obviously an aborted fetus cannot give consent to the use of its tissue, but should consent be obtained from its mother prior to an abortion? Would women be encouraged to have an abortion, knowing that the fetal eggs would be used for medical purposes? Of course, as Lee Silver argues, 'if the fetus is not a person, then the fetal ovaries can be seen as nothing more, or less, than tissues within a woman's body. If a woman asks a doctor to remove those tissues along with others from her body during an abortion, she has the right to determine whether they can be given to and used by other women' (1997: 172).

The HFEA launched a process of public consultation in 1994, but it rapidly became clear that there was strong opposition to the idea of fetal egg donation from the public as a whole and from Members of Parliament. In April 1994, weeks before the HFEA consultation was due to close, backbench MPs in an all-night sitting inserted a clause into an existing Bill, prohibiting fetal egg donation. Although some in the scientific community were outraged, and one commentator in the *British Medical Journal* described it as a 'roadblock in the path of medical science in Britain', it was clear that MPs had responded out of a deep sense of unease and revulsion. They reacted to the public mood which felt that medical science was driving the process of change too fast, and that creating life from an aborted fetus was a step too far, whatever the stated benefits might be.

Recent advances in reproductive technology

When IVF was first conceived by Steptoe and Edwards, it was intended for the use of mothers who had blocked Fallopian tubes, enabling an embryo to bypass the blockage and enter the womb so that implantation and development to maturity might occur. Today, IVF combined with other forms of reproductive technology can be used to treat a wide range of fertility problems. If the sperm and egg do not fuse spontaneously, a single live sperm can be picked up in a microscopically fine glass needle and injected directly into the egg cytoplasm under direct vision. This is the process christened ICSI (intra-cytoplasmic sperm injection), which has expanded rapidly following its development in 1992.

With ICSI it is possible to overcome infertility due to abnormalities in the concentration and quality of sperm. And by removing primitive developing cells from the testes of infertile men, and injecting their nuclear material into an egg, it is possible to create a baby using genetic material from men who produce no sperm at all. It is even possible to take immature cells (spermatogonia) from the testes and implant them into 'foster testes', where they can differentiate normally into fully active sperm which will retain the genetic material of the donor individual.

Frozen embryos

The 1990 Act which created the HFEA came into force in 1991. In order to minimize the complications which might result from indefinite storage of embryos, the Act stated that frozen embryos should be stored only for an arbitrary period of five years before they must be discarded. As the five-year deadline approached, on 31 July 1996, there was growing concern at the prospect of deliberately discarding a large number of viable embryos. In response, Parliament amended the Act to allow an extension of fetal storage to ten years, provided that couples gave specific consent. At the time it was estimated that there were a total of 52,000 frozen embryos in the UK, of which about 9,000 had been created before the Act came into effect and were therefore scheduled for destruction in July 1996 unless the parents could be contacted. The impending destruction of embryos was opposed by a number of groups, and some women volunteered to 'adopt' the embryos, becoming their legal guardians. Despite frantic attempts by fertility clinics to contact couples before the deadline expired, about 650 couples were uncontactable and their embryos were therefore destroyed.

The whole bizarre episode highlighted the confusion and ambiguity in the public response to the existence of thousands of embryos stored in flasks of liquid nitrogen around the country. How can we think of these beings? Are they merely bundles of cells, similar to tissue biopsies from cancerous growths stored in culture medium in a laboratory, or are they people, to whom we owe a duty of care and protection? Oliver O'Donovan points out that the processes of embryo creation and destruction should not be regarded as the 'old-fashioned crime of killing babies, but the new and subtle crime of making babies to be ambiguously human, of presenting to us members of our own species who are doubtfully proper objects of compassion and love' (O'Donovan 1984: 65). We shall return to the controversial question of how Christians should view the embryo in chapter 7.

Applications of IVF

Not only does reproductive technology itself cause concern. Equally problematical is the question of who should have access to it. At present the vast majority of IVF treatment cycles are performed for infertile couples who are either married or in a stable relationship. Liberal western governments, however, have concluded that they cannot legislate for or attempt to control the reproductive liberty of adult individuals. It is not necessary to complete a questionnaire, fill out a registration form or pass a simple examination before embarking on the process of conceiving a child! Even donor insemination is remarkably easy. Lesbian groups, for instance, have circulated self-help information on how to conceive using a sperm sample donated by an acquaintance and nothing more technologically elaborate than a syringe used for basting turkeys.

If human beings are capable of conceiving children naturally for any reason at all or none, on what logical grounds can we restrict the use of modern reproductive technology to those of whom we approve? In January 1998, the *Daily Express* reported that a sixty-year old grandmother called Tracy Williams had given birth following embryo donation. Apparently she had deceived doctors and counsellors at the private London Gynaecology and Fertility Centre, by claiming to be a younger infertile woman. In fact, she had three teenage grandchildren. Professor Ian Craft, Director of the Fertility Centre, has frequently defended the right of older women up to fifty-five to have children, provided that there was a loving relationship. Professor Robert Edwards, the pioneer of IVF, has also supported IVF in older mothers. 'In the last twenty years attitudes have changed so rapidly. Women are much younger in their later years and the biological evidence suggests the womb is capable of coping with pregnancy in the 50s. It is a cruel evolutionary trick that the ovaries stop producing eggs' (*Evening Standard*, 2 July 1997).

Parenthood by choice

Reproductive technology allows single women to have children without the need to find a partner. In the USA the support group Single Mothers by Choice provides information and runs workshops. *The Times* of 17 November 1997 carried a remarkable article by Christa Worthington, who had joined one of the local groups. She described how throughout her thirties and early forties she hoped to find the right man to be a husband and father. Now she was forty-eight years old. 'I am reinventing the world. There is, at the moment, no father for a child of mine, no husband for me, and what if there never is? I have had to stare this scenario in the face, and to my surprise it hasn't killed me. Instead I can have my life by claiming the decision of whether or not to become a mother.' As Christa contemplated seeking a sperm donor, she recognized she was braving the wrath of others. 'If I do pair my genetic material with that of an anonymous sperm donor, I will be accused of contributing to the breakdown of the family just as I manage to make one . . . Though infertile couples have the world's sympathy, discussion of the single women's journey to the edge of fertility is taboo.' Jane Mattes, the founder of Single Mothers by Choice, recognizes that 'there is a limit to fertility, even with money. You spend twenty years trying not to get pregnant: then you turn round and find that it's hard to conceive.'

'It's the lament of my generation,' wrote Christa Worthington. She described how prospective recipients listen to taped interviews from potential sperm donors or peruse binders of individual profiles, choosing the colour of the donor's hair and eyes. In the fertility clinic, 'crates holding frozen sperm in containers of liquid nitrogen are left like milk at the door'. Attracted to one man's profile, Ms Worthington rang the appropriate number but discovered that the sperm is 'sold out'. 'I think my donor's cute,' says her pregnant friend Ruth, and suggests they have siblings by the same man. Again, no more sperm is available. The article ends on a note of ambiguity: 'I really can't wait to see this kid, says Ruth . . . and we all fall silent thinking those old thoughts: Whose hair? Whose eyes?'

Surrogate pregnancies

With the use of surrogate mothers, new complexities have arisen. Novel family arrangements are common. In one case reported in the *Daily Mail*, embryos were created simultaneously from eggs and sperm provided by Tricia and her partner Julian. The embryos were frozen while a surrogate mother was sought. Eventually Teresa, a thirty-one-year-old administrator, agreed, and several embryos were thawed and implanted into Teresa's womb. A single pregnancy resulted and, after birth, baby Jennifer was given back to Tricia by Teresa. A year later, the remaining embryos were thawed and implanted into the womb of another surrogate mother, Gaynor. The second baby was born twenty-one months after her twin, and the two babies had no fewer than three biological mothers between them.

Although commercial surrogacy arrangements are illegal in the UK, it is not unheard of for British couples to employ the services of American agencies such as the Center for Surrogate Parenting and Egg Donation Inc. According to newspaper reports, couples can choose a surrogate mother from a list of 250 women whose pictures and details are provided. The total costs can exceed £40,000.

Having reviewed the range of issues raised by these developments in reproductive technology, in the remainder of this chapter I shall try to develop a Christian response.

Christian perspectives on reproductive technology
Lego kits

As we saw in chapter 1, our bodies used to be the last frontier of the natural world. But the development of reproductive technology seems to have broken for ever this last barrier. We do not have to accept the limitations of our bodies as they have been given to us. By understanding the molecular and biological mechanisms of which our bodies are constructed, we can learn how to manipulate them; we can improve on the Mark I old-fashioned design. The old technological dream of controlling and improving on nature, which stems from the period of the Enlightenment, can be extended to the design of the human body itself. This is what I have called the 'Lego kit' view of the human body. To recap: the essence of Lego construction is first that there is no internal or 'natural' order to a Lego kit, and secondly, there is no single purpose for which the kit is intended by its designers. From the point of view of the philosophical facts/values distinction, the Lego kit can be viewed as *all facts and no values*. It is delightfully value-free.

In the same way, because many modern scientists regard the human body as a complex mechanism generated by millions of years of random forces, they regard the structure of the body as value-free. We are liberated from antique taboos concerned with the dangers of tampering with the natural order. The difference between the 'natural' and the 'artefactual' has been obliterated; we are free to become our own designers.

Even in this technological Utopia, however, we are not completely free. There are some fundamental questions which responsible Lego users must ask of any new construction they produce. First, *does it work?* Does it satisfy the purpose which the constructor has imposed? Secondly, *is it safe?* Will the presence of this wonderful new construction adversely affect the constructor or others?

As the 'Lego kit' way of thinking has penetrated modern reproductive technology, it is not surprising that these are the dominant questions which are asked, as each advance becomes technically feasible. Already many ethicists have concluded that the only substantial objection to human cloning and asexual reproduction is the potential of physical harm to any children born as a result. In other words, it now seems fairly clear that it will work, but is it safe? Within the mentality of the Lego constructor, there are no other substantive questions to ask.

God's masterpieces

By contrast, as we saw in chapter 2, the Christian worldview takes seriously the concept of the natural order which penetrates both the physical structure of our bodies and the hidden ethical grain of our universe. Our bodies do not come to us as value-free. They are instead wonderful, original artistic masterpieces which reflect the meticulous design and order imposed by a Creator's will and purpose.

This concept is amplified and reinforced by the biblical doctrines of the incarnation and resurrection. The original design of human beings is not abandoned, despised or marginalized; it is affirmed and fulfilled. And in biblical, trinitarian thinking, through the advent of Christ, physical human nature has been assumed in a mysterious way into the Godhead. In the incarnation and resurrection of Christ as a *physical human being*, God proclaims his vote of confidence in the original created order. As we noticed earlier, the raised Jesus is recognized, eats and drinks. He is touched, and even carries the scars of the crucifixion, to show that he is not merely a spiritual phenomenon but is still a *human being*. The new humanity revealed in Jesus is the fulfilment, the final purpose for which the original humanity was always intended. Instead of starting afresh with a clean slate, in the resurrection of Christ God declares that for all future time he will sustain, redeem and transform the humanity that was originally made. The resurrection is God's final and irrevocable 'Yes' to humankind (see O'Donovan 1994: 53–58). If we take the biblical doctrines of the incarnation and resurrection seriously, we must conclude that the physical structure of our human bodies is not something we are free to change without very careful thought.

The flawed masterpiece

We must also, however, take seriously the reality of evil in God's world, the all-pervasive distorting and marring effects of the fall. As discussed in chapter 2, the original masterpiece, created with such love and embodying such artistry, has become flawed, defaced, contaminated, and is decaying from age. The reflection of God's character is distorted and partially obscured. But through the imperfections, we can still see the outlines of the original masterpiece. It still inspires a sense of wonder at the underlying design.

What is the responsibility that we owe to this flawed masterpiece? What is our duty as a human community? As we have emphasized, biblical ethics derives from biblical anthropology. What we must do is develop a fully orbed biblical understanding of who human beings are, within the natural order designed by God, so that we can then develop an understanding of what our duties are. If a biblical perspective on human beings views them as flawed masterpieces, then our responsibilities are to act as art preservers and restorers. Our duties are to protect masterpieces from further harm, and attempt to restore them *in line with the original artist's intentions*.

The ethics of art restoration

Just like doctors, responsible and professional art restorers must act according to a code of ethical practice. In a fascinating article entitled 'The ethics of conservation', Jonathan Ashley-Smith discusses the principles that should guide the professional restorer (Ashley-Smith 1994). He explicitly draws an analogy between his field and the field of medical ethics. 'To deny the practitioner the right to an ethical viewpoint is like denying the right of the doctor to withhold or prescribe dangerous drugs or denying the surgeon the right to refuse to undertake an unnecessary cosmetic operation.'

According to the UK Institution of Conservation Guidelines, 'Conservation is the means whereby the original and true nature of an artistic object is maintained.' The true nature of an object is determined by 'evidence of its origins, its original constitution, the materials of which it is composed and information which it may embody as to its maker's intentions and the technology used in its manufacture'.

So it is the *intention of the original creator* or artist which is normative. The restorer must use all the information at his or her disposal – X-ray analysis, historical records, sophisticated chemical tests and so on – to determine the object's original 'constitution', to assess what information the object itself embodies regarding the maker's intention. Only when the original creator's intention is revealed can the restorer decide what form of intervention is appropriate. Unethical restoration is the use of technology to alter, improve or enhance the appearance of the artistic piece. The ethical restorer must refuse any request to enhance the object, even if it means that valuable business is lost.

Art restorers are not free to change or improve the masterpiece as they like. They are not at liberty to improve on the original by adding an extra bit here or there. No, the restorer is free only to operate within the parameters fixed by the artist's original intention. Of course, provided they are operating within these constraints, restorers may decide to employ highly artificial and invasive technology. It may be necessary to replace an area of canvas with an artificial plastic substitute carefully modelled to resemble the original material. It may be necessary to remove the yellowed original varnish and replace it with a sophisticated polyurethane covering. The nature and invasiveness of the technology are less important than the aims of the restorer, to protect and maintain the 'original and true nature of the object'.

Of course, art restoration is only an analogy of the role of the doctor, and like all analogies it has limitations and difficulties. Nevertheless, I believe the analogy is helpful as we try to assess the mind-boggling possibilities raised by reproductive technology. The task of health professionals is to protect and restore the masterpieces entrusted to our care, in line with the original creator's intentions. We must use technology in a way which is appropriate to preserve and protect the original design, to maintain and preserve the creation order embodied in the structure of the human body. However tempting it may be, however spectacular the consequences which might result, we must not resort to unethical restoration. We are not free to improve on the fundamental design.

With each new advance in technology we have to ask the basic question: 'Does the use of this technology allow the artist's intention to be fulfilled, or is it changing the design at a fundamental level?'

Creation design in reproduction

In the original human design, making love and making babies belong together. Let me give a personal illustration. A number of years ago there was a junior doctor called John working in a London hospital. One day he met a stranger, a young lady called Celia, who happened to be a hospital administrator. One thing led to another and we fell in love and got married. Because we were two unique beings, our love was a unique entity, a strange mixture, part of me and part of her, invisible, spiritual, hidden in our hearts. Nobody had seen our love; it was private. And then after five years the most bizarre and amazing thing happened. Our invisible love took on physical form. It became flesh in front of our eyes; it became a baby whom we called Jonathan James. The unique combination of John and Celia became a physical reality. In fact, this miracle happened no fewer than three times. As we get to know our children, we recognize ourselves: the child is a bit of me and a bit of her, a unique expression of our love. What is more, if our children go on to have children of their own, the human gene pool will have been permanently altered. Even after John and Celia have gone, their unique love, their unique combination, will be enshrined for ever in the physical stuff of humanity.

Because, in God's design, making love and making babies belong together, genetics is important. DNA is the means by which a unique love between a man and a woman can be converted physically into a baby. Your genetic structure enshrines, embodies, makes physical, the unique loving combination of your father and mother. Not only that, but your genetic structure enshrines the countless conjunctions of your ancestors, the myriad love-makings of which you are composed. This is why, for adopted children, the task of tracing their physical parents and genetic roots may be so emotionally significant. Whatever our environment, however we are brought up, we can never escape the reality of our physical structure, the recognition that we are each a unique love-child, created by a unique combination of two unique beings. Our genetic structure expresses in a physical form the web of relationships out of which each of us has been created and into which we are being brought.

To the evolutionary biologist, sex remains something of a mystery (see, for example, Dawkins 1988: 268). It is a mechanism for increasing the random element in reproduction, shaking the dice in order to create novel combinations of genes and reduce the risk of harmful inbreeding. It seems that by mingling our genes randomly with other genes, we increase the chances that our own genes might make it to the next generation in a self-replicating body. But in Christian thought, sex is the way of constructing a unique baby to 'incarnate' a unique love. It is part of the creation order, and so, in theological language, the unitive and the procreative aspects of sex belong together.

But not everybody has been given this gift of making love and making babies. I want to be sensitive to the deep pain of those who long for children and find it impossible; those who long for their love to become incarnate and yet it does not happen. As we have seen, the pain of infertility is an overwhelming reality for many in our society. As a Christian community we need to learn to empathize, to be more sensitive to the deep but hidden pain of childless couples and individuals in our midst.

Begotten or made?

Although I have used the common phrase 'making babies', there is of course a world of difference between making an artefact, such as a house, and making a baby. In biblical thought, we do not *make* babies, we *beget* them. As Oliver O'Donovan pointed out in his London Lectures, *Begotten or Made?*, there is a profound thought which goes back to the Nicene Creed, formulated by the early church fathers. The Son of God was 'begotten, not made'. The wording of the Creed was intended to emphasize that the Son was 'of one substance with the Father'. Our offspring are human beings who share with us a common human nature. In God's design, we do not determine what our offspring are; we receive them as a gift, as beings who are equal with us at a fundamental level, in the same way that the Son is equal in being with the Father. By contrast, that which we make is *different* from us. It is an artefact, alien from our humanity, and is fundamentally at our disposal, a product of our *will* rather than of our *being* (O'Donovan 1984: 1). The danger of reproductive technology is that it subtly reflects and contributes to a change in our relationship to our own children. They become a product of our will, a commodity at our disposal.

The implications of reproductive technology

The Roman Catholic tradition of theology has tended to emphasize that each *sexual act* should combine these unitive and procreative elements. This is expounded in the document *Humanae Vitae* (1968): 'Because God has given marriage as a gift, he alone orders how the gift is to be used.' There is an 'inseparable connection established by God which man on his own initiative may not break, between the unitive significance and the procreative significance, which are both inherent to the marriage Act . . . an act of mutual love which impairs the capacity to transmit life which God the Creator, through specific laws, has built into it, frustrates his design which constitutes the norms of marriage, and contradicts the will of the Author of Life. Hence to use this divine gift while depriving it, even if only partially, of its meaning and purpose, is equally repugnant to the nature of man and woman, strikes at the heart of their relationship and is consequently in opposition to the plan of God and his holy will' (quoted by McCarthy 1997: 144).

Within this view, both contraception and any form of reproductive technology are seen as unacceptable because they divide these two aspects of sex; every act of sexual intercourse must be 'open' to the possibility of procreation, and no child may be conceived without a specific act of intercourse. It seems hard to defend this absolutist position on biblical grounds, and many Protestant theologians have argued that the unitive and procreative aspects of sex need to be held together within a marriage relationship *viewed as a whole*. It is not necessary for each sexual act to lead to procreation (McCarthy 1997: 155). Even when there is no attempt at contraception, only a small proportion of the individual acts of intercourse actually lead to the formation of a baby. The whole marriage can be viewed as an extended act which combines the unitive and procreative elements of sex. Sexual union forms an important but not exclusive part of the way in which a couple express their relational and procreative natures.

As Brendan McCarthy points out, this perspective may have significant implications for our view of reproductive technology (1997: 156–161). Just as we may argue that contraception is a method by which human beings use their God-given knowledge to help them to reproduce responsibly, so reproductive technology may be a means of allowing an infertile couple to express the procreative aspect of their marriage, even in the absence of a specific sexual act.

Is reproductive technology consistent with Christian beliefs?

Is it, then, appropriate for couples who are infertile to use the new technology, such as *in vitro* fertilization? As I have argued, we have to ask the question, 'Does the use of this technology allow the artist's intention to be fulfilled, or is it changing the design at a fundamental level?' In my view, IVF which is used to assist an infertile couple to have their own genetically related child may be regarded as a form of restorative technology. It is allowing the couple, in a sense, to bring together what the fall had separated – enabling them to express their love physically, in the form of a child which is genetically their own.

Even in the case where husband and wife provide the genetic material, however, there are very real anxieties about whether IVF is an appropriate use of technology. There is the intrusive effect of technology, and the implication that the child is an artefact or commodity created by technology – a product of human planning and ingenuity for the parents' use. There are the genuine risks of serious medical harm to the mother and to the child. There is the problem of what to do with spare embryos. Finally, there is the recognition that *in vitro* fertilization techniques have depended on the employment of many years of embryo research in the past. Even if we do not wish any embryos that we create to be used for research, we cannot escape the reality of the countless thousands of human embryos that have been intentionally destroyed in the past, in order to bring the technology to its current state of development. My own conclusion is that IVF may be acceptable for a married couple provided that no spare embryos are created, but that the possible negative consequences need to be very carefully considered before embarking on this course.

With embryo or sperm donation and with surrogacy, the unique genetic and biological link between parents and their children is broken. These procedures break the link between making love and making babies. Some have argued that this is already the case in adoption, which has always been regarded as a Christian alternative. Why should we not regard embryo or sperm donation as merely a form of antenatal adoption? There is a very clear difference, however, between a couple who voluntarily receive an *already existing* child into their family and a couple who consciously decide to *bring into being* a child who is at most only partly genetically their own. In the first case, an existing child is offered a good which he or she has previously been denied. In the other case, a child is brought into existence in order to provide a good which has previously been denied to a childless couple.

Gamete (embryo or sperm) donation may have far-reaching and unforeseen consequences in family dynamics and relationships. We may generate a profound ambiguity about the identity of the baby. Paradoxically, the ambiguity may be greatest when the child is genetically related to one member of a couple but not to another; for instance, in a child born by donor insemination. In this case, as the child develops it becomes apparent that he or she is half of the mother, but also half of a completely anonymous stranger. This child is not the love-child who should reflect our relationship, but rather a strange and hidden hybrid. Unbeknown to the child, this man who acts as a father is not the child's 'real' father – or is he?

Some have argued that sperm donation should be regarded as an act of simple altruism like blood donation. We do not regard a child who has received a blood transfusion as changed in any fundamental way by that process, so why should we not regard sperm donation in the same light? In my view it is naïve to imagine that blood donation and sperm donation are analogous. In God's design, sperm, and the DNA of which they are composed, are the means by which a unique love between a man and a woman can be converted physically into a baby. So the donation of sperm cells carries with it a profound significance which is not conveyed in the transfer of blood cells. I would argue that blood donation can be regarded as a form of technology which preserves the creation order, the integral design of humanity. It is an ethically acceptable form of 'art restoration'. By contrast, gamete donation is a form of technology which changes the design at a fundamental level by changing the relationship between a child and its parents.

Part of the ambiguity inherent in gamete donation is seen in the extreme emphasis which many parents place on the confidentiality of the process. Most couples seem desperately keen to hide the fact of gamete donation from other members of their family and from the child itself. Some will go to extraordinary lengths to ensure that no hint of this information could be released, even sometimes insisting that no mention of the genetic origins of the child is contained in medical records, or conveyed to other health professionals. Why do many parents go to such lengths to conceal the genetic origins of their child even if it involves extensive subterfuge? Is it because they sense that this information will somehow alter family and social perceptions of the child, and the child's perceptions of its parents? We should contrast this with the deep Christian instinct for openness and truthfulness in human relationships, especially within the intimacy and security of a family.

Similarly, surrogacy seems to raise profound ambiguities about an individual child's parenthood: 'Who exactly is my mother?' Brendan McCarthy, in his extremely detailed analysis entitled *Fertility and Faith*, argues that surrogacy may be viewed as an acceptable option for Christians, unlike gamete donation. He claims that, although it is normal for the woman who conceived a baby to continue to provide the environment of nurture and protection for the embryo, the connection between conception and nurture is not an essential one in principle. 'Unlike the connection between the unitive and the procreative aspects of sex, the connection between conception and nurture is a biological necessity. Where this connection is physically unsustainable, no principle is sacrificed if the nurturing element in an embryo's development is transferred to another woman as long as the genetic mother remains the mother of the child

. . . It is reasonable to see the dual aspects of sex as a matter of principle, but the connection between conception and nurture as a matter of expediency' (McCarthy 1997: 221).

I have to say that I find this argument unconvincing. If we take the creation order seriously, then there seem to be strong reasons to preserve the connection between conception and nurture. The very fact that it is a 'biological necessity' should make us ask why God made us this way. Surely the relationship of loving hospitality between the unborn child and its mother is a part of the creation design, the original artist's intention. In God's creation design, when a mother takes her newborn baby into her arms, she is receiving not a stranger, but a being who has shared her life for the preceding nine months. Already the relationship of security and love is established.

In my view, therefore, surrogacy is a technology which is at risk of changing the design at a fundamental level. Is it possible that the overwhelming desire to have a child may drive people to use technology unwisely? Perhaps we should be prepared to turn away from technology which is possible but unwise. Our desires to know, to probe the secrets of our human nature and to combat disease, are expressions of our God-given freedom; yet sometimes we must be prepared to say no to some of the possibilities of human freedom (Meilander 1997: 5).

What answer is there, then, for the infertile couple, for whom there is no possibility of a child without recourse to gamete donation or surrogacy? I have no easy solution. What I have to say may seem hard, and will be perceived by some as outrageous, an infringement of autonomy. But in a world which has so many sad, abused, abandoned and disabled children, is it possible that an infertile couple may find an alternative way to fulfil their deep, and God-given, desire for parenthood? Is it possible that by adoption or by fostering, by caring for the unwanted and the rejected in our society, there may be a better way than resorting to reproductive technology with all its risks and ambiguities?

I am in no position to criticize those who come to other conclusions. I and my wife have been given the gift of parenthood. How can I possibly empathize with the pain of childlessness? It is not for me to judge those who feel emotionally compelled to embark on the technological approach to making babies. And yet it seems that sometimes God calls individuals, in Oliver O'Donovan's words, to 'accept exclusion from the created good as the necessary price of a true and unqualified witness to it' (O'Donovan 1994: 96). By refraining from reproductive technology, a childless couple may bear witness to God's creation order while having to pay the price of exclusion from part of the blessings of that order. As a Christian community, we should learn to recognize and honour the painful sacrifice which such couples make.

In the next chapter we move from the pain of infertility to look at some of the problems which arise once a child is conceived: at developments in fetal screening, in which the unborn baby is tested for congenital abnormalities and diseases.

4. Fetal screening and the quest for a healthy baby

Although reproductive technology allows infertile parents to exercise choices in the process of conceiving a pregnancy, only a small percentage of all pregnancies are initiated in this way. At present the figure is about 1% of all pregnancies in the UK. By contrast, the use of medical technology in screening for fetal abnormalities is now widely practised, leading to a major change in the experience of pregnancy for many parents.

In the past, the mother's experience of pregnancy was usually fairly positive. Unless they were considering an abortion, most women looked forward to the coming of a new, mysterious being called a baby, about whom nothing was known. No decisions were necessary at this stage. As the baby grew, the parents' commitment to this individual grew. While parents knew that some babies would be born with a congenital disability, little or nothing could be done about this. But now technology has irreversibly altered the experience of pregnancy for modern parents.

The purpose of antenatal screening

When a woman tells her doctor that she is pregnant, one of the first questions the doctor will ask is, 'How do you feel about your pregnancy?' In other words, 'Do you really want to have a baby or do you want an abortion?' Right from the start the mother is offered choices. If she wishes to continue the pregnancy she will be offered a series of screening tests for abnormality in the fetus, depending on her age, family history and local practice. Tests are available for a long list of conditions, and, as genetic knowledge advances, the list is growing almost every week. There are about 4,000 known, simply inherited genetic disorders, and in the foreseeable future nearly all of them might be detectable by genetic screening of the fetus or embryo.

Most tests used in medicine are intended to guide treatment, leading to a cure or at least alleviation of a medical condition. In general, doctors have agreed that if no treatment is available, it is unethical to perform screening tests on apparently healthy people. But the ethical principles governing screening tests in pregnancy are rather different. A few treatments are available, but for the majority of abnormalities there is only one option on offer: abortion. And yet fetal screening is now being offered for all pregnant women in the UK. It is the only form of medicine in which doctors offer to treat a condition by eliminating the patient.

Although fetal screening for a range of common conditions, such as Down's syndrome and spina bifida, is being offered to all pregnant women in the UK, more detailed screening is employed in families where there is a particularly high risk of an abnormal child. Parents may have watched a previous child suffer because of a terrible congenital disease such as cystic fibrosis or muscular dystrophy. As genetic testing is now available for many of these conditions, some parents feel that they can risk embarking on a further pregnancy only because they know that there is the possibility of abortion if, tragically, the next fetus is found to be affected by the same condition.

At present there are only three widely available techniques which enable fetal cells to be obtained for detailed genetic analysis. *Chorionic villus sampling*, usually performed before the thirteenth week of gestation, involves the collection of a small sample of tissue from the developing placenta. *Amniocentesis*, usually performed later on, between the fourteenth and twentieth weeks of pregnancy, entails the sampling of amniotic fluid. In *cordocentesis*, a sample of fetal blood is obtained directly from the umbilical cord under ultrasound guidance. All are performed relatively late in pregnancy, leading to agonizing decisions about the termination of a comparatively mature fetus (see Moore 1997).

Two techniques currently under development are likely to transform the clinical practice of fetal screening. The first is the development of sophisticated cell-sorting methods to isolate fetal cells from the mother's circulation. In every pregnancy a minute number of fetal cells are dislodged from the placenta and are carried within the mother's blood stream. By identifying and isolating these cells, it will be possible to perform detailed genetic analysis on the fetus from a routine maternal blood sample, without exposing mother or fetus to risk. Technology will have overcome the physical barriers preventing genetic access to the fetus.

The other technological hope for the future is in the development of preimplantation diagnosis. Following the creation of an embryo by IVF, scientists have devised a way of extracting individual cells for genetic analysis. Once the embryo has reached the six- to ten-cell stage, the surrounding membrane is dissolved and a single cell is extracted for detailed genetic analysis. If the procedure is performed on each of the ten or so embryos created during a single cycle of IVF, the embryos which are free of a particular genetic mutation can be identified and then transferred to the carrying mother's womb. The same technique has been used to identify the sex chromosomes carried by each embryo in order to select embryos of the desired sex. Although preimplantation diagnosis is complex, invasive and expensive, it carries the advantage that no therapeutic abortion need be performed. The embryos which are found to be abnormal are not reimplanted, but discarded. Already, over a hundred children have been born worldwide, following preimplantation diagnosis and embryo selection. The use of this technique is likely to grow significantly over the next few years, encouraging parents to undergo IVF, not because of infertility, but in order to obtain the optimal chance of a healthy child.

Difficult choices

Unfortunately, an initial screening test may not provide the precise answer that is required. Instead, it usually leads inexorably on to another test, and then another, and so on. For example, the mother may have a blood test (such as the so-called Triple Test) to check for Down's syndrome. The result of this test enables the statistical risk of the syndrome to be calculated precisely. But how should she respond if the risk is increased compared to the general population? For instance, she may be told that there is a one in 200 risk of Down's syndrome, compared with an average risk in the population of approximately one in 2,000. If the risk is greater than an arbitrary value of one in 250 she will probably be offered further testing such as amniocentesis or chorionic villus sampling. This will provide a definitive diagnosis of a chromosomal disorder.

Unfortunately, these invasive tests carry a significant risk of causing a spontaneous miscarriage and fetal death. Even in skilful hands the risk in amniocentesis may be as much as one in 100. With chorionic villus sampling the risk may be as high as one in 50. The risk of accidentally causing the death of healthy fetus may thus be somewhat greater than the risk that the fetus is affected by Down's syndrome. So mothers are confronted with a choice between taking a risk with the life of their fetus and coping with uncertainty and anxiety for the remaining months of pregnancy.

Despite a great deal of interest and sensationalism created by the possibility of gene therapy, there are no new cures at present for the vast majority of genetic diseases, and such treatments as are currently available owe almost nothing to the new genetics. Instead, most recent developments have been in genetic testing, providing extremely precise information about the presence of genetic mutations, but offering no practical treatment except abortion for the devastating consequences that may follow.

One example is relevant to families in which there are several women who have had breast cancer. In 1990 a gene named BRCA1 was identified. Abnormal mutations in this gene are associated with a very high risk of breast cancer at some stage during life. It is now possible for a mother to screen her fetus for the presence of an abnormal BRCA1 gene, although the test is relatively expensive as the screening technology has been patented by a commercial company in the USA. But how should she respond if the gene probe shows that her fetus carries this mutant gene? Should she request an abortion in a fetus who might well have escaped cancer until late in life? Or should she knowingly bring a baby into the world with a genetic sword of Damocles hanging over her?

Growth in antenatal screening tests

The rapid growth in genetic knowledge is likely to mean that in the future, very many people will face similar dilemmas during pregnancy. The very existence of tests for fetal abnormality can create pressures to use the technology (Green & Statham 1996). From surveys it is apparent that, understandably, most women have little appreciation of the possible consequences of antenatal screening. In fact, when questioned after delivery, many are not aware that they have received blood tests for fetal screening at all. Although all women are supposed to receive counselling from health staff prior to fetal screening tests, in one study in a London teaching hospital 27% of women did not know they had received blood tests during pregnancy to detect spina bifida (Marteau *et al.* 1988). As the number of genetic tests increases, the problems of providing suitable counselling and information will become more intractable.

Most parents are initially reassured by knowing that the pregnancy is being monitored and that if there is anything wrong it will be detected and dealt with. They follow procedures presented to them by doctors and midwives because they wish to do the best for their babies. The fact that antenatal tests are routine means that most people assume that they are medically necessary and appropriate. Although staff are instructed merely to *offer* screening tests and to ensure that parents are informed about the options that are available, in practice parents often do not feel able to choose freely. They may not be given the appropriate information, or may not have understood the information which has been provided. The screening tests come with an aura of medical authority and respectability. It is as though someone else has already made the decision about their value and suitability for pregnant women. To decline the tests may seem to be acting irresponsibly, to 'go against medical advice'. Yet obstetric and midwifery staff are aware that they may be considered negligent if they fail to inform women of the availability of screening tests.

Effects of screening on the experience of pregnancy

What then have been the consequences of the widespread availability of antenatal screening on women's perception of pregnancy? Not surprisingly, the overwhelming effect has been one of increased anxiety. For many women, pregnancy has changed from a time of expectation to a time of worry. One study found that 79% of pregnant women were made anxious by the screening tests, and 20% described themselves as very worried or upset. The anxiety often persists even after a test has given a reassuring result, and several scientific studies have confirmed this (Green & Statham 1996: 146). Once those terrible fears about fetal abnormality have been raised, it is hard to put them to rest. Several studies have found that levels of anxiety in pregnant women who had been tested and received a reassuring result were no lower than levels of anxiety in women who had received no testing at all.

The sociologist B. K. Rothman, author of the important book *The Tentative Pregnancy* (Rothman 1986), argues that antenatal testing encourages women to view their babies as commodities that may be rejected if found to be substandard. The effect of fetal screening is that many mothers hold back from relating to their fetuses until tests have revealed that the baby is healthy. This is mainly to shield themselves from the pain of having to abort a baby they have come to love, and also because of a feeling that the fetus may be less than perfect. The pregnancy is tentative; some women do not tell anyone they are pregnant until the test results show that everything is all right, sometimes twenty weeks or more into the pregnancy.

Technology, then, has had the effect of encouraging a mother to distance herself from the child she carries. Instead of pregnancy being an inseparable attachment, which starts early on and grows throughout nine months, antenatal screening means that the relation of the mother and child now begins with separation and distancing and moves only later to attachment around the time of birth. Until late in pregnancy, some mothers hold themselves back from full commitment; they retain the option of walking away from their child. Interestingly, researchers have recently commented that there is no evidence that this understandable strategy does in fact reduce the psychological trauma if the test results are abnormal (Green & Statham 1996: 149).

Many parents look forward to the first ultrasound scan of their baby. It is the first chance to see their child, an event to be shared with the rest of the family. But what was supposed to be a wonderful experience may not be so. As one woman put it, 'Somehow when you go for a routine scan you can't believe that they'll find something so dreadful' (quoted by Green & Statham 1996: 143).

Several researchers have pointed out a strange paradox of human psychology. Health staff regard the purpose of antenatal screening tests as the detection of serious fetal abnormality. Thus when the test picks up an abnormality, this is in some sense a triumph. It is what the test is there for. Many mothers, by contrast, regard the purpose of antenatal tests as to provide reassurance that everything is all right. They decide to have the test to seek this reassurance. When the test picks up an abnormality they feel shocked and sometimes cheated, especially if they find that the only 'treatment' that the medical staff have to offer is abortion (Green & Statham 1996: 143).

One woman expressed her ambivalence about the testing process she had entered. 'If they'd handed her to me and said she was Down's I'd have been upset but I'd have got on with it; but once you've got into the testing trap you have to get to the end' (Green & Statham 1996: 150). 'The testing trap' – I am struck by the bitterness that lies behind those words. While health staff feel they are offering a positive service of benefit to women, not all women respond with gratitude. A number of women say that they feel pressurized by the system. The National Childbirth Trust recently performed a survey of mothers' experience of antenatal screening: 10% said that they felt pressurized to have tests and 7% said that they did not feel they had a real choice about whether to have the tests or not.

I don't think that the test for disability in the unborn child is presented as a choice. When I said I didn't want to be tested the doctor was shocked and she tried to talk me into it because it's an easy test, everybody gets it done nowadays, it's simple. But I don't think there is a choice. I think that we're pressurized into taking as many of these tests as are available (quoted by Shakespeare 1997).

I looked around the waiting room before my amniocentesis, wondering what poor soul was going to get bad news. I never dreamed it would be me . . . A few days later our family was ready to go out for dinner when the obstetrician called. I could hear in her voice that she had bad news. She said it was Down's syndrome. I felt like I was in a tunnel; it was like a bad dream. I started screaming, right there in front of my husband and the kids. I had to wait two weeks before I had an abortion. The baby was kicking. I thought I would lose my mind.

Once you get the results, every day your baby moves, you are dying inside.

When I walked into the abortion clinic with my wife, my first impulse was to turn around and walk out. The waiting room was full of teenage girls, who were presumably there to abort unplanned and unwanted pregnancies. And there we were, ending a pregnancy we had wanted so badly. We were in that waiting room for several hours. It was dreadful. (Quotations from Kohn & Moffitt 1994: 106–110.)

Psychological consequences of abortion for fetal abnormality

One can easily sense the pain and even desperation that lie behind those words. For many people the experience of abortion may be less traumatic than for those whose words are quoted above, and many feel a sense of relief as well as sadness. Yet several studies have shown that abortion for fetal abnormality is associated with a high incidence of depression in both parents, with guilt at being responsible for the decision-making and loss of self-esteem because of the conception of an abnormal fetus. The highest risk of problems occurred when parents were young or immature or if there was infertility subsequently (Green & Statham 1996: 151). Of course, there is terrible pain when a major malformation is discovered after birth. This too can bring depression and feelings of failure. The experience of caring for a handicapped child may be devastating and can lead to family break-up, but it seems that the feelings of guilt, self-accusation and sense of responsibility for causing the death of an unborn child are often greater.

> We chose to have an abortion because I know Down's syndrome children can be born with physical as well as mental handicaps and that they can suffer greatly. And we had to look at how we would care for a handicapped child when we were sixty. But I didn't want to accept that part of my decision was selfish, that I didn't want a less-than-perfect child. Then when we went to the parents' support group other couples said they blamed themselves for not being strong enough to deal with an abnormal child. When they said this, it was like a dagger through my heart, because I knew it was true for me, too. I cried for two solid days, but I had to face my guilt. Those feelings are there, and if you don't get them out, they eat away at you.

> I think about it every day, even just for a second. But life has to go on. (Quotations from Kohn & Moffitt 1994: 116–117.)

In a two-year follow-up of couples who had undergone terminations of pregnancies affected by fetal abnormalities, 20% of the women interviewed still experienced regular bouts of crying, sadness and irritability (Marteau & Anionwu 1996: 134). Fathers may be as deeply affected as mothers. 'One father who, having been through years of infertility, had then aborted a baby with Down's syndrome was deeply shaken. He found it difficult to be around children and gave up some friends and favourite recreational activities because he knew children would be present' (Kohn & Moffitt 1994: 113).

In Britain, the society ARC (Antenatal Results and Choices, formerly SATFA) was formed to provide emotional support and counselling for parents facing this experience, and provides a range of literature and information. In families with inherited disorders, the decision whether to abort an affected fetus when parents already have one living child with the same condition can be particularly agonizing. Undergoing an abortion on an affected fetus may feel as though one is rejecting the existing child. One parent said that she was not able to accept prenatal testing because she wanted to avoid having to say in effect to her six-year-old disabled son, 'We've got another one like you so we're getting rid of it' (Green & Statham 1996: 145). Other parents feel that, having witnessed the suffering of a previously affected child, they have no option but to request an abortion, and feel thankful that they were able to take this route, despite their distress.

What about those parents who declined screening and then had to face the reality of bringing up a disabled child? How did other people relate to them? A study in the UK found that 'Geneticists, obstetricians and the general public were more blaming towards mothers who gave birth to a child with Down's syndrome, having declined screening, than they were to mothers who had not received screening' (Marteau & Anionwu 1996: 135). Some ethicists have suggested that mothers who have discovered that their fetus carries a lethal abnormality, such as the severe chromosomal disorder Edwards syndrome, have a duty to obtain an abortion. In his book on genetics at the start of life entitled *The Perfect Baby*, Glen McGee states: 'There can be no question that a couple who find out that their infant is sure to suffer and die incurs special responsibilities, and among those responsibilities may be one to abort. From time to time, genetic testing will suggest a duty to abort' (McGee 1997: 93).

Notice the phrase 'a duty to abort'. Over the last thirty years we have moved imperceptibly from abortion as an option in extreme circumstances, through abortion as an option on request, to a duty to abort. This is what technology can do to the experience of pregnancy.

Professional views of genetic screening

But what about the health professionals? What do they feel about the programme of fetal screening? Here is one description of the aims of prenatal diagnosis, given by Professor Marcus Pembrey, a distinguished geneticist at Great Ormond Street Hospital in London:

(1) to allow the widest range of informed choice to women and their partners at risk of having a child with a genetic disorder
(2) to provide reassurance and reduce the level of anxiety associated with reproduction
(3) to allow couples at risk of a genetic disorder to embark upon a family, knowing that, if they wish, they may avoid the birth of seriously affected children through termination of an affected pregnancy
(4) to prepare a couple who wish to know in advance that their child is affected in order that they can continue the pregnancy prepared, and to ensure early treatment for the child (Pembrey 1996: 78).

Obstetricians and geneticists draw a sharp distinction between giving people information, and letting them make their own decisions on the basis of the information that has been conveyed. In essence this is a version of the distinction between facts and values which is a feature of much modern philosophical thought (see later in chapter 11). The duty of the clinician or counsellor is to convey the scientific information about screening – the facts, which are objective, neutral and value-free – without making any recommendation. The individual patient is then free to make up her own mind about the values she wishes to follow – to exercise informed choice, individual autonomy free from coercive influences of any kind. This is the philosophical perspective which lies behind the practice of so-called 'non-directive counselling'.

Yet when professionals attempt to counsel non-directively, they are aware of grave difficulties. Many, if not most, patients actively seek directive advice. They are uncomfortable with the liberal concept of unfettered individual freedom and autonomous choices. One of the commonest questions asked of professionals is, 'What would you do in my place?' – described as the 'terrible question' by an experienced counsellor. Refusing to give advice may impede the counselling relationship of trust and openness, and is often interpreted by the patient as a lack of care. In some cases a strange struggle ensues, with the patient trying to force professionals to say what their own recommendation would be, and the counsellors desperately trying to 'act professionally' and hence not to reveal their own opinions.

Faced with this experience, some have concluded that the whole goal of non-directive counselling is flawed. 'It is questionable whether non-prescriptive counselling is really possible . . . no single story, however balanced, can ever be neutral or value free' (Shiloh 1996: 86). 'So-called non-directive genetic counselling . . . is just as dangerous as paternalistic medicine. The physician is unavoidably engaged in the care of parents and patient, and must work toward disclosing all the information available, including his own opinions' (McGee 1997: 93). It seems that the fact/value distinction does not work in practice. It fails to fit with reality – with the way the world and human beings are made.

Most obstetricians and geneticists are strongly in favour of fetal screening with the option of abortion, as they see it as a way of preventing suffering for parents and for children. It is unlikely that the considerable resources that have been allocated to antenatal diagnosis would have been allocated if the main aim was reassurance or psychological preparation for abnormality. Geneticists recognize that the new technology carries with it 'an enormous potential for the avoidance of serious genetic diseases and congenital malformations', in the words of another distinguished scientist, Professor Sir David Weatherall (quoted in Green & Statham 1996: 144). For the foreseeable future, however, this potential will be realized only if parents are prepared to have abortions when affected fetuses are detected. And with advances in genetics, many more tests are likely to become available. As the number of genetic disorders that can be detected during pregnancy continues to grow, more and more couples will face decisions about terminating affected pregnancies.

Some doctors say that fetal screening enables the 'prevention' of disability. Antenatal screening is just another example of preventative medicine. But this is a novel redefinition of the word 'prevention'. To be strictly accurate, prenatal screening and termination do not prevent disability; they eliminate disabled individuals.

Financial implications of antenatal screening

In many countries, large amounts of money and resources have been put into making fetal screening widely available. The *British Medical Journal* of 26 July 1997 reported that screening has become available for a genetic condition which causes mental disability, called the fragile X syndrome. Although the technology has been available for some time, there has been some reluctance to screen for the disorder in the NHS because of the lack of conclusive evidence of its likely effectiveness and cost. The syndrome affects about one in 4,000 boys and one in 8,000 girls. At an estimated cost of over £90,000 for each case detected, routine antenatal screening for the syndrome is three times as expensive as that for Down's syndrome. But this must be offset against the costs of lifetime care for a child with fragile X syndrome, which exceed £700,000. The report's authors conclude, therefore, that screening for the syndrome is both accurate and *cost-effective* (my emphasis), and should now be considered for inclusion in a national screening programme (*BMJ* 1997: 315:208). Later in the same year, however, a *BMJ* editorial by another geneticist, Dr Angela Barnicoat, questioned whether antenatal screening for the condition was appropriate in view of the relatively good outcome of female fetuses and the demands of counselling pregnant mothers identified as being at risk (*BMJ* 1997: 315:1174–1175).

Of course, fetal screening can also lead to expenditure, due to the cost of litigation. In the Introduction we looked at the case of Reece O'Sullivan, a child with spina bifida whose parents were suing the hospital because of a 'wrongful life'. In another case, Sandra Hurley successfully sued her doctors because they did not give her accurate information about her baby's risks of Down's syndrome and the possibility of amniocentesis. In the event, her son Matthew did have Down's syndrome and Mrs Hurley claimed that the burden of bringing him up led to depression and the break-up of her marriage. Her lawyer told the court: 'She is utterly devoted to Matthew but this cannot obscure or dilute the enormous burdens to her' (*The Guardian*, 29 April 1977). The financial sums involved in so-called 'wrongful life' claims can be huge, as parents can claim for the cost of raising and educating a child who would not have been born but for a doctor's negligence. It seems that, as a result of the promotion of antenatal screening tests, it is now relatively common for parents to blame health professionals when a child is born with a genetic disorder. This may well lead to poorer psychological adjustment, and it has been suggested that the availability of prenatal screening may therefore be adversely affecting the adjustment necessary for parents caring for affected children. Similarly, antenatal screening employs large amounts of scarce Health Service resources, sometimes for questionable gains. One programme for the detection of fetuses with blood diseases such as thalassaemia, after screening no fewer than 18,907 people, detected four affected pregnancies, of which just one was terminated (Marteau & Anionwu 1996: 135).

Attitudes of disabled people to antenatal screening

Until recently the voice of disabled people in our society has been marginalized and their views have scarcely reached public attention. But things are changing. One eloquent voice is that of Tom Shakespeare, an academic sociologist at Leeds University. In a paper entitled 'Choice and Rights: Eugenics, Genetics and Disability Equality', Shakespeare gives a counterblast to the conventional medical wisdom about genetic screening of fetuses. 'Politicians, scientists and doctors alike must realize that disabled people do have a particular interest in prenatal testing and should therefore be systematically involved in the public debate' (Shakespeare 1997).

Tom Shakespeare happens to have a severe congenital condition called achondroplasia, which causes abnormal bone growth and restriction of body growth. It is a form of short stature which can be detected by ultrasound in the later stages of pregnancy. If it is detected, as a chance finding on a late scan, for example, abortion may be offered. Not surprisingly, Shakespeare has a view about this. Many disabled people 'oppose screening because it is very difficult to support a practice which would have prevented one's own existence'. We need to take the views and opinions of disabled people into account, including those of people with learning difficulties and communication problems. 'People with severe intellectual impairments may not be able to contribute directly to the debate on screening . . . Just because a person is unable to articulate their views and concerns clearly does not mean that their life isn't worth living.' 'Disabled people are not consulted on matters which affect us: professionals, unrepresentative charities and governments all make decisions about disability, without considering that the best experts on life as a disabled person are disabled people themselves' (Shakespeare 1997).

Shakespeare argues that it is disingenuous for scientists and clinicians to claim that the development of genetic science is neutral and value-free. Science is part of society and scientists have to take responsibility in influencing how scientific information and technology are applied. Scientists must be held to account for their own beliefs and practices.

The term 'eugenics' can be defined as 'the science of improving the population by control of inherited qualities'. Shakespeare argues that many geneticists have views which might qualify as eugenicist on this definition. They believe that genetic testing is a good thing because it allows people to have healthy babies instead of unhealthy ones. Hence they place a negative value on people with certain conditions, and see it as socially desirable to prevent the birth of certain fetuses. Similarly, many obstetricians seem to be highly directive in persuading patients to have an abortion in the presence of fetal abnormality. Surveys of obstetricians have suggested that the majority favoured termination in a number of severe conditions including spina bifida, Down's syndrome, Huntington's disease and muscular dystrophy, and a minority favoured termination in less severe conditions including cystic fibrosis, sickle-cell anaemia, achondroplasia and haemophilia (Marteau *et al.* 1993). By offering genetic technology to identify affected fetuses and encouraging individual choices in favour of abortion, Shakespeare argues, many obstetricians are promoting eugenic selection. Although he is not opposed to abortion in general, defending the woman's 'right to choose', he maintains that the law should not make a special case for abortion because of fetal impairment. 'Everyone carries mutant and potentially harmful genes . . . the law should not discriminate between impaired and non-impaired fetuses.'

According to Shakespeare, many people decide to abort an affected fetus because of the uncaring attitude of society to disabled people. 'The decisions underlying selective termination of affected fetuses are often about the social implications of bringing up a disabled child, not a eugenic unwillingness to bring disabled people into the world.' Instead of promoting antenatal screening, we should be ensuring better provision of welfare services and financial benefits to parents of disabled children, in order to make it easier for parents to decide to continue such a pregnancy. 'To the extent that prenatal interventions implement social prejudices against people with disabilities they do not expand our reproductive choices. They constrict them' (Hubbard, quoted by Shakespeare 1997).

A woman who decided to continue her pregnancy following a diagnosis of spina bifida wrote of her own experience. 'Every time there was a knock at the door or a letter we thought, "Here's another lecture." They kept saying things like it was wrong to keep the baby . . . it would be wicked . . . They meant well, but . . .' (Farrant, quoted by Shakespeare 1997).

In 1987 an author called Christy Nolan won the Whitbread Book of the Year prize for his autobiography *Under the Eye of the Clock*. At the prize-giving ceremony, there in a ballroom in London, surrounded by the glitterati of the literary world, was a young profoundly disabled man in a wheelchair. He had typed the entire book by means of a pointer attached to his forehead. Because he was unable to speak, his mother read his acceptance speech. This is part of what he said:

> You all must realize that history is in the making. Tonight a crippled man is taking his place on the world literary stage. Tonight is my night for laughing, for crying tears of joy. But wait, my brothers hobble after me

hinting. What about silent us? Can we too have a voice? Tonight I am speaking for them . . . Tonight is the happiest night of my life. Imagine what I would have missed if the doctors had not revived me on that September day long ago. Can freedom be denied to handicapped man? Can *yessing* be so difficult that, rather than give a baby a chance of life, man treads upon his brother and silences him before he can draw one breath of this world's fresh air?'

Increasingly, disabled people are perceiving fetal screening as a form of social discrimination against them. It is a technological means by which the healthy majority implement social prejudices against the minority with disability. Why should we argue that the life of an individual with Down's syndrome is not worth living, and that such a person is merely an intolerable burden on his or her parents, the community and the state? Is this not a new form of discrimination? Instead of discriminating on the basis of skin colour or country of origin, a discrimination called racism, we are now guilty of discriminating on the basis of chromosomes: 'chromosomalism'.

In 1995, Dominic Lawson, the editor of the *Spectator*, became the father of a baby called Domenica with Down's syndrome. He wrote a moving article in the *Spectator* of 17 June 1995 about his experience. He described his emotions of anger at the cold, professional way in which the doctor outlined the features of Down's syndrome, the intense, almost physically painful, love that he felt for his daughter, and his sense of grief at the losses which Domenica will suffer as a result of her physical and mental disability. He expressed his anger that 'a whole industry has been developed to make it increasingly improbable that children like Domenica Lawson will be allowed to live . . . This is nothing less than state-sponsored annihilation of viable sentient fetuses. In the People's Republic of China, the authorities wait until such children are born naturally before starving them to death. In Hitler's Germany, even before the final solution to the Jewish "problem", the Nazis were exterminating wholesale the mentally retarded. In this country the weeding-out process is done before birth, and only with the parents' consent. I do not think, however, that this constitutes a triumph for democracy. To the extent that this policy is more than half-baked eugenics, it is, to take the most charitable interpretation, based on the utilitarian idea that the child born with a physical or mental handicap will be an unhappy person, so unhappy that he or she would have been better off dead. One only needs to state this proposition to understand how presumptuous it is.'

Describing himself as an atheist, he argued strongly for the principle that all human life should be protected. 'The sanctity of life is not just some kind of abstract, obscure principle. A life is a life, and every life can be filled with all kinds of positive things and real happiness.'

It is not only those with a Christian or other religious faith, then, who react against the abortion of affected fetuses. There are many people in our society who have deep intuitions that the destruction of potentially disabled fetuses is not the best way for our society to develop and flourish. For many, the noble aim of medicine has become subverted into 'half-baked eugenics'. These are the words of feminist writer Meg Stacey: 'Tidying away some hereditable diseases will not make society tidy, nor will it eliminate suffering. Has the time perhaps come when it is necessary to revise the scientific goal to one which would work with nature rather than attempting to beat it?' (Stacey 1996: 345).

We shall look at Christian responses to the issues raised by fetal screening in chapter 7, but in the next chapter we examine in more detail some recent advances in human genetics and the opportunities and challenges that they bring.

5. Brave new world: the new genetics

Developments in biotechnology since the late 1980s have contributed to a remarkable sense of uncertainty among policy-makers and so-called opinion-formers. There is a sense of being cut loose from familiar ethical moorings, a feeling of unease at the runaway technological development coupled with ethical relativism which threatens to engulf us all. If it is technically feasible to generate an unlimited supply of human embryos for research, should we prevent it, or encourage it? If it is possible to choose the sex and to enhance the genetic potential of our children, should this be opposed or regulated? If it is possible to clone organisms from human embryos which will provide vitally needed human tissue, or genetically matched organs for transplant, why should we oppose it? When the potential medical and human benefits are so enormous, what possible grounds can be found to resist?

In this chapter we consider some recent developments in genetic technology and ask how Christian thinking can be brought to bear in this rapidly changing field.

Sex and race selection

One of the many options which has become available for parents is the selection of the sex of their future child. In a recent public lecture, philosopher John Harris has argued neatly that within a liberal secular worldview, parental choice should be paramount. Parents should be able to choose the sex of their child, rather than leave it to chance. 'Either the sex of your child is morally significant, in which case it's much too important to be left to chance, or it's morally insignificant, in which case it doesn't matter if we let parents choose.'

The logic is impeccable. Leaving something as important as the sex of your future child to chance makes no sense at all in a secular universe. It makes sense only in a theistic worldview, where a child can be regarded as a mysterious gift and not as a product of human planning and ingenuity. And yet the UK Human Fertilization and Embryology Authority is still strongly opposed to sex selection, except on strictly medical grounds, where it may be used to avoid sex-linked diseases. Although there are pragmatic reasons to oppose sex selection, such as a possible shift in the balance of males and females in society, it seems that the main reason for this opposition is because choosing the sex of one's child still *feels* wrong, at least to most of us. It goes against a basic intuition of many in our society. But for how long?

According to a 1997 news item, a British doctor, Paul Rainsbury, has set up a clinic in Naples to allow couples to choose the sex of their baby for social reasons. Dr Rainsbury planned to use a laboratory in Riyadh, Saudi Arabia, to carry out preimplantation genetic selection on embryos. The embryos of the selected sex would then be reimplanted in Naples. He expected his clients to be mainly Asian, and that 80% of them would choose boys. Dr Rainsbury said: 'My hope is that any criticism will disappear as people come to understand why we have decided to use existing medical science to help those who face intense personal pressure to produce babies of a specific sex. Offering sex selection as part of infertility treatment was always going to come. It was simply a question of who was going to be first to grasp the nettle' (*GenEthics* 1997: 16:10).

Of course, sex selection using preimplantation diagnosis is a high-tech version of a process which has been going on for thousands of years. There are many people across the world who 'face intense personal pressure to produce babies of a specific sex'. In India, pregnant women are often forced by relatives to undergo antenatal tests such as high-resolution ultrasound scanning, or even amniocentesis, to identify the sex of their fetus. If it is found to be female, an abortion is performed. A report in the *British Medical Journal* of 13 August 1994 estimated that at least 50,000 female fetuses a year were aborted in India for this reason. Most of these abortions happen in private abortion clinics and sex-determination shops, of which there are two thousand in Delhi alone. Large profits are made from sex-determination tests, and, although legislation has recently been passed in the Indian Parliament to outlaw the practice, it is difficult if not impossible for the state authorities to control. In Delhi alone, it was estimated that 70% of all abortions were cases of female feticide. 'Girls are seen as an economic burden by parents because they need a dowry for marriage. They are also seen as a potential embarrassment because they are vulnerable to sexual harassment.' The effects of female feticide and infanticide have changed the population balance so that there are only 927 women for every 1,000 men.

In 1994 a black woman in Italy received an embryo created from white sperm and egg donors because she wanted to have a white child, who she felt would be free from the prejudice a black child would face. Although many opposed this practice, John Harris defended it on the grounds of individual autonomy. 'Previously people have got gametes from their procreational partners and that's been treated as the norm. Technology has given us the power to change that.' For Harris, the key issue is the right to choose. After all, he points out, when people request gametes of the same race they are making a race choice. 'It seems suspect that when people choose the same race gamete they are not choosing the race of their child. Why should it be more problematic to choose a different gamete?' (quoted in *BMA News Review*, May 1994).

Preimplantation genetic analysis and embryo selection

At present, preimplantation genetic analysis and selection of embryos are restricted to the detection of childhood diseases – such as sickle-cell anaemia or cystic fibrosis – that are regarded as having a severe impact on quality of life. The rapid increase in the identification of disease-predisposing genes, however, will enable scientists to detect genetic variants that have a less severe impact on a child's life, such as predispositions to obesity, diabetes, heart disease, asthma and various forms of cancer. It seems likely that genetic variations which increase resistance to infective diseases will also be identified. The identification and modification of genes which may predispose to 'socially desirable characteristics' is much more speculative and still belongs to wilder reaches of science fiction. The speed of progress in molecular genetics and reproductive technology, however, is enough to dispel complacency.

A distinction is commonly made between *negative* selection against embryos which carry genetic variations likely to cause a disease, and *positive* selection in favour of embryos which are found to carry genetic variations which are socially desirable. In reality, the distinction is less clear than it seems at first. If we choose not to select an embryo with a genotype likely to cause a disease, should we refuse to select an embryo whose genotype will make him or her an unaffected carrier of the disease, but who may pass it on to any future offspring? Should one select for a genetic variation which is found to be associated with a *reduced* risk of disease compared with the general population? Of all the embryos available, why not select the ones that have the least risk of disease and the best chance of future well-being?

Lee Silver predicts that embryo selection is here to stay, at least in American society, where the majority 'hold fast to the overriding importance of personal liberty and personal fortune in guiding what individuals are allowed and able to do'. Although embryo selection is currently used by a tiny fraction of prospective parents to screen for a tiny number of disease genotypes, 'with each coming year, the power of the technology will expand, and its application will become more efficient. Slowly but surely, embryo selection will be incorporated into American culture, just as other reproductive technologies have been in the past . . . Environment and genes stand side by side. Both contribute to a child's chances for achievement and success in life, although neither guarantees it. If we allow money to buy an advantage in one, the claim for stopping the other is hard to make, *especially in a society that gives women the right to abort for any reason at all'* (Silver 1997: 224–225, my emphasis).

Cloning and nuclear transfer

On 23 February 1997, the news of the creation of Dolly the sheep transfixed the world media and the scientific community alike. Dolly was created using DNA taken from a cell-line cultured from a mammary-gland cell from an adult sheep. The nuclear material was transferred into an unfertilized egg from which the original nucleus had been removed. The newly created embryo was then inserted into the uterus of another sheep, where it grew into Dolly – whose genetic structure was identical to the sheep from which the mammary-gland cell was taken (*Nature* 1997: 385:810–813). Although cloning using cells from embryos had been reported previously, the scientific community was surprised and even shocked that it was possible to use nuclear material from an adult cell.

Commentators and ethicists seized on the possibility that the same procedure could be undertaken on humans. It was not a new idea. Aldous Huxley, in his novel *Brave New World*, had introduced the concept to a mass audience. 'Bokanovsky's Process . . . one egg, one embryo, one adult – normality. But a bokanovskified egg will bud, will proliferate, will divide. From eight to ninety-six buds, and every bud will grow into a perfectly formed embryo, and every embryo into a full-sized adult. Making ninety-six human beings grow where only one grew before. Progress' (Huxley 1932: 17). In 1970 Alvin Toffler produced his influential book *Future Shock*, which predicted: 'One of the more fantastic possibilities is that man will be able to make biological copies of himself . . . Cloning would make it possible for people to see themselves anew, to fill the world with twins of themselves' (Toffler 1970: 197). Woody Allen brilliantly parodied the idea in his movie *Sleeper*, where a surgeon, transported 200 years into the future, is given the task of cloning the recently deceased leader from his nose, which had been kept alive for the purpose. Ira Levin's *The Boys from Brazil* was based on the use of cloning in a conspiracy aimed at duplicating an army of neo-Nazi thugs.

With these nightmarish ideas in the public consciousness, it is hardly surprising that the public response to Dolly's creation was so intense. Many scientists working in the field of mammalian genetics and embryology are dismayed at the unwelcome attention directed at their research. Some have tried to calm the fears by playing down the possibility of human cloning. Lord Winston, the eminent reproductive specialist, said there was 'absolutely no possibility whatsoever that human beings could be cloned in the near future' (quoted in the *Daily Mail*, 26 February 1997). Others said that there was no clinical reason why anyone would want to undertake human cloning, and that even if individuals wanted to clone themselves or someone else, they would never find trained professionals willing to do it.

Such anodyne statements are unlikely to be totally reassuring. There seems to be no reason to doubt that the technology will be applicable sooner or later to human cells. The equipment and facilities are standard in laboratories and assisted-conception clinics around the world. There are thousands of professionals who possess the necessary skills to undertake experiments leading to human cloning. Following the announcement of Dolly's birth, US Senator Tom Harkin complained about the 'irrational' opposition to human cloning: 'It is wrong and demeaning to human nature for government to try to stop or limit human cloning experiments. Human cloning will take place and it will take place within my lifetime. It holds untold benefits for humankind in the future, such as the replacement of babies who die after birth, and the creation of genetically identical tissue for transplantation' (*GenEthics* 1997: 16:10).

Where the visions of Huxley and Levin are misleading is that the technology is unlikely to be used in the foreseeable future by totalitarian governments or neo-Nazi dictators. Instead, the demand for human cloning will come first from the strictly medical arena. It is important to make a distinction between reproductive and non-reproductive cloning. *Reproductive cloning* is designed to produce a fetus which will grow into a separate individual. *Non-reproductive cloning* is intended to produce a human embryo which can then be manipulated to generate genetically identical stem cells for medical purposes. No embryonic development beyond the fourteen-day stage will occur and thus, in this case, no developed individual will result.

Genetically matched stem cells offer the prospect of remarkable new treatments for a range of medical diseases. Blood, skin, muscle and brain cells could be grown in the laboratory and implanted without the need for anti-rejection treatment, because of the identical genetic match with the patient. If we are prepared to accept the generation, manipulation and destruction of human embryos, we may have access to an unparalleled range of new treatments for inherited, degenerative and cancerous diseases. At the time of writing, the UK Human Fertilization and Embryology Authority has commenced a process of public consultations on whether non-reproductive cloning should be allowed.

Reproductive cloning, too, carries the possibility of medical benefit. For instance, the success of bone-marrow transplantation for leukaemia depends critically on the availability of a genetically matched donor. Sometimes, when bone-marrow transplant remains the only hope of treatment, a prolonged search of related and unrelated donors fails to find a suitable match, condemning the leukaemia sufferer to death, without the prospect of a cure. The cloning of a child from genetic material taken from the leukaemia sufferer would provide a genetically matched donor for a bone-marrow transplant. Is it wrong for a couple to use reproductive technology to have a second child who will not only be loved for himself or herself, but will also have the capability of saving their first child's life?

Informal surveys conducted by organ-transplantation centres suggest that it is not unheard of for couples to have another child by normal means in order to act as a potential donor for an older sibling, although this is rarely acknowledged in public (Silver 1997: 113). The availability of cloning would enable parents to reproduce knowing that an exact genetic match would result.

Another suggested use of nuclear-transfer techniques is to prevent the inheritance of rare disorders (affecting a component of the cell known as the mitochondria) which are passed on in the cytoplasm of the mother's egg. If the nuclear DNA from the mother was inserted into a donor egg from which the nucleus had been removed, followed by IVF, it would be possible for the mother to have a genetically related child without the risk of mitochondrial disease being passed on to the next generation. A third possible scenario is that of the mother who, after giving birth to a baby, receives chemotherapy for cancer, which means that she becomes permanently sterile. If her baby were then to die, in a tragic accident for example, cloning from cells taken before or even after the baby's death would enable her to have another child who was still genetically her own.

Cloning might even allow lesbian couples to share biological parentage of a child, and avoid introducing alien genes into their relationship. One member of the couple could provide the donor cell, and the other the unfertilized recipient egg. The newly formed embryo could then be introduced into the uterus of the second woman, allowing the child to be biologically related to both women (Silver 1997: 116).

Gene therapy

The first human gene-therapy trial started in Los Angeles in September 1990, when children with a severe immune deficiency due to lack of a vital enzyme were treated with specially engineered viruses carrying the gene to enable synthesis of the missing enzyme. So far, gene therapy has had only limited success due to formidable technical difficulties. In order for the therapy to have a permanent effect, it is necessary for the genetic modification to take place in the stem cells, which are self-replicating. In this way, the therapeutic effect will last the life of the individual. Scientists and ethicists have agreed that genetic manipulation of germ-line cells (those leading to eggs or sperm) should not be performed, as the genetic modification will be passed on to children and on into future generations, with unforeseeable consequences. In order to prevent accidental modification of germ-line cells, genetic manipulation of the early embryo has been forbidden by the Human Fertilization and Embryology Authority, and by other regulatory bodies.

Nevertheless, Dr French Anderson, who was involved in the first trial in 1990, has proposed trials of gene therapy in fetuses with immune deficiency or inherited blood disorders (*New Scientist*, June 1998: 12). By concentrating treatment in the very early stages of life, there is a greater chance of obtaining genetic modification of the stem cells before permanent damage to the body has occurred.

Public acceptability of genetic technology

Many genetic scientists believe, in private, that there will be a gradual acceptance of human genetic selection and manipulation by the community as a whole. They point to the initial media furore and ethical disquiet that have greeted many advances in medical technology over the last few decades. In 1966 two American reproductive specialists wrote presciently about fertility treatments: 'Any change in custom or practice in this emotionally charged area has always elicited a response from established custom and law: horrified negation at first; then negation without horror; then slow and gradual curiosity, study, evaluation, and finally a very slow but steady acceptance' (quoted by Silver 1997: 75).When news of the first successful IVF treatment reached the media in 1978, there were editorials calling for the abandonment of all research on 'test-tube babies'. Now the technique has gained broad acceptance within the community. Many scientists believe that the main role of official bodies such as the Human Fertilization and Embryology Authority is to gauge the public mood and ensure that approved activities remain within broad limits of public acceptability. In the *BMA News Review* of May 1994, Peter Brinsden, medical director of Bourn Hall Assisted Conception Clinic in Cambridge, put forward this view: 'I think ethics is what the public is comfortable with.'

At the same time, it may be argued that ultimately governmental control of reproductive technology is doomed to failure. Small clinics can be set up in any part of the world, including off-shore islands. Many people in our society have an overwhelming desire to raise healthy children, and, in a free-market economy, the financial rewards that are available for those who satisfy that desire are enormous. As Silver puts it, 'If there are people who desire reprogenetic services, there will be others willing to provide them . . . Whether we like it or not, the global marketplace will reign supreme' (1997: 11).

Promises and dangers of the new genetics

Even if we penetrate the hyperbole, there is no doubt that the new genetics offers real promise for the future. First, there is the possibility of new biological insights which will have far-reaching consequences for medicine. By understanding the complex links between genetic variations and the complete range of human diseases, scientists are already discovering new insights which are likely to lead to completely new medical treatments. Secondly, gene therapy, despite disappointing results so far, clearly has great potential for the future. Thirdly, genetic analysis may enable genetically vulnerable individuals to be identified early in life, so that exposure to damaging environmental factors can be avoided.

But at the same time there is a dark side to genetic technology. Widespread use of genetic screening is likely to lead to increased stigmatization of genetically abnormal individuals. In the past, medicine has been limited in both diagnostic precision as well as therapeutic possibilities. What new genetic understanding provides is a very much more precise means of predicting the future, while the possibility of any specific genetic treatment remains many years away. For some individuals the ability to predict the future may be a curse as much as a blessing. The identification of a genetic mutation may mean that an individual is unable to obtain a job, purchase life or health insurance, obtain a mortgage, or find a marriage partner.

Increased antenatal screening may lead to loss of respect for, and victimization of, the disabled and their parents. The use of genetic techniques to select and enhance embryos may encourage parents to regard their children as commodities. Commercial exploitation of genetic information will allow large multinational corporations to exert enormous financial pressures on individuals and on healthcare systems, including the National Health Service. Limited access to expensive genetic and reproductive technology may exacerbate social tensions between wealthy and poor people in our society. In the same way the technology may concentrate limited resources on the diseases of wealthy groups and divert resources away from low-tech solutions to the diseases associated with poverty and deprivation. New gene therapies may have unexpected physical side-effects and life-long consequences. Finally, unscrupulous politicians and dictators may be tempted to use the technology to increase control over their people, to engage in eugenic social engineering or even to use genetic 'bombs' to wipe out unwanted racial groups. In the words of C. S. Lewis, 'Man's power over nature turns out to be power exercised by some men over other men' (Lewis 1978).

Christian responses to genetic technology

How can we respond to these issues from the perspective of the Christian worldview? What are the fundamental principles which should inform our thinking and our practice? As we try to think Christianly about developments in genetics, we must steer between two fallacies.

On the one hand there is the fallacy of *genetic determinism*. This is the popular fallacy of the simplistic biological reductionist. According to this view, genetics explains everything. I am programmed by my genes as a computer is programmed by its software. Everything I am, everything I do, is determined, a product of an immutable genetic code which was randomly generated at my conception. This attitude is encouraged by much of the sensationalism generated by the media and by some of the genetics industry itself. The implication is that detailed genetic analysis and the introduction of gene therapy will usher in a new age of health, wisdom and benevolence. Similarly, much of the shock-horror publicity about advances in genetics encourages a popular belief in genetic determinism. It implies that once scientists have unravelled the entire human genome, they will have insight into all the mysteries of the human condition and will be able to control and manipulate human beings at will. The furore generated about the possibility of human cloning is another example. When Dolly's birth was announced, a number of journalists and commentators speculated that if a genetically identical individual was created in this way, it might not be a real human being and would have no 'soul'. Again, this is nonsense. Identical twins conceived naturally are 'clones', and yet no-one would suggest that they are anything less than human.

The truth is that genetic determinism is both scientific rubbish and spiritual idolatry. Human beings are far greater than the product of their genes. At a physical and psychological level, we are formed continuously by the interaction between our physical and genetic structure and the constantly changing environment to which we are exposed. At a spiritual level, we have a unique relationship with God who calls us into existence and into relationship with him.

The opposite fallacy is that of *philosophical dualism*, which says that my physical body and structure are of no importance compared to the real me, the immaterial thinking mind and spirit. My genetic structure is irrelevant to my identity. I am free to manipulate the physical structure of my body and its genetic code at will because my identity is defined by my mind, or by my relationship with God. Dualism has obvious attraction for biological scientists and doctors who have Christian beliefs. It allows us to participate in biological research or in reproductive and other forms of biotechnology without having to be too concerned about the spiritual consequences. After all, biological science and medicine deal only with the physical stuff of humanity, whereas the true identity and value of human beings lie in their relationship with God.

But dualism, like determinism, is based on a fallacy, on a false view of reality. Orthodox Christian thought has always affirmed that in the complex and mysterious unity which constitutes the human person, *both* the physical structure of my body *and* the immaterial spiritual aspects of my being are important and inextricably intertwined. The givenness of my genetic inheritance, expressing in a physical form the web of relationships into which I have been born, is as much a part of my identity as my mind and my personality. Certainly the body matters and certainly my genetic heritage is important in determining my identity, but I am not merely programmed. The human self, known and loved by others and by God himself, is greater than my genes.

If genetic inheritance is important, then, how should we think about medical treatments which manipulate the genetic code? Within the perspective of medicine as art restoration, is gene therapy an appropriate form of technology for 'flawed masterpieces'? In my view, genetic manipulation which is intended to be *restorative*, re-creating a damaged length of DNA, or replacing an abnormal gene variant with a normal counterpart, seems consistent with normal medical practice. The aim is to preserve and restore the artist's original design. There seems to be no fundamental difference between providing artificial thyroid hormone for a patient with congenital hypothyroidism and replacing a segment of DNA with a new portion, so that the patient is able to synthesize his or her own thyroid hormone. Both actions are aimed at preserving the original design. Therapy which is intended to be *enhancing*, however, aimed at producing children with stronger limbs, better growth and quicker brains, seems to me to step over the limits of human responsibility. Enhancing gene therapy attempts to improve on the original design. But Christians must take creation order seriously. Within ethical art restoration, the intention of the original artist must be normative.

Of course, the distinction between restorative and enhancing therapy is not always clear-cut. What about gene therapy which was intended to lead to an improved resistance to infectious diseases, such as HIV infection? Should this be regarded as therapy that is restoring the original design, or is it a fundamental change? Because of the impact of new genetic technology, Christians will need to reflect more deeply on the natural order given at creation. What does it mean to be human? What are the limits laid down by the physical structure and the moral order of our creation?

Similarly, the selection of embryos to ensure the desired sex or genetic make-up of a child seems fraught with problems. In the original creation order, a child can be seen as a gift, a mysterious other who is equal to us in status and significance. But with embryo testing and selection, the child becomes a commodity, the one we have chosen, reflecting our wishes and desires. This seems to me to change the nature of parenthood. It is to surrender to the controlling spirit of the age. Modern parents are in danger of being control freaks. We want to control and design our children to fulfil our deepest desires. We want to live out our unfulfilled expectations in them. But a biblical perception of parenthood teaches us that we must let go. Although we have a responsibility to protect, nurture and educate, we must also *respect* out children. In the words of Gilbert Meilander, 'we are very reluctant to let the mystery of personhood – equal in dignity to our own – unfold in the lives of our children'. Instead, 'we need the virtue of humility before the mystery of human personhood and the succession of generations. We need the realization that the children who come after us are not simply a product for us to mould' (Meilander 1997: 45).

I have no neat solutions or obvious panaceas to the challenges and questions which genetic and reproductive technology raises. We need to struggle together as a Christian community to understand more clearly the rapid changes which are occurring in our midst and to discern how to respond from a position of Christian faith. Here are some broad outlines of a Christian response.

First, I believe we are called to *empathize* with the deep and hidden pain of childless couples, and of families devastated by genetic illness. It is the reality of this hidden pain and the quest for technological solutions which drive the research and development in the new genetics. It is the failure of practical caring in our society which often seems to drive a desperate quest for technological fixes to the painful realities of the human condition.

Secondly, the Christian community is called to *challenge* the reductionist, 'Lego kit' mentality which is starting to pervade modern society and the healthcare systems within it. We need to oppose and inform the naïve and dangerous concepts of genetic determinism perpetrated by the media. At a social level, we need to challenge the economic and political power base which new genetic technology is creating, and demand democratic accountability, transparency and justice in the actions of those who control the technology.

Thirdly, I believe we have an urgent need to develop a more profound *understanding* of what it means to be a human being, created in God's image, contaminated by evil, yet affirmed and redeemed by the Christ event – the incarnation, death and resurrection of Jesus of Nazareth. We need renewed input from theologians and biblical scholars who can reflect on the nature and implications of the created order and our role within it. At the same time, we need the insights and practical experience of doctors, geneticists and reproductive scientists who can build a bridge between the biblical world and the world of modern science.

Fourthly, we need to *present* an alternative biblical worldview to our society: a worldview that regards human beings as wonderful but flawed masterpieces, rather than randomly generated, self-replicating organisms; a worldview which encompasses wonder, respect, empathy and protection for the weak and vulnerable in our society; a worldview which takes the physical structure of our bodies seriously while pointing to a greater reality, a deeper healing, and a hope which transcends the grave.

Finally, and perhaps most importantly, I passionately believe that we as a Christian community need to demonstrate the reality of our belief in the value of every human life through *practical caring*.

We shall return in more detail to these five themes in later chapters, but now we turn from the ethical dilemmas raised by recent genetic advances to the painful issue of the unwanted pregnancy and the ancient ethical debate about abortion and infanticide.

6. Abortion and infanticide: a historical perspective

At first glance, abortion (the intentional termination of pregnancy with the destruction of a fetus) and infanticide (the intentional killing of a newborn baby) seem starkly different. Yet, as we shall see, on both historical and ethical grounds they belong together. Our aim in this chapter is first to look at the ancient history of abortion and infanticide, and secondly to review the contemporary scene.

Abortion and infanticide in the ancient world

'If you don't know where you are going,' Archbishop William Temple once said, 'it is sometimes helpful to know where you have been' (quoted by Ferngren 1987a). As moderns, we tend to imagine that our problems are unique to our generation. Yet the debate about abortion and infanticide is an ancient one in the history of western civilization and in the history of the Christian church. By delving into some musty history, we may gain a fresh perspective on the debate which is still raging.

Both abortion and infanticide have been common practices since the earliest records of human history. Far from being confined to primitive, unsophisticated communities, both were well-known in the cosmopolitan and advanced civilizations of ancient Greece and Rome (Gorman 1982). In the city states of Greece and throughout the Roman Republic, abortion was widely available. It was a service provided by both professional and amateur abortionists and by some physicians. The methods included manipulation of the abdomen and uterus, herbal medications given by vaginal pessaries or by mouth, and a range of surgical techniques using tools specially designed for the purpose.

In most regions, abortions were readily available, although at a price. They were therefore more common among wealthy women than among the poor. Probably the commonest reason for obtaining an abortion was so that a woman might conceal illicit sexual activity, but it is well attested that wealthy women would obtain abortions merely to preserve their figures and their sexual attractiveness (Gorman 1982: 15).

The practice of abortion was endorsed by many prominent philosophers and writers. In discussing the role of women in his ideal *Republic*, Plato stated forcefully that pregnant women above the age of forty years should have an abortion, presumably because of an increased risk of maternal death and fetal abnormality. Aristotle, in his work *Politics*, recommended both infanticide and abortion if there was a risk of a 'deformed child', or if there was already an excess number of children in a family. He recognized, however, that infanticide by exposure of normal children might not be acceptable in certain regions, and therefore recommended an abortion in these cases:

> On the ground of number of children, if the regular customs hinder any of those born being exposed, there must be a limit fixed to the procreation of offspring, and if any people have a child as a result of intercourse in contravention of these regulations, abortion must be practised on it before it has developed sensation and life: for the line between lawful and unlawful abortion will be marked by the fact of having sensation and being alive (see Wyatt 1996: 8).

A major concern of the leaders of Greek city states was overpopulation leading to famine and social breakdown. Both abortion and infanticide were seen as entirely rational and reasonable approaches to this danger. The attitudes to babies and children within the classical Graeco-Roman world were startlingly different from our own (see Amundsen 1987). Contemporary Graeco-Roman society was fundamentally hierarchical. At the top of the pile were the élite: politicians, philosophers, athletes. Next down were ordinary decent working men: farmers, soldiers, tradespeople. Further down were women. And then there was the riff-raff: children, slaves, the disabled, the leper, and other undesirables. It was a society that prized athleticism, strength and what were called the 'masculine virtues', so it was natural for children to be despised because of their weakness, dependence and immaturity. The significance and worth that society tended to place on an individual child were in proportion to his or her future contribution to the state as an adult.

Like abortion, the intentional killing of malformed or unwanted newborn babies, by exposure, strangling or drowning, for instance, was widespread. In fact, the practice was so common that one contemporary historian, Polybius, writing in the second century BC, concluded that it had contributed to the serious depopulation that had occurred in Greece at the time. There were no laws prohibiting the killing of malformed or sick infants, and even healthy newborn babies were frequently unprotected by legal statute or social custom. Infanticide was such a natural and common event that it is mentioned frequently in comedies and plays of the period (Amundsen 1987).

It seems that the majority of philosophers and writers of this time supported both abortion and infanticide. In Plato's *Republic*, infanticide is regarded as essential to maintain the quality of the citizens. 'The offspring of the inferior and any of those of the other sort who are born defective, they will properly dispose of in secret, so that no-one will know what has become of them.' For Plato, children were valued according to their approximation to the ideal adult. They must be 'malleable, disposed to virtue and physically fit'.

Aristotle supported a law to ensure the compulsory exposure of all malformed babies: 'As to exposing or rearing the children born, let there be a law that no deformed child shall be reared.' Seneca, in his treatise *On Anger*, wrote, 'Mad dogs we knock on the head; the fierce and savage ox we slay; unnatural progeny we destroy; we drown even children who at birth are weakly and abnormal. Yet it is not anger, but reason that separates the harmful from the sound.'

In the Roman monarchy and republic, power was enshrined in the head of the family, the *paterfamilias*. He had, quite literally, the power of life and death over all his lawful possessions, in other words his slaves, children and wife. The earliest Roman law code permitted a father to expose any female infant he wished, and a deformed baby of either sex. Interestingly, abortion came under greater official disapproval than infanticide. This was probably partly because it involved a risk to the mother's life and health, but also because it allowed married women to commit adultery without being discovered by their husbands, and perhaps because it was a common practice of professional prostitutes. The secret performance of an abortion on a woman without the knowledge of her husband was viewed as a major offence against the 'property' of the husband. Nevertheless, abortion was extremely common in Rome and its dependent states from the first century BC onwards. Handbooks on techniques for abortion circulated quite freely and were read by rich women and prostitutes. The emperor Domitian (AD 51–96) had a clandestine affair with his niece Julia. She became pregnant and Domitian commanded her to have an abortion – a procedure which tragically resulted in her death (Gorman 1982: 19–32).

Within the orthodox medical world, gynaecology developed as a separate discipline, and a number of female physicians specialized in this art. Soranus, a Roman physician in the first and second centuries AD, wrote the earliest known treatise on gynaecology, which is still available. He maintained that abortion to conceal adultery or to maintain feminine beauty was improper, but that it was permissible to save the woman's life. He also included a chapter entitled 'How to Recognize the Newborn that is Worth Rearing'. In it, Soranus gives practical advice for midwives on the assessment of newborn babies immediately following delivery. First, the mother's health during pregnancy should be assessed, together with the gestational age of the infant. Subsequently, the newborn baby is examined to see if 'when put on the earth it immediately cries with proper vigour', and also to ensure that 'it is perfect in all its parts, members and senses; that its ducts, namely of the ears, nose, pharynx, urethra and anus, are free from obstruction; that the natural functions of every member are neither sluggish nor weak; that the joints bend and stretch; that it has due size and shape and is properly sensitive in every respect . . . And by conditions contrary to those mentioned, the infant not worth rearing is recognized' (quoted in Wyatt & Spencer 1992).

Not all the classical philosophers and writers approved. In particular, the Hippocratic Oath prohibited the use of a pessary to procure an abortion, and we shall return to this later in chapter 11. But it is clear that both abortion and infanticide were widely accepted.

It is possible to identify three underlying assumptions in the culture of the time. First was the belief that the value of an individual human life was not inherent, but was acquired some time after birth. No fetus or newborn child had an intrinsic right to life after birth. Secondly, it was assumed that the value of a life lay primarily in its usefulness, partly to the parents, but especially to the state as a future citizen. The healthy fetus or newborn baby was a future farmer, soldier or mother, provided that it was accepted as a useful member of society with the possibility of making a worthwhile contribution. Thus the value of the fetus or the newborn resided entirely in its *potential* to make a future contribution to society. Failure to make a contribution to society rendered one worthless. Finally, there was the generally accepted belief that health and physical wholeness were essential not only to survival but also to human dignity. In a culture that gloried in the 'masculine virtues', the weak, the disabled and the malformed were always likely to be seen as less than fully human.

If abortion was regarded as wrong, it was generally because of the risk to the mother's life, which clearly was of value to the state, or because of the infringement of the father's property rights or the rights of some other interested party. If infanticide was wrong, it was because of the risk of depopulation. No author seems to have raised the possibility that there was an *intrinsic* value in the life of a fetus or even of a newborn baby. It is clear that the apparent value to society of an unwanted fetus or a malformed or diseased newborn was minimal. It is interesting that whereas abortion was criticized from time to time, it appears that the morality of killing sickly or deformed newborns was hardly questioned. It is perhaps understandable that the care of sick or defective babies appears to have been of no concern to the medical profession, and that the physicians of that period concentrated their efforts on the older children and adults whose lives were of obvious value and significance.

The Judaeo-Christian world
The Old Testament period

The Jewish world of the same period displayed a radically different attitude to the fetus and newborn infant. There is no doubt that this stemmed from the teaching of the Old Testament law, the Torah. In the next chapter we shall return to the biblical teaching in more detail, but here we shall sketch the outlines. At the heart of the Jewish law was the doctrine of the image of God. Every human being, newborn or adult, deformed or healthy, slave or free, had an *intrinsic* value as a unique expression of God's image. As we have seen, the Torah taught that the deliberate destruction of any human life was an affront to the dignity of God (Gn. 9:6). The Mishnah, which enshrined traditional rabbinic teaching, declared that God created but a single man in order to teach humankind that 'whoever destroys a single individual God imputes it on him as if he had destroyed the entire world, and whoever saves the life of a single individual God imputes it on him as if he had saved the entire world' (Ferngren 1987a).

In ancient Jewish thought the high value attached to human life extended to the fetus, which was the unique creation of Yahweh, formed for his own purpose. Nevertheless, the protection afforded to the fetus was not absolute. The rabbis taught that it could be destroyed before birth if it was necessary to save the life of the mother. But from the moment of birth, once the head had emerged from the body of the mother, the baby was regarded as a full member of society with the same rights and protection as any fully grown person.

The second element in the condemnation of abortion and infanticide was the requirement given by God for the strong to protect the defenceless. Although the Torah does not contain many specific references to fetuses or babies, there is no doubt that they were seen as especially vulnerable and therefore among those whom God was concerned to protect from abuse. The pagan ritual of sacrificing children was explicitly condemned in the Old Testament law (Dt. 18:10), and the practice of infant exposure was, not surprisingly, viewed with abhorrence within Israel. Yet it was a sufficiently common practice in the surrounding nations to be referred to by the Old Testament prophets. In the book of Ezekiel, the infant nation of Israel, rejected by the surrounding nations, is graphically compared to a newborn baby 'thrown out into the open field, for on the day you were born you were despised', and lying on the ground 'kicking about in your blood' (Ezk. 16:4–6).

Philo, a well-known Jewish apologist writing at the time of Christ, confirmed the orthodox Jewish view of child exposure when he stated that 'infanticide undoubtedly is murder, since the displeasure of the law is not concerned with ages but with a breach to the human race'. The Roman historian Tacitus, who frequently commented in his writings on the strange and exotic practices of foreigners, felt that the unusual attitude of the Jews to newborn infants was worthy of comment. With an unmistakable air of astonishment, he wrote that infant exposure was unknown among Jews; in fact, 'they regard it as a crime to kill any recently born child' (quoted in Wyatt & Spencer 1992).

Jesus and the early church

Jesus affirmed the Old Testament view of the significance of babies and young children, and in some senses he took a more radical position. Living in our modern child-orientated society, we find it hard to appreciate just how revolutionary was Jesus' teaching that unless we become like a little child we cannot enter the kingdom of God (Mt. 18:1–4). Jesus taught that the 'welcoming' of a little child in Jesus' name was equivalent to welcoming Christ himself and the Father who sent him (Mt. 18:5; Mk. 9:36–37). Conversely, those who caused a little child to 'stumble' would be punished with great severity (Mt. 18:6). Unlike the Jewish religious teachers of the day, Jesus emphasized the importance of children, and it is obvious that he had a special affection for them. He rebuked his disciples for preventing children from coming to be blessed by him, and went out of his way to make time for them (Mt. 19:13–16; Mk. 10:13–16).

Although there is no explicit reference to abortion and infanticide in the New Testament, the term *pharmakeia* and its cognates are found in lists of evil practices which are incompatible with Christian truth (*e.g.* Gal. 5:20; Rev. 21:8; 22:15). *Pharmakoi* is normally rendered 'sorcerers' or 'those who practice magic arts' in translations of the New Testament. *Pharmakeia* refers to the use of drugs, and is the root of our words 'pharmacy' and 'pharmaceutical'. But it was in fact a technical term which may well refer to the employment of herbal potions to poison or to obtain an abortion (Gorman 1982: 48).

The *Didache* and the *Epistle of Barnabas* are early Christian treatises on practical Christian living which date from the first two centuries AD. They contrasted two ways to live: the way of light and the way of darkness. The way of light is the way of neighbour-love and care for human life in all its forms. The way of darkness included murder, adultery, sodomy, fornication, the use of magic, and child destruction by abortion or infanticide. Abortion and infanticide are seen as clear examples of offences against the two great commandments referred to by Jesus: love of God and love of the neighbour (Gorman 1982: 49–50).

The early Christian writer Clement of Alexandria wrote with vehemence against the inhumanity of abortion. He said that those who, 'in order to hide their immorality, use abortive drugs which expel the matter completely dead, abort at the same time their human feelings' (Gorman 1982: 51–53). The early church fathers uncompromisingly attacked the contemporary Graeco-Roman morality with its acceptance of the elimination of unwanted human life and its cruelty to the weak and despised.

The Christian apologists of the first three centuries defended themselves against the three common charges of atheism (because they disbelieved in the official gods of the Roman state), incest (from their emphasis on brotherly love) and cannibalism (from a misunderstanding of the eucharist). In response to the charge of cannibalism they emphasized their horror of bloodshed, pointing out that Christians have renounced murder in all its forms – and linking together gladiator contests, animal fights, infanticide and abortion (Gorman 1982: 53–54). Whereas the Romans drew a distinction between abortion and infanticide, early Christians tended to speak of them both as 'parricide'. In the Roman world 'parricide' was the term for the killing of a parent or close relative, and it was regarded as the most shocking of crimes, because it was the most unnatural (Gorman 1982: 58–59; Ferngren 1987b: 55). It is very significant that Christians applied this scandalous term to both abortion and infanticide, equating the destruction of an unwanted child to the murder of a close relative.

Early church responses to abortion and infanticide

The consistent Christian teaching of the first three centuries, then, was total opposition to the pagan practices of abortion and infanticide. But the early Christians did not stop at opposing these practices; they saw the need to create practical alternatives. The rescue of orphans and foundlings was regarded by early Christians as a particular Christian duty, since in many cases it involved saving those babies who had been exposed by their parents. As the local population got to know about these Christians with their 'crazy' ideas, it was apparently quite common for mothers to leave their unwanted babies at the doors of churches in the hope that they would be cared for. Christians frequently adopted foundlings into their families, as shown by inscriptions on tombs; but as the numbers grew, Christian orphanages were set up in the third and fourth centuries (Ferngren 1987a).

It is fascinating to see how the laws of the Roman Empire gradually changed in the third and fourth centuries, at least partly in response to the growing Christian witness in their society. In the third century, several laws were passed to restrict abortions and to control the supply of abortifacient drugs. As Christianity was recognized as an official religion of the Roman Empire, following the conversion of Constantine in AD 312, attitudes to infanticide changed too. In 318 Constantine made it a punishable offence for a father to kill his child, and in 331 he decreed that those who raised exposed children could legally adopt them. In 374 infanticide and infant exposure were made punishable by law and all parents were required to care for their own offspring. Subsequently, Justinian extended the protection of newborns by prohibiting their subjection to any form of servitude by those who rescued them. Christian hospitals began to be established towards the end of the fourth century, and many of the hospitals had a section (called the *brephotropheion*) specifically set apart for foundlings (Ferngren 1987a).

In summary, the consistent teaching of the Old and New Testaments and of the early church fathers is, first, that the value of the lives of all human beings, including fetuses and newborn babies, is *intrinsic* to their creation by God. Secondly, there is an overwhelming duty on the followers of Christ to act with neighbour love towards the weak and vulnerable in society.

Abortion in the modern world

As we turn to the battleground which abortion has become in our society, our Christian task is to listen first and to understand, to empathize. Only in this way shall we be able to speak with integrity, authenticity and Christlike compassion.

In Britain, as in most countries, intentional abortion was illegal from the medieval period. The Offences Against the Person Act of 1861 made abortion a felony with a maximum sentence of penal servitude for life. The Infant Life (Preservation) Act of 1929 made it an offence to 'destroy the life of a child capable of being born alive'. The Act made a gestational age of twenty-eight weeks the point at which there was *prima facie* proof that this stage had been reached. The only exception allowed under the 1929 Act was an abortion carried out in good faith to preserve the life of the mother.

In 1938 the eminent gynaecologist Aleck Bourne was prosecuted for performing an abortion in a fourteen-year-old girl who had been raped by several soldiers. He was subsequently acquitted and the judge stated that there was no essential difference between protecting the mother's life and protecting her health, and therefore abortion was lawful if carried out to prevent the woman from becoming a 'physical or mental wreck'. The effect of this judgment was to cause a steady increase in abortions performed in the UK. Interestingly, Aleck Bourne became increasingly concerned by what he saw as the abuse of psychiatry in the practice of certifying that many pregnant women were at risk of profound mental disturbance. He strongly opposed the 1967 Act and became a founder member of the Society for the Protection of the Unborn Child.

Despite the fact that abortion was being practised on a small scale by gynaecologists, it was not widely available, except for the privileged few who had the wealth and the necessary contacts to obtain an abortion privately. Yet everybody knew that a large number of criminal abortions were being performed by 'back-street' abortionists, who could be found in every part of society. Many women suffered from the consequences of criminal abortion, with the risk of serious infections and infertility, and a few died. In the nature of things, the exact number of criminal abortions was not known, and estimates have varied wildly. Probably the most authoritative estimate is that from a 1966 report from the Royal College of Obstetricians and Gynaecologists, which concluded that the annual number at that time was about 14,600, although other estimates were much higher. In 1967 the number of maternal deaths which were known to be due to criminal abortion was thirty-two.

The 1967 Abortion Act

David (now Lord) Steel introduced his Private Member's Bill to reform the abortion law in 1966, and it was passed in 1967. It seems clear that the motivation of David Steel and many of the original framers of the Bill was genuinely humanitarian. The great concern that was expressed at the time was the need to prevent the litany of death and misery from criminal abortions and illegal abortionists, and to provide a legal remedy for the victims of rape and those found to be carrying seriously malformed infants. The abortion debate was also coloured by the thalidomide tragedy, in which hundreds of fetuses were severely damaged by a sedative taken by their mothers. Medical abortion was seen as a way of reducing the number of severely handicapped children being born every year. Another quoted reason was to reduce the terrible evil of child abuse (which was being increasingly recognized by paediatricians) by reducing the number of unwanted children.

Some of the 1967 Bill's supporters claimed that it would not make abortion easily available, but rather that it would reform and clarify the law, enabling doctors to carry out abortions in 'hard cases' without fear of prosecution. Interestingly, the radical liberal argument, that women had the right of abortion on demand out of respect for their moral autonomy, was not a feature of the parliamentary debate. David Steel stated explicitly that '. . . it is not the intention of the promoters of the Bill to leave a wide-open door for abortion on request'.

Twenty-five years later, the *BMA News Review* (October 1992) carried an article by David Steel in which he wrote: 'through my Private Member's Bill I sought to create a positive state of law, whereby two medical practitioners could lawfully balance the rights and conditions of the mother against the assumption of the right of the fetus to develop to full life'.

Although the 1967 Act was amended by Parliament in 1990, the core of the legislation remains unchanged. In its current form it states that an abortion is legal if two doctors agree in good faith on one of the following grounds:

A The continuance of the pregnancy would involve risk to the life of the pregnant woman greater than if the pregnancy were terminated.

B The termination is necessary to prevent grave permanent injury to the physical or mental health of the pregnant woman.

C The continuance of pregnancy would involve risk of injury to the physical or mental health of the pregnant woman, greater than if the pregnancy were terminated.

D The continuance of the pregnancy would involve risk of injury to the physical or mental health of any existing child(ren) of the family of the pregnant woman, greater than if the pregnancy were terminated.

E   There is a substantial risk that if the child were born it would suffer from such physical or mental abnormalities as to be seriously handicapped.

Or in the rare conditions of a genuine medical emergency:

F   To save the life of a pregnant woman.
G   To prevent grave permanent injury to the physical or mental health of the woman.

Abortion statistics

The Abortion Act came into force in 1968 and the numbers of legal abortions rose steadily, from 54,000 in the first complete year to over 169,000 in 1974. Abortions peaked in 1990 at 186,000, with a slight decline since then to 163,000 in 1995. Between the Abortion Act's becoming effective in April 1968 and the end of 1995, 4,212,193 legal abortions were carried out in England and Wales.

Although the intention of the original supporters of the Bill may not have been to allow abortion on request, the wording of the Bill was capable of remarkably elastic interpretation. In particular, because the risk to the mother of a completely normal delivery at term is greater than the risk of an early abortion, ground C can be interpreted to allow abortion in any pregnancy. In fact, it is very difficult to envisage a situation in which an abortion would not be 'legal' under the current wording of the Act.

Legal abortions in 1995 (England and Wales residents)

Ground A	126
Ground B	2,387
Ground C	136,928
Ground D	13,051
Ground E	1,823
Grounds F and G	0

The peak age at which women have an abortion is the twenty to twenty-four age group; in 1995, over twenty-five per 1,000 women (2.5%) in this age group had an abortion. In the sixteen to nineteen age group, 2.1% of all women had an abortion. In women under the age of sixteen, 3,270 abortions were performed. Of those who had abortions in 1995, 66% were single. Eighty-nine per cent of abortions were performed at less than thirteen weeks' gestation, and only just over 1% at more than twenty weeks. Just over 1% of abortions were performed because of clause E, a 'substantial risk' of a child who is 'seriously handicapped'. Fewer than one abortion in a thousand is performed because of a risk to the life of the mother (*Population Trends*, Spring 1997, and *Abortion Statistics*, 1995, Office for National Statistics).

The reality of the current situation in the UK is that abortion is available for most women on request. The apparent intention of the 1967 Act is being widely flouted, even if doctors can claim to remain within its precise wording. At present, approximately one in five of all established pregnancies ends in abortion. What this means in practice is that abortion touches virtually all of us in the UK society, in one way or another.

The experience of abortion

The personal reality of abortion was revealed in a moving article in the London *Evening Standard* of 8 August 1996, following fresh media controversy over selective abortion in a twin pregnancy. Eight women in London talked about their own experience.

In our office we all said that we had friends who had had one [an abortion]. We all knew that for many of us, the friends we were talking about were actually ourselves. I told no-one at the time of my abortion and never have since. Many women block it out of their minds. They are the lucky ones. I don't regret it but I know that I will feel stigmatized for the rest of my life. My boyfriend is a medical student, but there was no way I could tell him . . . the operation was over quickly and I blocked it out of my mind.

I find it very difficult to even admit to myself now that I have had three abortions . . . I had the first two when I was very young. Then I grew up and blocked them out of my mind. I had just started a new job when I got pregnant. I was thrilled. I couldn't believe my husband's reaction. He said he couldn't cope; he had just lost his job. I had another abortion. Throughout I wanted someone to stop me. We separated six months later.

I had lived with my partner for four years. We were talking about breaking up so I didn't tell him. So I found myself in the clinic alone . . . it was incredibly depressing. The image of that room still haunts me . . .

I can remember every detail about telling him [my boyfriend]: me fiddling with my study notes, him laughing and saying we could get married – he thought that solution was so unbelievable . . . we split up . . . I was elated afterwards because it was all so easy. But after that I fell into a real depression. My [new] boyfriend and I are now trying for a baby and I hope like hell we can have one. I know this is pathetic, but I feel that if I don't get pregnant it will be a punishment.

I had two abortions in my twenties . . . The second abortion occurred after I knew I was going to split up with my boyfriend. I was incredibly practical about it. But then I met Jeff. We lived together for three years and talked about having a baby. But when I told him that I was pregnant, all he said was that this wasn't the time, we need to be more financially stable. I was devastated . . .

When I read those accounts, I feel a profound sadness at the sense of silent despair and grief carried by so many women in our society. It is as though abortion is a deep scar penetrating through our society. The statistics demonstrate just how many younger people in our community are touched by it, although for most the pain is never revealed, not even to their closest friends and confidants. This is why the violent rhetoric of the public abortion debate is so unhelpful, if not positively damaging. Whenever the evils of abortion are declared in a harsh and condemnatory fashion, it is as though a knife is being silently twisted in the hearts of so many who listen.

I also feel deeply ashamed for my gender: ashamed at the cynical psychological abuse perpetrated by men on women who find themselves in the exquisitely vulnerable position of an unwanted pregnancy. The tragic irony is that abortion on request, effectively legalized by the 1967 Abortion Act, was hailed by feminists as empowering women and liberating them from patriarchal oppression. In fact it has become a means for others, principally men, to exploit and manipulate pregnant women. It seems that many women in our society have abortions, not from an exercise of free choice – unconstrained autonomy as expounded by the philosophers – but because they fear that their partner will abandon them if they persevere with the pregnancy. The very availability of abortion on demand means that, in practice, women must provide their partners with a reason, not for having an abortion, but for the reverse; they are required to demonstrate an adequate reason for *continuing* with their pregnancy. The prominent feminist lawyer Professor Catharine MacKinnon agrees that liberal abortion rules allow men to use women sexually with no fear of any consequences of paternity. Against the reasoning that abortion should be regarded as a private matter for women to decide, she argues that this supposes that women are really free to make decisions for themselves within the private space they occupy. In fact, she insists, women are often very unfree in the so-called private realm. Men often force sexual compliance upon them in private (Dworkin 1995: 52). In the brutal language of another feminist, a liberal abortion policy allows men 'to fill women up, vacuum them out, and fill them up again' (quoted by Dworkin 1995: 53).

The emotional consequences of abortion

In June 1994 a private Parliamentary Commission chaired by Lord Rawlinson published a report entitled *The Physical and Psycho-social Effects of Abortion on Women*. The report concluded that there were very few reliable figures on the incidence of psychological distress and psychiatric illness in association with abortion. Most women experience immediate feelings of relief, but subsequent distress and remorse seem to be common, particularly around the time that the baby should have been born, and in subsequent pregnancies. For understandable reasons, if they encountered problems, many women were reluctant to return to the clinic where an abortion was performed, and formal post-abortion counselling was uncommon.

Hospitalization because of psychiatric illness after abortion was low, but it was estimated that around 10% of women had symptoms of psychiatric illness in the short to medium term after abortion. The report also concluded that both pre- and post-abortion counselling was often inadequate, and recommended the further development of counselling agencies which were clearly independent of the medical services. The Commission also recommended that there should be a waiting period of one week between the first visit to a doctor at which abortion is considered, and the actual operation. This would alleviate some of the time pressure on the decision, and allow more time for reflection, an opportunity to weigh up the longer-term consequences of an abortion, and the consideration of possible alternatives.

The desire to minimize the psychological trauma of abortion has led to divergent views on how to improve practical abortion arrangements. Those in favour of a liberal abortion policy have argued that abortion should be made as straightforward and uncomplicated as possible. In June 1997, Dr Tim Black, the Chief Executive of Marie Stopes International, announced the creation of a walk-in, walk-out abortion service in dedicated clinics which would be set up in major cities in the UK. The abortion procedure costs £285 and takes about ten minutes. It would be possible for women to leave the clinic after sixty minutes. Dr Black aroused media controversy by stating that it would be a 'chance for working women to have an abortion in their lunch hour'.

Here is another example of medical science being employed as a quick technological fix to meet complex human and social issues. The adverse implications of an unwanted pregnancy in our modern society are due to a complex mix of psychological, relational, social, financial, employment and gender issues. Abortion seems to offer a neat, apparently uncomplicated technological solution to a complex problem. But, as so often, the solutions offered by technology come with a high price tag, one which is tragically in excess of £285.

The well-known American feminist Naomi Wolf has recently published an uncompromisingly honest account of growing up as a young woman in the sexually liberated atmosphere of Los Angeles in the 1960s, entitled *Promiscuities* (Wolf 1997).

If you were sleeping casually with someone, you were supposed to take care of all birth-control arrangements . . . Birth control and abortions 'belonged' to the girls . . . Most boys didn't like it if you dragooned them into helping with contraception . . . It was the mere thought that we could become pregnant that would turn boys off. By extension, we understood, we should dispose of our potential maternity the same way we were supposed to 'go on' the Pill: efficiently, without revealing any distasteful hint of it to boys. The mere biological fact of our ability to become pregnant was, for women of our age, the secret to be discreetly dealt with that menstruation had been to our mother's generation (Wolf 1997: 196).

Wolf goes on:

Among the events described by the women I interviewed, it was only the accounts of their teenage abortions that they insisted on confiding anonymously, compartmentalized from the rest of their stories. Out of all the difficult sexual events the women experienced, it was the abortions alone that seemed, even twenty years later, just too painful to integrate . . . (1997: 197).

One of the women recounted the story of her abortion at seventeen:

I did get pregnant. I really wanted to have the baby, but I was so in love with my boyfriend that to protect him I had an abortion. It really devastated me. We were so young . . . Logically I thought, OK, this is what you do in this situation. I had no idea what the emotional ramifications would be. It was the strong, smart, emancipated thing to do. We had no idea of the enormity of it. We were just kids (1997: 197).

Adoption figures

Adoption has always been an alternative to abortion when a mother feels unable, for whatever reason, to raise and care for her baby. The number of legal adoptions in the UK was rising in the 1950s and 1960s and reached a peak of 24,800 a year in 1968, the year that the Abortion Act became effective. Since then the number of adoptions has been falling steadily year on year, and in 1995 the number fell to 5,800, less than a quarter of the 1968 figure. This means that in 1995 an unwanted fetus was twenty-eight times more likely to be aborted than to be offered for adoption. Perhaps it is inevitable that as abortion has become more common and socially accepted, the number of babies being offered for adoption has fallen. Yet this trend has meant that it has become progressively more difficult for childless couples to adopt a child. Of course, adoption is not without problems, and adopted children may suffer complex emotional difficulties in later life. But the lack of babies for adoption has undoubtedly contributed to the pressure on health professionals and medical services to develop and provide new techniques and treatments to help infertile couples.

In the modern gynaecology ward, it is not uncommon to find patients who have been admitted for infertility treatment side by side with others who have been admitted for an abortion of a healthy fetus. To the nursing and medical staff it sometimes seems as though half the world is desperately trying to have a baby while the other half is equally desperately trying to get rid of one. This is the practical reality of what philosophers have called the 'right to procreative autonomy'.

Late abortion or 'feticide'

The Human Fertilization and Embryology Act 1990 amended the 1967 Abortion Act. The gestational age at which abortion could be carried out under the 'social' reasons (grounds C and D) was reduced to twenty-four weeks, because of advances in neonatal intensive care which meant that babies beyond this gestational age were now able to survive. Abortion for strictly 'medical' reasons (grounds A, B, E, F and G), however, could now be carried out at *any* gestational age, up to and including term.

Thus abortion can be performed at any stage of pregnancy if 'there is a substantial risk [undefined] that if the child were born it would suffer from such physical or mental abnormalities as to be seriously handicapped [undefined]'. The wording of the Act seems deliberately vague, allowing considerable latitude for interpretation by doctors and lawyers. What exactly is a 'substantial risk'? In private conversation an experienced lawyer told me that a court would probably conclude that a risk of 10% was within the definition of 'substantial'. Similarly, the definition of 'serious handicap' is open to considerable variation in interpretation, and might include abnormalities such as achondroplasia or even cleft palate, although a recent report of the UK Royal College of Obstetricians emphasized the need for caution in the application of the law (RCOG 1996).

In 1995, seventy-four abortions were performed beyond a gestational age of twenty-four weeks, because of fetal abnormalities. The range of abnormalities included congenital hydrocephalus and chromosomal abnormalities, of which the commonest was Down's syndrome. Although late feticides are uncommon compared to the large numbers of 'social' abortions performed each year in the UK, nevertheless they cause great unease to obstetricians, paediatricians and to the staff of neonatal intensive-care units. The paradox is that late feticides may be performed only in major NHS hospitals, and it is those same hospitals which have seen dramatic improvements in my own specialist area of intensive care for premature babies. As a society we seem to think that trying to save a tiny baby's life is worth thousands of pounds, even if, sadly, the baby will survive with some long-standing problems. And yet if the baby is still in the uterus it can be a very different story.

The practice of late feticide has led to a somewhat surreal situation. Imagine the scene in two adjacent operating theatres in a major NHS hospital. In one operating theatre a group of highly trained professionals is engaged in a sophisticated medical procedure with the sole aim of salvaging an unborn baby whose life is seen as precious and uniquely valuable. Paediatricians and neonatal nurses are present to resuscitate the infant immediately after birth and commence sophisticated intensive care. Yet in the other operating theatre a group of highly trained professionals is engaged in a sophisticated medical procedure with the sole aim of destroying an identical baby who is seen as disposable and whose life has effectively been rejected by both parents and society.

The contradictory activities in the two operating theatres may collide in an even more startling way. Suppose the fetus in the second operating theatre, instead of being killed within the womb, should accidentally be delivered alive. There is now a living but critically unwell baby whose life is technically protected both by law and by traditional medical ethics. Do the doctors have a duty to preserve his or her life now that the baby is delivered? Should the paediatricians from the first operating theatre be called to initiate intensive care of this baby who, just moments previously, was under sentence of death? How is it possible for one medical system, one body of law and one society to encompass and approve of such mutually contradictory procedures? It seems to me that one way of understanding this paradox is to recognize that it is as if the two operating theatres are functioning under two mutually contradictory ethical traditions. In the first operating theatre the view of the newborn is derived ultimately from the Judaeo-Christian tradition, whereas in the second the ethical viewpoint is much closer to the ancient Graeco-Roman perspective.

And what is the ultimate reason for the different activity in the two theatres? Answer: the wishes of the parents. In fact, it is ultimately the wish of the mother alone, as in this particular area fathers have few legal rights. This is the philosophical principle of autonomy, the right to choose within a liberal society, being worked out in practice.

In response to public and professional unease, and cases such as that of Jacqueline James (to which we referred in the Introduction), the UK Royal College of Obstetricians and Gynaecologists published guidelines entitled *Termination of Pregnancy for Fetal Abnormality* in January 1996. The document makes rather grisly reading:

Abortion . . . is the deliberate termination of a pregnancy for the benefit of the woman. The intention of an abortion is that the fetus should not survive – that the process of abortion should result in its death. A fetus that is born alive becomes a 'child' even if the reason for the birth was a legal abortion procedure. A deliberate act that causes the death of a child is murder . . . Consequently a doctor could be accused of murder when the deliberate act in question was the performance of a lawful abortion by a method that was followed by a live birth and the subsequent death of the child, perhaps because of immaturity. Consequently a legal abortion must not be allowed to result in a live birth. Within defined limits the law allows the destruction of a fetus but not of a child.

The fetus is entitled to respect throughout the pregnancy. Up to twenty-six weeks' gestation the method of abortion should be selected to minimize the physical and emotional trauma to the woman. After twenty-six weeks it is not possible to know the extent to which the fetus is aware. So, in the later weeks of pregnancy, methods used during abortion to stop the fetal heart should be swift and should involve a minimum of injury to fetal tissue.

As these quotations reveal, the procedure of medical feticide in a mature fetus is disturbingly close to an execution. I have witnessed at first hand the psychological unease and distress which may be caused not only to parents but also to health staff who are involved, sometimes rather unwillingly, in these distressing procedures.

A survey of obstetricians in the UK found that over 95% would perform an abortion at beyond twenty weeks of gestation for Down's syndrome or spina bifida. The percentages of those who would perform an abortion beyond twenty-four weeks were 13% for Down's syndrome, 21% for spina bifida and 64% for anencephaly (Green 1995). Thirteen per cent also agreed with the statement that 'The state should not be expected to pay for the specialized care of a child with a severe handicap in cases where the parents had declined the offer of prenatal diagnosis'. The opposite view, that late abortion is justified only for conditions which are inevitably fatal, has also been forcibly stated by several obstetricians (Chervenack *et al.* 1995). It is clear that many obstetricians feel uneasy about agreeing to a request to perform a late abortion under these circumstances. The widespread availability of abortion of perfectly normal fetuses for social reasons, however, may mean that some obstetricians find it hard to refuse to perform an abortion at the parents' request when the fetus is abnormal.

Recent philosophical reflection on abortion and infanticide
Ronald Dworkin

In chapter 1 we looked at Professor Ronald Dworkin's book *Life's Dominion: An Argument about Euthanasia and Abortion*, a highly influential and beautifully written exposition of a modern liberal position. It is important to understand that Dworkin is writing out of the American experience of violence and social unrest over abortion. He is concerned that these deep-rooted divisions in society will continue to fester, leading ultimately to civil breakdown and widespread violence. How can we live together as a society when we differ about such a fundamental issue as whether the life of a fetus is sacrosanct?

According to Dworkin, there is only one answer: we must agree to disagree. He argues that although abortion is an extremely divisive issue in western societies, in fact nearly all members of those societies hold fundamental convictions about the sacred and 'inviolable' nature of human life. It is just that we have very different ideas of what that 'sacredness' consists in (Dworkin 1995: 68–101).

Dworkin argues that we differ about the importance of the natural and the human contributions to each individual life. The 'conservative' position sees the sacredness of human life in its natural creation, in its biological origin and make-up. By contrast, the 'liberal' position perceives the sacredness of any individual human life in terms of the human investment and contribution which that particular life represents.

Dworkin writes strikingly of the process of self-creation which a human life entails. As soon as a pregnancy is planned, creative decisions are being made,

> . . . because a deliberate decision of parents to have and bear a child is, of course, a creative one. Any surviving child is shaped in character and capacity by the decisions of parents and by the cultural background of community. As that child matures, in all but pathological cases, his own creative choices progressively determine his thoughts, personality, ambitions, emotions, connections and achievements. He creates his life just as much as an artist creates a painting or a poem . . . We can – and do – treat leading a life as itself a kind of creative activity, which we have at least as much reason to honor as artistic creation. The life of a single human organism commands respect and protection, then, no matter in what form or shape, because of the complex creative investment it represents, and because of our wonder at the divine or evolutionary processes that produce new lives from old ones, at the processes of nation and community and language through which a human being will come to absorb and continue hundreds of generations of cultures and forms of life and value, and, finally, when mental life has begun and flourishes, at the process of internal personal creation and judgment by which a person will make and remake himself, a mysterious, inescapable process in which we each participate and which is therefore the most powerful and inevitable source of empathy and communion we have with every other creature who faces the same frightening challenge (Dworkin 1995: 83–84).

Therefore, in Dworkin's view, 'conservatives' view the destruction of human life as wrong because of the intrinsic or innate value of life. 'Liberals' view the destruction of human life as wrong because of the frustration of all the human contribution to that life. There is a spectrum of belief between those who put all the emphasis on the intrinsic element of the sanctity of life and those who put all the emphasis on the human contribution to the sanctity of life.

He illustrates this by giving the example of a young single woman who has an unwanted pregnancy and who has to face either an abortion or abandoning her education to care for the child. The 'conservative' person views the abortion as wrong because it frustrates the intrinsic natural value of the human life of the fetus. The 'liberal' regards continuing the pregnancy as wrong because the life of the fetus has had very little human contribution and therefore its destruction causes little frustration of human life. Moreover, the forced abandonment of the mother's education frustrates her life and is therefore an offence against the 'sacredness' or inviolability of her life. So an abortion should be performed to respect the sanctity of the mother's life! 'It may be more frustrating of life's miracle when an adult's ambitions, talents, training, and expectations are wasted because of an unforeseen and unwanted pregnancy, than when a fetus dies before any significant investment of that kind has been made' (1995: 92–93).

It is the difference in conservative and liberal conceptions of the sacredness of human life that leads to very different views about the morality of abortion. Dworkin then goes on to argue that at root, the difference between the 'conservative' and the 'liberal' position is a religious or spiritual difference (1995: 91–101). Our beliefs about what the sacredness of human life consists in are at the heart of how we view ourselves and other human beings. As we saw in chapter 1, Dworkin argues that the atheistic secular liberal's system of beliefs has 'a place in the life of its possessor parallel to that of the religious person's belief in God' (1995: 155). The liberal's beliefs affirm an essentially religious idea, that the importance of human life transcends subjective experience. Both the secular liberal and the Christian believer hold religious or spiritual beliefs about human life. It is just that they differ in those beliefs. Dworkin hopes that this insight will mean that real community is possible across deep religious divisions. 'We might hope for even more – not just for greater tolerance but for a more positive and healing realization: that what we share – our common commitment to the sanctity of life – is itself precious, a unifying ideal we can rescue from the decades of hate' (1995: 101).

If beliefs about abortion are essentially religious beliefs, then the modern state should not *coerce* its citizens to adopt one particular set of beliefs. Arguing from major constitutional debates taking place, particularly in the USA, Dworkin concludes that the right of privacy of individuals gives them the right of procreative autonomy (1995: 158). Because beliefs about abortion are fundamentally religious issues, the state must allow citizens to exercise freedom of religion. 'If we have a genuine concern for the lives others lead, we will also accept that no life is a good one if lived against the grain of conviction, that it does not help someone else's life to force values upon him he cannot accept . . .' (1995: 168).

Dworkin puts forward a hypothetical example. Suppose that in some country or state a majority of voters decide that it shows *disrespect* for the sanctity of life to *continue* the pregnancy if there is severe fetal malformation. 'If a majority has the power to impose its own views about the sanctity of life on everyone, then the state could *require* someone to abort, even if that were against her own religious or ethical convictions' (1995: 159). We would rightly think that was intolerable. But Dworkin says that the argument applies with equal force in the opposite direction. A government just as seriously insults the dignity of a pregnant woman when it forces her to continue a pregnancy against her deeply held convictions. The democratic majority should not be able to *coerce* people to act against their 'religious' beliefs.

This brings Dworkin to his conclusion. Modern liberal societies have shown how different religious groups can live together by differentiating between 'public' matters and 'private' matters. The laws of the state are able to direct and coerce citizens on public issues, but freedom of conscience must be allowed on private matters. Private matters are those which are a matter of individual preference and belief. By removing religion out of the public sphere and putting it in the private sphere we are able to live together in harmony despite our religious differences. We can respect one another's differences without threatening social harmony. Since beliefs about abortion (and, for that matter, euthanasia) are essentially religious beliefs, they should be removed from the public sphere and placed in the private sphere. We can respect one another's ethical views as essentially religious differences. If a liberal society is going to survive, the law must allow abortion whenever a mother's individual autonomy demands it (1995: 167).

The hypothetical example of the two operating theatres side by side, mentioned above, is a startling illustration of procreative autonomy being worked out in practice. Dworkin would argue that the existence of the two mutually contradictory operating theatres is a triumph for the democratic principle of individual autonomy. The procedure in one operating theatre is likely to be based on the 'conservative' philosophical view that the value of a fetal life is intrinsic. The adjacent operating theatre is working on the alternative 'liberal' philosophical position. In any genuinely democratic society, both operating theatres should be made available. Any individual woman is free to decide which operating theatre she opts for and thus whether she wishes her fetus to be saved or destroyed. You pay your money and you take your choice.

There is clearly some force to Dworkin's arguments. We do have to live together as a pluralistic society, in which there are deep divisions in religious and philosophical beliefs. But deep down, many of my professional colleagues and many other lay people in our society feel uneasy about the situation in the two operating theatres. Can a society survive in which such totally contradictory activities are being officially approved and carried out with state help? Can a society survive in which some state employees are saving lives and other state employees are destroying identical lives? What kind of vision of society is this?

Does it make no difference to me what practical decisions you make about the ultimate value of life, and *vice versa*? Is society just a collection of private individuals all doing their own thing? The very fact that disabled people like Tom Shakespeare and Christy Nolan want to protest against the abortion of affected fetuses is evidence that this is an inadequate view of society and of the value of human life. It seems to me that the liberal individualistic concept of society as a series of autonomous individuals is a modern mythical construction. It does not fit with reality and it does not fit with our deepest human intuitions.

As we have seen in chapter 2, the Christian perspective on society is very different. Christian thinking views us as locked together in mutual dependence with bonds of loyalty and responsibility to each other. Of course, we may differ fundamentally in our beliefs, and we may have unique attributes and personalities, but even so we are not just a collection of autonomous individuals. What I do affects you, and what you do affects me. If we treat the abnormal fetus with contempt it does have an undeniable effect on disabled people in our midst. In Christian thought, human beings are one family, and the rules that should govern our relationships are family rules – rules of duty, loyalty, responsibility and care for all of God's creation.

Peter Singer

As we saw in chapter 1, to Professor Peter Singer it seems self-evident that the life of a fetus is worth less than the life of a healthy adult, and that the life of a handicapped child is not as valuable as that of a healthy child. Neither the fetus nor the newborn baby can be regarded as a 'person', an autonomous, choosing individual. Singer admits that there are some differences between the fetus and the newborn baby, in that the baby is no longer dependent on the mother's body and that if the baby is unwanted by the mother, it can be cared for by someone else who does want it (Singer 1995: 211). Ultimately, however, both abortion and infanticide are acceptable options. The parents' choice, their free, autonomous decision, is central. If they want the baby to live, that's fine, but if they do not wish their baby to survive, it is morally acceptable to get rid of it, either before or after birth, provided we do it cleanly and painlessly. Singer quotes with approval the case of a baby called John Pearson who was born with Down's syndrome in Derby General Hospital in June 1980 (Singer 1995: 121). When Molly Pearson, John's mother, was given the news, she wept and said to her husband, 'I don't want it, Duck.' The baby was under the care of the respected paediatrician Dr Leonard Arthur, who prescribed 'nursing care only', together with regular doses of a potent analgesic. The death of John on the fourth day of life led to a celebrated murder trial. The charge was subsequently changed to attempted murder, and after complex legal argument Dr Arthur was acquitted.

To Singer it is inexplicable and irrational that we are prepared to abort a fetus with Down's syndrome, but are not prepared to kill a newborn baby with the same condition. He argues that this is merely a curious quirk of a society influenced by Judaeo-Christian religious ideas. 'Killing unwanted infants or allowing them to die has been a normal practice in most societies throughout human history and prehistory.' It was not only ancient Greek and Roman societies that practised infanticide. Anthropologists confirm that most forms of human societies have approved of the killing of unwanted babies. 'We find it in nomadic tribes like the Kung of the Kalahari desert, whose women will kill a baby born while an older child is still too young to walk . . . Japanese midwives who attended births did not assume that the baby was to live; instead they always asked if the baby was "to be left" or "to be returned" to wherever it was thought to have come from. Needless to say, in Japan as in all these cultures, a baby born with an obvious disability would almost always be "returned" ' (Singer 1995: 214). 'Even in nineteenth-century Europe, unwanted infants were given to foundling homes run by women known as "angel makers" because of the very high death rates that occurred . . . It is worth knowing that from a cross-cultural perspective, it is *our* tradition, not that of the Kung or the Japanese, that is unusual in its official morality about infanticide' (1995: 129, Singer's emphasis). Yet Singer sees an increasing public acceptance of some forms of selective medical infanticide in western societies. 'Thousands of years of lip-service to the Christian ethic have not succeeded in suppressing entirely the earlier ethical attitude that newborn infants, especially if unwanted, are not yet full members of the moral community' (1995: 130).

As Singer recognizes, our own society has been heavily influenced by Judaeo-Christian concepts of the value of fetal and newborn life. In our next chapter we examine the biblical basis of this perspective and ask how it can be applied practically to the painful issues of antenatal screening and abortion.

7. When is a person? Christian perspectives on the beginning of life

When we turn from the complex and painful dilemmas raised by abortion, infertility treatments and antenatal screening to the world of the Bible, we are again struck by the gulf between the biblical world and our own. We cannot look for proof-texts which will provide neat answers to these complex problems. Sometimes Christian writers and teachers have attempted to construct a complete edifice of teaching about abortion on a single text, such as Exodus 21:22–24, which deals with accidental injury to a pregnant woman. We shall consider this passage later, but it is not where we should start. Instead, we must attempt to immerse ourselves in the biblical worldview, to view the world as the biblical writers saw it.

We begin with creation design – the way we are made. As we saw in chapter 2, in orthodox Christian thought we are all unique and we are all special in God's eyes because we are made in God's image. Each human being is 'lacking a very little of God' (Ps. 8:5, literally), a unique masterpiece of God's creation – flawed, imperfect, damaged, but a masterpiece nevertheless.

As we have seen, in much recent philosophical thought, the right to be treated with dignity, the right to be protected, the right to be regarded as a 'person', is a right which has to be earned. It is as though every human has to pass a test before he or she is regarded as 'one of us', a member of the moral community. Are they aware of their own existence as 'continuing selves'? Are they able to choose, to exercise autonomy? Do they display 'morally relevant characteristics'? To be regarded as 'persons' depends on their function, on what they can do.

But in the biblical Christian worldview no human being needs to earn the right to be treated with respect or dignity. Our dignity is *intrinsic*: it lies in the way we have been made, in how God creates us, remembers us and calls us to himself. Biblical ethics, the way we are called to treat one another, is derived from biblical anthropology, the way we are made.

God's creative involvement with human beings extends to fetal life

The biblical narrative insists that God's creative activity does not commence at the moment of birth. Instead, God is intimately involved in the hidden and mysterious process of fetal development within the womb. This is seen most clearly in Psalm 139, which is a wonderful and moving meditation on the awesome intimacy between God and a human individual. The psalmist starts with a profound awareness of God's presence, an unsettling sense that God has invaded every aspect of his life.

> O LORD, you have searched me
>   and you know me.
> You know when I sit and when I rise;
>   you perceive my thoughts from afar.
> You discern my going out and my lying down;
>   you are familiar with all my ways.
> Before a word is on my tongue
>   you know it completely, O LORD.
> You hem me in – behind and before;
>   you have laid your hand upon me.
>
> (Ps. 139:1–5)

The extent of the divine knowledge is wonderful, bringing a sense of security in God's all-encompassing presence. But this presence is not entirely welcome. There is an element of ambiguity in the psalmist's response; a very human sense of emotional claustrophobia. It is as though he is saying, 'This is all very well, but could you please get off my back, God? I need a little space.' So the psalmist embarks on a thought experiment. Is there any place in the cosmos where he could escape from God's all-invading presence? No. The search for emotional space is doomed to failure.

> Where can I go from your Spirit?
>   Where can I flee from your presence?
> If I go up to the heavens, you are there;
>   if I make my bed in the depths, you are there;
> If I rise on the wings of the dawn,
>   if I settle on the far side of the sea,

> even there your hand will guide me,
>   your right hand will hold me fast.

> (verses 7–10)

If there is no place in the cosmos where the psalmist can evade God's presence, perhaps there is a place in his personal history. Perhaps if he goes back far enough into his personal origins he can find a space, a time, when, for once, he was free from the claustrophobic presence of God. But no; even if he traces his life story back to his own mysterious origins in the womb, he discovers God's presence.

> For you created my inmost being;
>   you knit me together in my mother's womb.
> I praise you because I am fearfully and wonderfully made;
>   your works are wonderful,
>   I know that full well.
> My frame was not hidden from you
>   when I was made in the secret place.
> When I was woven together in the depths of the earth,
>   your eyes saw my unformed body.
> All the days ordained for me
>   were written in your book
>   before one of them came to be.

> (verses 13–16)

Wonderfully and terrifyingly, the search for a space away from God is doomed to failure. The narrative of a human life is invaded by God from its intrauterine origins. Of course, this is poetry and not a textbook of embryology. The fetus is seen as woven together as on a divine loom, hidden in the depths of the earth. The psalmist was not a fool. He knew that babies were not dug up like potatoes from the soil. But in the Old Testament world, virtually nothing was known about the biological processes which occurred in the womb. In a world where abdominal surgery was unheard of and post-mortems were taboo, what was actually happening within the pregnant abdomen was a complete mystery. People knew that a man and a woman had intercourse and nine months later out popped a baby, but what happened in between was an enigma, one of the greatest riddles of human existence. In the words of the Preacher:

> As you do not know the path of the wind,
>   or how the body is formed in a mother's womb,
> so you cannot understand the work of God,
>   the Maker of all things.

> (Ec. 11:5)

By contrast, we know a great deal about the biological process of fetal development. Antenatal ultrasound, in particular, allows us the privilege of seeing what the psalmist could only dream of. Many parents, myself included, have experienced a mysterious thrill at the first glimpse of their unborn child. It is a glimpse into the hidden creation chamber where God is bringing another wonderful but flawed masterpiece into existence.

What then can we learn from Psalm 139 about God's involvement with the unborn child? How can we relate this ancient poetry to the world of the ultrasound scan and the assisted-conception unit? John Stott, in his book *Issues Facing Christians Today* (Stott 1990: 315–317), helpfully draws out three headings.

First is *creation*. The clear emphasis of the passage is on God's individual and minutely detailed creative activity within the womb. This is not just an anonymous deterministic biological mechanism, a routine proliferation of cells. Molecular biology is uncovering many of the cellular mechanisms which control the formation of the human organism, but we must avoid a crude biological or genetic determinism. While the biological mechanisms are ticking away, the divine artist is creating a unique masterpiece.

It seems to me that the psalmist is consciously echoing the creation narratives of the first chapter of Genesis. The womb is dark, mysterious, the secret place; the action occurs in the depths of the earth; the body is unformed. This is the secret creation chamber of the infinite God. Inside this womb is a microcosm of the miracle of the creation of the universe. God's guiding hand is creating; God's voice is calling a unique being into existence and into relationship with him. God is the potter who is working the unformed clay; God is the artist weaving his unique tapestry on the divine loom. That is why we must treat even the fetus with wonder. One possible reading of the Hebrew of verse 14 is: 'I praise you because, being made, I am wonderful.'

Second is the theme of *covenant*. Throughout the psalm the writer is self-consciously using the language of covenant, unconditional commitment. God the Creator is in covenant relationship with the psalmist. 'You *know* me, God.' This is not just an intellectual awareness, because of course God knows everything. This kind of knowledge implies a committed, intimate involvement, as when Adam *knew* Eve in the act of sexual intercourse (Gn. 4:1, literally). 'Your eyes saw my unformed body.' 'You *knew* me, you were involved with me.' The emphasis is not on fetal awareness of God, as if the psalmist were saying, 'I knew you were there, God, in the womb.' No; what matters is that God knew the fetus. God was involved. 'God was calling me into existence and into a relationship with him.' Here is an example of a unilateral covenant based on God's grace; a covenant of creation which God initiates and maintains.

Third is the theme of *continuity*. The psalmist meditates on his own personal history, the narrative of his unique, individual life. There is the past ('you searched me'), the present ('you know when I sit and when I rise'), the future ('your hand will guide me, your right hand will hold me fast'), and the antenatal history ('when I was woven together in the depths of the earth'). The psalmist looks back to his mother's womb and says, not that there was a mysterious being in there which later became 'me', a person, but 'That was me in there.' I, the adult human, am in direct continuity with the fetus. This is all *my* story, the narrative structure of a human life.

These same themes can be traced in many parts of the Bible. In the book of Job, the common creation of all human beings in the womb is used as a symbol of the need for equality and justice in human relationships. 'Did not he who made me in the womb make them? Did not the same one form us both within our mothers?' (Jb. 31:15). The suffering servant of Isaiah also refers to God's intrauterine call: 'And now the LORD says – he who formed me in the womb to be his servant . . .' (Is. 49:5). Here are the same themes of creation, covenant and continuity.

The fetus is an actor within the human drama

Doctor Luke records in his gospel a homely incident: the excited meeting of two pregnant women, to share their experiences. Mary, having just received the visitation from the angel and being in the earliest stages of pregnancy, hurries excitedly to visit her relative Elizabeth, also pregnant, but close to term. 'When Elizabeth heard Mary's greeting, the baby leaped in her womb and Elizabeth was filled with the Holy Spirit. In a loud voice she exclaimed: "Blessed are you among women, and blessed is the child you will bear! But why am I so favoured, that the mother of my Lord should come to me? As soon as the sound of your greeting reached my ears, the baby in my womb leaped for joy' (Lk. 1:41–44).

I have sometimes wondered why, out of all the eye-witness accounts of Jesus' life which Luke must have accumulated before he wrote his gospel, he chose to record such a common-place domestic occurrence. Was it because he wanted to emphasize that Jesus' earthly ministry commenced even before birth? At first glance there are only two people in that room in Zechariah's home. But Luke implies that in fact there are four: Elizabeth and the unborn John, Mary and the unborn Jesus. John leaps for joy at Jesus' presence only a few weeks after Jesus' conception, in the same way that lepers and paralysed men and blind beggars will leap for joy as Jesus passes by in future.

Jesus shares the narrative of a human life, including all the stages of fetal life. He has become like us, as the letter to the Hebrews says, 'in every way' (Heb. 2:17). In fact, to use a phrase of Paul Ramsey, Jesus was a fellow fetus – or, in the words we have quoted already, 'Jesus has been with us in the darkness of the womb as he will be with us in the darkness of the tomb' (Meilander 1997: 30).

Luke uses the same Greek word, *brephos*, for the unborn John as he does for the newborn baby Jesus (Lk. 2:12) and for the little children who were brought to Jesus for his blessing (Lk. 18:15). The consistent witness of the biblical material is that the fetus is part of the human drama, a hidden actor on the human stage; one whom God is creating in secret, calling into existence and into relationship with himself. The same concept of continuity throughout all the stages of the human narrative is evident in the Apostles' Creed, which states that Jesus was 'conceived by the Holy Spirit, born of the Virgin Mary, suffered under Pontius Pilate, was crucified, dead, and buried . . . [and] rose again'.

The status of the embryo and early fetus

Is there a biblical distinction between the early stages of conception and the later fetus? Some, such as Professor R. J. Berry, have argued that biblical material such as Psalm 139 can be used only to argue in retrospect. If I know that I exist, then I know that God must have been involved with me when I was a fetus. 'Once a person exists, one must reckon with his or her whole life history as a linked sequence of divinely guided and appointed processes and events. But Psalm 139 says nothing whatsoever about those who are not "persons"' (Berry 1996: 73). In other words, we cannot use this psalm or similar passages to argue that God is involved with *every* fetus or embryo, including the numerous embryos and fetuses which are spontaneously lost during the early stages of prenatal development.

As Professor Berry and other distinguished commentators, such as Professor Gordon Dunstan (Dunstan 1984), have pointed out, there is a long-standing Christian tradition which made a distinction between a 'formed' and an 'unformed' fetus. The story is rather tortuous, but it remains an important feature of contemporary Christian debate. The historical evidence strongly suggests that ancient Judaism was opposed to deliberate abortion, except in rare cases of obstructed labour, when it was performed in order to save the mother's life (Gorman 1982: 34). The Exodus law, however, did contain a statute dealing with accidental injury to a pregnant woman (Ex. 21:22–24). A literal translation of the Hebrew is as follows:

> If men strive together, and hurt a woman with child, so that her fruit depart, and yet no injury follow, he shall surely be fined, according as the woman's husband shall lay upon him; and he shall pay as the judges determine. But if any injury follow, then thou shalt give life for life . . .

The problem is that the meaning of the text seems fundamentally ambiguous. The phrase 'her fruit depart' could refer to miscarriage leading to fetal death, but it could also refer to premature birth with survival of the baby (as in the New International Version's translation). Similarly, the 'injury' could mean injury to the mother or to the baby.

When the Hebrew text was translated into Greek in the third century BC (the Septuagint version), the Greek words for 'unformed' and 'formed' were substituted for the phrases referring to injury. Thus the statute prescribed a fine for the loss of an 'unformed' fetus but the death penalty if there was loss of a 'formed' fetus. This fitted with the Greek philosophy of Aristotle, who drew a distinction between (first) the early embryo, which had first a vegetative followed by an animal nature, and (second) the fully formed fetus, which was recognizably a human being, and which therefore had a 'rational' or 'intellectual' soul (Dunstan 1984).

The early church fathers seem to have been divided on whether to accept a difference in the significance of the destruction of an unformed or a formed fetus. Basil wrote that 'A woman who deliberately destroys a fetus is answerable for murder. Any fine distinction as to its being completely formed or unformed is not admissible among us' (quoted by Dunstan 1984). By contrast, Augustine accepted the distinction. 'If what is brought forth is unformed but at this stage some sort of living, shapeless thing, then the law of homicide would not apply, for it could not be said that there was living soul in that body, for it lacks all sense, if it be such as is not yet formed and therefore not yet endowed with its senses' (quoted by Dunstan 1984). The same tradition was accepted by Aquinas and other medieval theologians.

The subject remains a matter of painful controversy and debate between Christians. A number of modern theologians and Christian doctors have argued that this ancient moral tradition should be preserved. In their view, the embryo or early fetus cannot be regarded as a human individual, and does not become worthy of respect and protection until later in pregnancy. They point to other evidence from modern embryology and genetics to support this view. It is now thought that more than 50% of all embryos created naturally following sexual intercourse fail to implant and are lost as early miscarriages. Sometimes the mother may not even be aware that she was pregnant. Some early embryos split spontaneously, leading to the formation of identical twins. Very rarely, two separate, non-identical embryos which have formed at the same time may fuse to form a single embryo. Most of the material which makes up the early embryo does not even go to form the future fetus, but instead becomes the placenta and the other supportive structures which are subsequently lost. Even the crucial step of fertilization, with the formation of a new genetic identity, does not happen instantaneously, but takes place over a matter of hours; the nuclear material from the sperm and the egg remains separate within the one-cell embryo, and fuse totally only following division and formation of a two-cell structure.

In view of this evidence, how can the human embryo and early fetus be regarded as a unique human individual worthy of respect and protection? Professor Donald MacKay argued that in the development of the fetus a critical level of complexity was required before the fetus could be considered a 'conscious personal agency'. In particular, a degree of brain development allowing self-regulation and information processing was necessary (see account in Stott 1990: 319–320). Professor Gareth Jones similarly argues that the early fetus should be regarded as a 'potential' person with only limited rights to protection. 'The fetus is on its way to becoming an actual person and, by the later stages of fetal development, may have most of the characteristics of personhood' (D. G. Jones 1984: 175).

The implication of this argument is that early abortion, although always painful and less than ideal, may be a Christian action, the lesser of two evils, an act of compassion, and even, at times, a Christian duty (D. G. Jones 1984: 174–184). Similarly, the creation and destruction of human embryos in research, in order to help more mature human beings, can be seen as worthwhile, provided that significant benefits are likely to accrue in medical advance for the benefit of humanity.

From a personal point of view, as a medical student and junior doctor in the 1970s I became convinced by this argument. I felt that abortion in many different circumstances could be seen as an act of compassion, the lesser of two evils. But over the years, as my clinical experience and theological under-standing grew, I became increasingly uneasy. Could the intentional destruction of even the early fetus really be consistent with a Christian worldview? What were the arguments that led to my change of heart?

Arguments in favour of protecting the embryo and early fetus

First, I have become convinced that the traditional distinction between the formed, human fetus and the unformed, sub-human fetus is not a biblical concept, nor is it consistent with modern biological understanding. It derives ultimately from a dualistic Greek philosophy which regarded the essence of humanity as consisting in a rational, thinking, feeling soul. The soul is seen as a distinct, immaterial entity which is implanted in a physical body at a certain stage of fetal development. This does not fit with the thought-forms of the biblical worldview. The interpretation of the statute in Exodus 21 remains unclear, but in my opinion it cannot be used with integrity to support this distinction. Further, the statute clearly deals with compensation following *accidental* injury, and cannot be applied to the morality of intentional abortion. It seems that Christian thinkers such as Augustine and Aquinas were using Aristotelian ideas of animation at a later stage of pregnancy, because that was the best empirical information that was available. Today, vast improvements in scientific information have made the distinction obsolete. There is no stage in fetal development which represents a biological discontinuity and which might be interpreted as the transition from an animal to a human form. If there is any discontinuity in the formation of the human individual, it seems to be around the time of fertilization, when a unique human genetic code is created, or implantation in the wall of the womb, when the embryo starts to develop the essential support structures to survive and develop into a mature fetus (see Meilander 1997: 30–31).

Secondly, it is pointless to expect biology to reveal conclusively the point at which God's covenant involvement with a human individual commences. Biology and genetics can only suggest certain points at which personal identity may commence. Oliver O'Donovan argues that we cannot demonstrate that a person exists by scientific testing for various attributes or capacities, such as rationality or responsivity. Instead, 'we discern persons only by love, by discovering through interaction and commitment that this human being is irreplaceable' (O'Donovan 1984: 59). In order to know one another as persons we must adopt a mode of knowledge which is based not on objective scientific analysis, but on love. 'This implies a commitment in advance to treat all human beings as persons, even when their personal qualities have not yet become manifest to us' (1984: 66). We do not know whether any one particular embryo or fetus will survive the hazards of embryonic development and intrauterine life, to emerge as a responsive individual whose personal qualities we can identify, but this does not absolve us from the responsibility to demonstrate a moral commitment in advance to treat each embryo or fetus as though destined to manifest its personality in future. We must 'approach new human beings, including those whose humanity is ambiguous and uncertain to us, with the expectancy and hope that we shall discern how God has called them out of nothing into personal being' (1984: 66). The biblical theme of continuity between intrauterine and extrauterine life is entirely consistent with this attitude of prior moral commitment.

Thirdly, the thrust of historic biblical theology places the emphasis on what human beings *are* by creation, in the stuff of their being, and not on what they can *do*, on their attributes or functional abilities. It is not necessary to assess what the fetus can do, or to look for central nervous system functionality or responsivity, in order to discern the evidence of God's involvement or covenant commitment. God's grace revealed in the Christian gospel is precisely love towards the unresponsive. The covenant relationship of loving commitment does not depend on reciprocity. As parents, we commit ourselves in love to our children long before they are able to respond with self-awareness to that love. As we saw in our brief exploration of Psalm 139, the critical issue is not whether the fetus is aware of God, but whether God is aware of and committed by grace to the fetus.

Fourthly, the Bible views all human beings as called by God to share in his life. When God calls us he calls us *as persons*; he calls us by name. We cannot think of God calling us in any way other than in a personal way. Similarly, we cannot think that there was a time in our personal history when we were outside the call of God. In other words, within the confines of our human existence there was never a time when God was not calling us. As Brendan McCarthy puts it: 'If God calls us, as the Christian faith asserts, then he must have called us, as well as the Old Testament prophets, while we were still in our mother's wombs' (McCarthy 1997: 122). (In fact, since God is outside of time he knows and calls us even before our conception, as in Je. 1:5.) So our unique human personality derives from God who calls us by name, and God's call is present from the beginning of our human existence. It is a strange thought that even the embryo has a name, a unique identity, in the sense that no animal or inanimate object has a name, but it is consonant with the biblical worldview. God's creation of a unique human being constitutes God's call to enter into fellowship or communion with him.

Fifthly, Christian thinking emphasizes our responsibility to be neighbourly, to exercise a duty of care and protection for vulnerable, weak and defenceless human beings. In the Christian understanding of community, we are locked into bonds of loyalty and responsibility even to those who appear alien to and different from us. The embryo and early fetus seem to represent *par excellence* those vulnerable human beings to whom we owe a special duty of care and protection.

Finally, if we recognize a deep uncertainty and ambiguity about the moral significance of the embryo or early fetus, we have to ask: 'What is an authentically Christian response to this deep ontological uncertainty?' Surely an appropriate response is to vote in favour of protection and against intentional destruction. It is a standard principle of medical ethics that if there is any significant degree of uncertainty about life-and-death issues (for instance, in deciding whether to withdraw life-sustaining treatment where the prognosis is hopeless), then we should 'play safe'. We vote in favour of life, and against death. It is only if we are certain *beyond any reasonable doubt* that there is no hope of survival, that the outlook is hopeless and there is no reasonable hope that our therapy can be helpful, that we can consider the removal of supportive treatment. In the same way, it seems to me that if there is reasonable doubt about the moral status of the embryo or early fetus, then we should vote in favour of protection. Perhaps we can never know with any certainty how God regards any individual embryo or fetus. That profound uncertainty does not give us licence to treat the embryo as a being who is at our disposal. We need an authentic Christian response to uncertainty.

Theological themes and the human embryo

The human embryo is a unique type of being. It is *sui generis*. We cannot think of it simply as a baby who happens not to have been born yet. Neither can we think of it as merely a biological mechanism, a collection of genetic material and intracellular apparatus, a blob of jelly, which happens to have the potential to become a baby. We have to create a new category of thought for this being. It is neither an unborn baby nor a blob of jelly. It is a human embryo – unique, different in kind from anything else in our experience.

And in thinking biblically about this strange entity, we must hold on to two familiar tensions which crop up repeatedly in Christian theology. First, we must retain the *tension between the physical and the immaterial*. All human beings have a physical aspect (they are constructed out of the physical stuff of genetic codes, biochemical engineering, intricate plumbing and miles of electrical wiring) and an immaterial aspect (they are persons who mysteriously reflect God's character, strange Godlike beings who love and are loved, unique individuals each with a unique life history, known by God and destined for eternity). These two aspects of our being are locked together in our humanity. We are, *at one and the same time,* fully physical and fully immaterial. The existence of a physical human body is a physical sign that an immaterial person is present. That is the way God made us – as 'disgusting hybrids' with the different and apparently contradictory aspects of our being locked together. The reductionist says that human beings are *really* sophisticated self-replicating survival machines which happen to have achieved self-consciousness. The philosophical dualist says that human beings are *really* spiritual beings who happen to be attached to a body for the period of their existence. Biblical anthropology has to resist both of these alternatives. Human beings are, at one and the same time, fully physical and fully spiritual beings. We hold the two realities in tension.

It is a tension which is familiar to biblical theology. We see it in the doctrine of the incarnation: Jesus was at one and the same time completely human and completely divine. We see it in the doctrine of inspiration: the words of the Bible are at one and the same time the words of human writers and the words of God. We see it in the doctrine of the sacraments: the bread and wine, and the baptismal water, are physical elements and at the same time pointers to a hidden spiritual reality.

When we think of the embryo within a biblical worldview, then, we must regard this strange being as having both a physical and an immaterial reality. Indeed, I wonder if we cannot think of the embryo within a version of sacramentalist theology. At one level the embryo is just biology. It is a collection of genetic material and cellular machinery. But at the same time it is a physical sign of an immaterial or spiritual reality, a sacrament of a hidden covenant of creation – a sign that God is bringing forth a new, Godlike being, a unique reflection of his character, a being to whom he is locked in covenant commitment. God is bringing into existence another person and calling him or her into relationship with himself. So we cannot treat the human embryo with contempt because it is 'just' a minute blob of jelly, any more than we can treat the written words of the Bible with contempt because they are 'just' human words. These particular physical words are special; they have a unique spiritual significance. This particular physical blob is special; it is a sign of God's creative covenant.

This also has implications for the way we think biblically about the human genetic code and the molecules of DNA from which it is constructed. The biblical revelation views human beings as sons and daughters of Adam and Eve. As we saw in chapter 2, modern genetic analysis suggests that we must treat the biblical narrative with due seriousness. Human beings are both theologically and, it seems, in genetic reality a single extended family. Not only do we carry the mysterious image of God, we also carry the image of our distant grandparents, Adam and Eve. We have an *organic solidarity* with Adam. This is the meaning of the biblical phrase 'in Adam'. There is an unbroken line of descendants through which each of us can trace our origins to Adam. But what is the physical counterpart of this organic solidarity? How was Adam's image passed on through each generation down to us? The answer is the human genetic code. DNA is the physical means by which God has enabled Adam's likeness to be passed faithfully on to each generation. Of course, the biblical concept of being 'in Adam' implies much more than just possessing a particular genetic code, but nevertheless, in the physical and spiritual unity which comprises a human being, it is the human genome which is the physical sign that we are Adam's offspring, that we are 'in Adam'. This particular configuration of DNA molecules is the physical counterpart of a human person, a physical sacrament which points to a hidden, spiritual mystery. And it is at fertilization that the particular configuration of the human genome is created. It is at fertilization that the image of Adam is passed on to the next generation. Even the early embryo is a being 'in Adam'.

The thinking which draws a distinction between the embryo or early fetus and the later mature fetus tends to verge towards dualism. It implies that the early fetus is merely a physical being and 'therefore of little consequence until the spiritual bit, the soul, or the responsive mind enters. In other words, it splits the indissoluble biblical link between the physical and spiritual realities. A very early human being can be just a physical entity with no spiritual element. Since it is only the spiritual bit of humanity that really matters, the purely physical stuff of which the embryo is constructed may be regarded as disposable or used for research. I am increasingly convinced that we should resist the creeping philosophical dualism which splits the physical aspect of the fetus from the spiritual.

The second biblical tension which we have to retain is the *tension between the 'already' and the 'not yet'*. The embryo is just one example of the tension which runs through the whole of human existence. We are already human beings but, in Christ, we are also becoming something else. We have not yet arrived at our final destination, which is to become fully human. We are becoming more of what we already are. John Stott quotes the words of ethicist Paul Ramsey: 'The human individual comes into existence as a minute informational speck . . . His subsequent prenatal and postnatal development may be described as a process of becoming what he already is from the moment he was conceived' (in Stott 1990: 321). Seventeen centuries previously, Tertullian expressed the same thought: 'The future man is a man already; the fruit is already present in the seed' (*Apology*, quoted by McCarthy 1997). Again this is a familiar tension in Christian theology. We have been saved by God's grace, but in God's grace we have yet to experience the full reality of that salvation. It is the same tension which holds together the two biblical senses of the image of God. All human beings are made in God's image, but Christ himself is the unique image of God. We are already made in God's image, but in God's grace we are being transformed to become like Jesus, the image of God. We are becoming what we already are.

The language of potentiality, when applied to the embryo, tends to be confusing rather than helpful. What does it mean to be a 'potential person'? When used by philosophers it tends to mean 'not yet a person'. Because the fetus is not yet a person, we are not required to treat it as if it were a person. This kind of thinking cuts between the 'already' and the 'not yet'. It breaks the biblical understanding of human life, which holds that all human beings are in a process of becoming what we already are. In the embryo we encounter something which is the same as ourselves, although not yet the same. But why should this be so? Why should human beings be caught in an indissoluble link between the 'already' and the 'not yet'? The answer lies in the grace of God. In John Stott's words, 'It is God's grace which confers on the unborn child, from the moment of its conception, both the unique status which it already enjoys and the unique destiny which it will later inherit. It is grace which holds together the duality of the actual and the potential, the already and the not yet' (Stott 1990: 321).

Human intuitions about abortion

In my own quest for a Christian understanding of the unborn child, it is not only the theological and biblical arguments which have influenced me. I have been deeply struck also by the profound intuitions about abortion which many people in our society reveal, including many who have no Christian or religious faith. I spoke recently to a BBC producer who was making a major television documentary about abortion. She had interviewed a considerable number of women and doctors by way of background research. She told me in private that she had been struck by the fact that when talking about abortion, the doctors and other professionals were careful to use medical language such as 'termination of pregnancy', in order to avoid giving offence. By contrast, virtually all the women she had spoken to had talked about 'killing their babies'. In her view, the women were much more honest than the doctors about the emotional implications of medical abortion.

In a foreword to their book *Pregnancy Loss, A Silent Sorrow*, American bereavement counsellors Ingrid Kohn and Perry-Lynn Moffitt, writing from an entirely secular perspective, discuss the language they have chosen to use:

This book was written to provide guidance, comfort, and hope to all parents who have experienced an unwanted pregnancy loss, including those who have ended an impaired pregnancy. We considered using terms such as 'fetus' and 'embryo' when discussing abnormal pregnancies and abortions, realizing this language was more in keeping with a pro-choice stance. In the end, we continued to refer to the 'unborn baby'. We felt compelled to acknowledge this common grief: *no matter what the cause of their loss, bereaved parents mourn for someone who was dear to them, someone who was supposed to be their 'baby'*. If the words we chose are imperfect, they still represent our sincerest attempt to give expression to this universal sorrow (Kohn & Moffitt 1994: viii, my emphasis).

Elaine Storkey, in her meditation on the experience of Mary, the mother of Jesus, expresses the intuitive sense of wonder and the emotional demands of pregnancy from the mother's perspective.

Pregnancy is itself a symbol of deep hospitality. It is the giving of one's body to the life of another. It is a sharing of all that we have, our cell structure, our bloodstream, our food, our oxygen. It is saying 'welcome' with every breath, and every heartbeat. And for many mothers that welcome is given irrespective of the demands made on one's own comfort, health or ease of life. For the demands of this hospitality are greater than almost any of our own. And the growing fetus is made to know that here is love, here are warm lodgings, here is a place of safety. In hiding and in quiet the miraculous growth can take place . . .

   This is one of the reasons why the decision for abortion is such a painful and heavy one. Of course there are those who have been taught by our culture to present themselves to the clinic with barely a second thought, accepting the sterile terminology of the hospital for what they are about to do: 'a termination of pregnancy'. Yet for many other women who have had an abortion there has been anxiety and grief and a sense of loss. In spite of all the reasons which directed them to take this step, some feel guilty of a deep betrayal of trust. They could not find within themselves the hospitality that was needed to sustain this life . . . (Storkey 1993: 34).

Whenever we contemplate abortion for a malformed or unwanted fetus, we are sending a message of rejection. We are saying that we do not wish to accept this new other, or to offer basic human hospitality. Although the desire to spare a child from suffering is motivated by genuine human compassion, the act of abortion seems the opposite of a loving welcome. The sense of unease is frequently expressed by mothers who plan to undergo an abortion in these circumstances. 'Once you get the results, every day your baby moves, you are dying inside.' This, of course, is why disabled people, represented by Tom Shakespeare and Christy Nolan, react so violently to the practice of genetic screening and therapeutic abortion of affected fetuses. It strikes at the heart of our intuitions about humanity and human community. By contrast, Joseph Pieper helpfully defines the essence of love: 'love is a way of saying to another person, "It's good that you exist; it's good that you are in this world"' (quoted by Meilander 1997: 49).

I therefore find myself driven by the thrust of the biblical material, by theological arguments and by the undeniable reality of widespread human intuitions about abortion, to the conclusion that we owe a duty of protection and care to the embryo and the early fetus as much as to the mature fetus and newborn baby. Even the earliest stages of human development deserve respect and protection. There is no point from fertilization onwards at which we can reliably conclude that a human being is not a member of the human family, one who is known and called by God, one with whom we are locked in community.

Fetal screening

I have argued that the destruction of even an impaired or abnormal fetus is inconsistent with a Christian worldview. As a result, I think that we should resist the tendency, noted in chapter 4, for modern pregnancies to become 'tentative'. The very existence of fetal screening and the availability of abortion until even late in pregnancy tend to imply that the commitment of parent to child is tentative or conditional. In some ways, it seems to me that fetal screening offers a false hope, a technological mirage. It seems to offer the anxious parents the possibility of the security and confidence that their baby will be 'all right'. But the sad and unpalatable truth is that no technology can offer this confidence to parents. No technology can guarantee that unpredictable problems and disabilities will not arise after birth. As B. K. Rothman put it, 'The possibility of spending the rest of one's life caring for a sick or disabled child can never be eliminated by prenatal testing. I worry about women who say that they only dare have children because prenatal diagnosis is available. Motherhood is, among other things, one more chance for a speeding truck to ruin your life' (Rothman 1986: 252). Anxiety about our children is, sadly, a reality of being a parent which no amount of technology can assuage. It is part of the human condition.

But if in my view abortion for fetal abnormality falls short of genuine Christian compassion, does this mean that all fetal screening is valueless? What about the argument that fetal screening is helpful because it allows us to prepare ourselves psychologically for a disabled baby? This argument sounds good in theory, but in practice it may be less valuable than it seems. Certainly my own clinical experience is that the weeks of waiting for the birth of a baby who is known to be impaired may cause increasing anxiety and psychological distress rather than benefit. In some cases it seems as if the medical knowledge provided by fetal screening has harmed the normal relationship between parents and newborn child. Why is this? I would like to speculate that in the original creation order, we are so designed that we start to love our unborn baby as a mysterious unknown, as a gift given in secret, before we meet him or her face to face at birth. Gilbert Meilander expressed this perspective well: 'Perhaps the time of pregnancy will be better spent learning to love the child we have been given, before we evaluate and assess what our child is capable of' (1997: 55).

I want to emphasize that this does not mean, of course, that all fetal screening and antenatal care is valueless. On the contrary, many of the tests offered by obstetricians and midwives, including antenatal ultrasound, congenital infection screening and antibody tests, allow treatable problems to be identified, so that the fetus can be helped and supported. What I feel deeply uneasy about are the tests for fetal conditions when the only available 'treatment' is abortion. Many pregnant women do not realize that they are being tested for conditions, such as Down's syndrome, for which the only option is abortion. They need to ask for information before the tests are performed and make clear their wishes to the hospital staff.

Hard cases

We cannot, of course, escape the very few hard cases where there seems to be an overwhelming argument in favour of abortion. What about the dying mother, the rape victim, the conjoint twins, or the twelve-year-old pregnant child? In the case of the mother who is dying from the effects of pregnancy, it has been argued that death has already entered the pregnancy. It is not a matter of deciding whether a death should occur, but rather of deciding whether death should strike the fetus alone, or both the fetus and the mother. In this extreme example it seems that an abortion may be acceptable, although deeply painful. As Meilander put it, 'we cannot require a mother to build the human race by destroying herself' (Meilander 1997: 35). In practice, with modern obstetric care, it is very rare for a mother's life to be severely threatened by a pregnancy. Moreover, it may well be possible to delay termination of the pregnancy until the twenty-fourth or twenty-fifth week, when the fetus can then be delivered and offered a reasonable chance of survival with modern neonatal intensive care.

In the tragic case of the rape victim, again we can perceive a terrible conflict between fetus and mother. Although the fetus has, of course, no personal responsibility, its continued existence within the woman may constitute for her an embodiment of the original attack upon her person. There may be an understandable and overwhelming desire to get rid of any vestige, any reminder, of the assault. Surely an abortion is the loving and Christian response? Even in this painful case, however, there is an argument for continuing the pregnancy. For to perform an abortion may be perceived, emotionally and unconsciously, as the perpetration of yet another assault on a woman who has already suffered terribly. To the long-lasting emotional consequences of rape are added the complex emotional traumas of deliberate abortion. How can the healing love of Christ be brought into this terrible agony? It seems impossible to give a general answer which will fit each case. Similar arguments apply to the issue of the schoolgirl pregnancy. Although abortion seems a neat solution – a technological fix for a complex social dilemma – experience shows that it may have long-lasting, unpredictable and deeply scarring effects on all those involved.

One of the strange paradoxes of the human condition is that because of unwanted pregnancies, extremely young women are frequently confronted with the option of abortion without the emotional maturity to comprehend the life-long significance of their decision. As Naomi Wolf ruefully commented, 'We had no idea of the enormity of it. We were just kids.' It may take years of experience of life for some to come to terms with the human significance of abortion. Those who counsel women with post-abortion trauma will say that this is not unusual.

Finally, there are rare and distressing hereditary conditions in which medical treatment seems unable to save children from appalling and uncontrollable suffering and progressive deterioration which are heart-breaking to watch. If the diagnosis can be made by DNA analysis before birth, is abortion always wrong? How can the love of Christ be demonstrated practically for parents confronted with these painful dilemmas? I shall discuss the tensions faced by Christian health professionals who are trying to help patients face these dilemmas in chapter 11, but now we consider options other than abortion.

Practical alternatives to abortion

My own personal belief, strengthened by over twenty years of clinical experience, is that *nearly always* there is a better alternative to the unwanted or abnormal pregnancy than abortion. It is the way of practical support for the mother and for the unwanted child. This way is costly, emotionally, practically and financially. It is not an easy way, because the truth is that there is no quick and easy technological fix for the ultimate dilemmas of the human condition. Practical, supportive caring is not an easy alternative. But I am convinced that it is a better way. It is also an essential response if we Christians are not to be guilty of hypocrisy. Unless Christians are in the forefront of providing practical care and support for those with unplanned pregnancies, and for parents struggling with the implications of bringing up a disabled or impaired child, then our supposed commitment to the sanctity of human life is deeply suspect.

One of the most promising developments in this field is the rapid expansion of pregnancy crisis centres, particularly those under the leadership of CARE for Life. In ten years this organization has established almost a hundred crisis pregnancy centres throughout the UK. Each centre aims to provide free pregnancy testing, skilled counselling, clear information on all the options available, practical support (including short-term housing and other practical help) and time to explore all the conflicting emotions and long-term implications which an unplanned pregnancy brings. Help, support and counselling are not restricted to those with unplanned pregnancies, but are also made available to those who have experienced abortions or suffered other forms of pregnancy loss, such as miscarriage or stillbirth. The centres are staffed almost entirely by female volunteers, and vary greatly in their age, size and location. The centre in Basingstoke, one of the longest-established, sees approximately one thousand women each year and has eighteen volunteer counsellors. Women are referred by family doctors or local churches, or come as a result of personal recommendation or advertising (Minnis 1996).

Pregnancy crisis centres represent a wonderful, authentically Christian response to the problem of the unplanned pregnancy. At their best they demonstrate all the finest qualities of Christian caring – practical, costly, down-to-earth, realistic, unglamorous, empathic, respectful, sacrificial. Giving practical answers to human need, it is a way that fits with the deepest intuitions of many in our society. Yet much more needs to be done, in widening the geographical and social penetration of the centres, improving the quality of the counselling, offering better practical support for mothers and families before and after their child's birth, helping to secure suitable employment, granting financial help, providing personal support links with local Christian communities, gaining the confidence of medical and other health professionals, and raising awareness among the general public. I am convinced that the Christian community represents a vast and still largely untapped resource for caring in our society. Here is an unparalleled opportunity for ordinary Christian people to demonstrate the practical reality of the gospel to hurting people in our midst.

Postscript

Maybe someone reading these words is oppressed by feelings of guilt or failure from a past experience. It is not my intention to judge others who have felt compelled to request or to perform an abortion in extreme circumstances. Maybe you pressurized your partner, your friend or your child to have an abortion. Maybe you were confronted by the existence of a terribly malformed baby and felt there was no alternative to abortion. I am painfully aware that many people carry deep burdens of secret pain and, maybe, guilt, in this area – burdens which they may feel completely unable to share with others. If this refers to you, then please get help. Make the first step by finding a trusted Christian counsellor or friend to whom you can unburden your heart. Remember that human beings do not divide up into the guilty and the innocent. I am guilty. We are all guilty. Rather, human beings divide into the forgiven and the unforgiven. In Christ we can find a new beginning. Maybe, in God's grace, your painful experience can be transformed slowly and miraculously – redeemed by God's power – so that it becomes a source of help and healing for others.

8. The dying baby: dilemmas of neonatal care

The effects of advances in medical technology, which we considered in earlier chapters, are nowhere more obvious than in the development of intensive care for newborn babies. The survival of extremely preterm infants born at twenty-four to twenty-five weeks' gestation, almost four months before term and weighing just 500–700 grams (1 to $1\frac{1}{2}$ lbs) is now commonplace. Many babies with profound and even bizarre congenital malformations (such as exomphalos, in which the bowel grows outside the abdomen) may be surgically treated at birth, leading to healthy survival into adulthood. But medical advances such as these are not bought cheaply, in personal, social or financial terms. For parents and family there is the trauma of watching helplessly as their child struggles week after week under the burden of intensive-care procedures. For the National Health Service the bill is up to £1,000 per baby per day. The total cost to the NHS of providing intensive care for very preterm infants alone was estimated in 1993 at between £42 million and £70 million per annum (Griffin 1993), and the figure is likely to be substantially higher now.

Ambivalence towards abnormal or premature babies

Those of us who care for newborn babies are frequently aware of an uncomfortable ambivalence which many people feel towards the abnormal or preterm infant. On the one hand, our society is highly sensitized towards the needs of babies and children. Charities and individuals donate hundreds of thousands of pounds to buy intensive-care equipment. Prominent publicity campaigns feature dramatic pictures of babies festooned with intensive-care machinery. Newspapers and television run prominent articles on the newest 'gee-whizz' medical technology as well as heartwarming human-interest stories about the latest child survivor. Parents and visitors to neonatal units are frequently moved to tears by the sight of tiny babies struggling for life and the concentration of resources and expertise devoted to their care. Behind this public interest and support lies more than sentimentality. Babies, especially those who are sick and vulnerable, are seen by many as infinitely precious beings, unique and defenceless individuals who are to be nurtured, cared for and protected.

But an entirely contradictory view towards the abnormal or preterm baby is also widespread, although frequently unspoken. According to this perspective, however deeply we may be moved by the abnormal baby's plight, we have to realize that he or she is in reality one of 'Nature's rejects', the unfortunate consequence of a complex biological process which is frighteningly fallible and prone to accidents. If Nature in her wisdom has decided that this particular baby has no viable future and should be discarded, who are we to use the panoply of modern intensive-care techniques to thwart her wishes? Why waste scarce financial resources and emotional energy on this individual? Far better to ensure that the baby does not survive, and suggest to the parents that they try to have another.

This view has several hidden assumptions. First, the implication is that sick or abnormal newborn babies are disposable, unlike adults or older children who require medical care. In other words, there is no fundamental duty upon the rest of society to preserve their lives. Secondly, in distinction to adults who have a unique character and life history, the sick baby has no genuine individuality or personality. 'It' cannot be regarded as a person, and so each baby is viewed as fundamentally *replaceable*. Another infant can always be conceived to substitute for the abnormal and unwanted one. Thirdly, there is the implicit acceptance of what might be termed a eugenic biological imperative, a desire to preserve the human gene pool and eliminate harmful genes. To believe that 'Nature knows best' is to believe that only the fittest should survive. The parents may have a 'selfish' wish to ensure the survival of their sick or abnormal baby, and this is understandable, but from a strictly biological perspective it may be fundamentally against the best interests of humanity as a whole. From this perspective the whole enterprise of neonatal intensive care for abnormal or premature babies can be seen as misguided, wasteful of scarce resources and ultimately futile. It is 'against Nature' – a modern version of medical hubris.

As we have seen, some bioethicists, such as Peter Singer, reinforce this attitude by arguing that newborn babies are not full members of the human community and that their lives may be taken, if this seems to be in the best interests of the community as a whole. It would be misleading to suggest that all or even the majority of modern ethicists would give wholehearted support to the position of Singer or Harris. They represent an influential but extreme position within the spectrum of attitudes among contemporary philosophers. Nevertheless, their views seem logically consistent with their basic philosophical presuppositions, and demonstrate the radical implications of a rigorously utilitarian approach to the newborn baby.

Treating babies with respect

Mother Theresa used to tell of the work of her Sisters of Charity in the slums of Calcutta. Every day the sisters would scour the streets to pick up the dying beggar, the abandoned baby found in a dustbin, the leprosy victim. She described in graphic detail the appalling degradation of those she found: the live maggots in the wounds, the stench, the pathetic courage. Where did the sisters find the motivation which drove them to this level of caring? Was it pity for these miserable scraps of humanity? This is what she once said: 'It is more than pity that motivates us, it is compassion mingled with *respect*.'

Here again is the theme of respect which we noted in chapter 2. But how can anyone possibly respect a being who has sunk to such degradation and filth? Mother Theresa used to give a spiritual answer to this down-to-earth question. She quoted the parable of the sheep and the goats in Matthew's gospel: 'I was hungry and you gave me something to eat, I was thirsty and you gave me something to drink, I was a stranger and you invited me in, I needed clothes and you clothed me, I was sick and you looked after me . . .' 'Lord, when did we see you hungry and feed you . . .?' 'I tell you the truth, whatever you did for one of the least of these brothers of mine, you did for me' (Mt. 25:31–46).

Mother Theresa was saying, in effect, 'This is Jesus.' Jesus was present, in what she used to call 'a distressing disguise' (Mother Theresa 1975: 87). When we care for the abandoned and rejected of society, we are 'tending the wounds of Christ'. That is why we respect them, and treat them with dignity. 'Here on the streets, in the unwanted children, in the broken body of the leper, in the dying beggar, we see Christ, we touch him and we care for him.' A Hindu social worker once described the difference between their official activities for the poor and those of Mother Theresa. 'We do it for something, but you do it for someone . . .' (1975: 50). That is the heart of Christian caring. It's the reason for the note of respect which I believe is the hallmark of authentic Christian compassion.

Mother Theresa's thought has affected me deeply as I have reflected on my work as a paediatrician. I have come to realize that I am called to treat this tiny body, struggling for life, covered in tubes, attached to complex machinery, with the same tenderness, the same sense of wonder, the same *respect*, that Mary and Joseph showed as they cared for their little bundle in a stable two thousand years ago. The Christian doctrine of the incarnation teaches that Jesus was a baby – not a sentimental, sugar-candy, Christmas-card cherub, but a real baby, who dribbled down his front and had dirty nappies; a baby who fitted with the medical definition: 'a gastrointestinal tract with no sense of responsibility at either end.'

Christian caring for babies cannot be sentimental and airy-fairy. It must be down to earth, realistic and practical. It must be rooted in the stuff of our physical humanity. Yet at the same time it should display the distinctive qualities of the way in which Christians should care for all members of the human community: wonder, respect, empathy and protection.

Advocacy for the vulnerable

Treating babies with respect means that we cannot treat even the extremely premature baby as less than a full member of the human community. Babies are our neighbours, who deserve 'respect-love' with all its sacrificial demands. Instead of a eugenic concern that only the fittest should become members of society, we should be concerned to ensure the survival and the protection of those who are the most vulnerable. The risk of exploitation can come from parents and relatives who may put their own interests above those of their child, from doctors or managers who may wish to use their patients to increase power or academic status, or from healthcare purchasers who wish to redirect funds to other patient groups because of political expediency or utilitarian convictions. Our duty as Christians is to act as advocates on behalf of all the weak in our society, to ensure that their voice is heard and their interests are preserved.

When should intensive treatment be withdrawn?

Treating babies with respect does not, however, mean that we are obliged to provide intensive treatment in every conceivable condition, to attempt to prolong life even when there is no prospect of recovery. In the Introduction we reviewed the tragic story of Samuel Linares, a baby with no prospect of recovery who was receiving intensive care for months, but whose doctors felt unable to switch the machines off to allow death to occur. In the end it was Samuel's father who was compelled by compassion and desperation to take the law into his own hands. In my view this case represents a terrible failure of modern medical care. It was a failure on the part of Samuel's doctors, whether from fear of litigation or for some other reason, to recognize the point where medicine had changed from a source of healing and restoration and instead had become a technological monster, even a strange form of child abuse. Treating babies with respect means that we must learn to let go; we must learn to recognize the point at which medical treatment becomes futile and abusive, and the burdens of treatment exceed the benefits.

How do we balance the burdens and benefits of intensive medical treatment? If it is apparent that there is no hope of meaningful long-term survival, and that intensive support is merely prolonging the process of dying, withdrawal of medical treatment, following full discussion and with the agreement of the parents, is most consistent with a genuine respect for the dignity of the individual. Techniques such as ultrasound scanning of the brain can give vital information about whether brain injury is present in the critical few hours and days after delivery. Although it may not be possible to foresee the long-term outlook with complete reliability, it is becoming increasingly possible to predict the likely long-term consequences for the individual. How should this information be employed in making decisions about the appropriateness of intensive care for the sick newborn?

In assessing the consequences of brain injury or abnormality, a Christian perspective places special importance on the value of relationships. As we saw in chapter 2, it is the human capacity for relationships which is at the heart of our identity. Richard McCormick put it like this: 'In Judaeo-Christian perspective, the meaning, substance, and consummation of life are found in human relationships, and the qualities of justice, respect, concern, compassion, and support that surround them' (quoted in Higginson 1987). As we try to assess the consequences of brain injury, then, in my view the critical issue is not the degree of physical handicap which may result, but the likely capacity to enter meaningfully into relationships with family and friends, with the community, and ultimately with God himself.

Therefore, brain injury which causes impaired mobility or loss of vision or hearing, but in which sufficient brain function is retained for some capacity for loving human relationships, does not in my view constitute adequate justification for the withdrawal of intensive care. The benefits of medical treatment are likely in most cases to outweigh its burdens. By contrast, brain injury of such severity that no capacity for meaningful relationships is apparently possible can be regarded as reducing human life to mere biological survival. This is likely if there is global destruction of cortical and subcortical structures in both cerebral hemispheres. In a similar category come brain malformations involving a generalized failure of development of the cortex or subcortical connections. While the presence of such brain injury would not prevent the infant from being regarded still as a human being worthy of respect and dignity, it does raise questions about the appropriateness of prolonging survival by intensive medical and technological support. It is open to question whether the burden to the individual of prolonged and unpleasant intensive care outweighs the possible benefit that such treatment can bring. In this case, provided there is a consensus between healthcare staff and parents, it is justifiable to withdraw intensive treatment with the realization that death is very likely to follow. The intention is not to end life, however, but to withdraw futile treatment, although doctors and parents can foresee that death may occur as a result of this action. If, as sometimes happens, the baby does not die as a result, then compassionate caring, with provision of feeds and symptom relief, is continued.

This approach does not mean that the intrinsic value of a baby's life is reduced because of severe brain damage; this would contradict the basic Christian stance I have defended earlier. The presence of severe brain damage may, however, reduce the possible benefits of intensive care and invasive medical treatment relative to their considerable burdens. We are not at liberty to decide whether a life is futile or not. We can, however, decide whether intensive treatment is futile or not.

This argument may also be applied to the continuation of intensive care in adults with very severe brain injury, such as Tony Bland, whose story was discussed in the Introduction. In the case of Tony Bland, however, it must be recognized that the issue at stake was not the withdrawal of intensive life-support measures and artificial respiration, but rather the withdrawal of tube feeding. This raises different questions, which will be discussed in chapter 10.

Techniques like brain scans, which allow the extent of brain injury to be assessed, do not of course solve the painful ethical dilemmas concerning the appropriateness of intensive care for a malformed or critically sick newborn, but they provide objective information which can be discussed in detail with the parents and with other concerned individuals, and on which ethical decisions about intensive care can be based. In this way, respect for the dignity and worth of the individual baby, and concern for his or her best interests, can be translated into practical decisions about medical care.

Care of the dying baby

When health professionals and parents recognize the point at which intensive treatment should be withdrawn, it is important to realize that although medical treatment may stop, caring must never stop. In essence, we must provide the highest quality of terminal care for dying babies, just as we should provide terminal or palliative care for every dying adult. In my view, every baby deserves a minimum level of care by virtue of his or her birthright as a human being.

First, we must provide adequate pain and symptom relief. We have a duty to use medical and nursing care to ensure not only that pain is adequately treated but also that distressing symptoms such as breathlessness and convulsions are controlled. Secondly, except in extreme cases where there is no possibility of absorption through the bowel, we should provide food and fluids; allowing babies to die from starvation and dehydration is not compatible with treating them with respect. Finally, and equally importantly, we must ensure that the dying baby receives 'TLC', tender loving care. Cuddles, where possible from the mother or other close relative, physically demonstrate the wonder, respect and empathy which we owe to each baby. All other treatments, such as antibiotics and intravenous nutrition, need be given only if the likely benefits will exceed the burdens of the treatment. But the short list of symptom control, food and TLC is the minimum that every baby deserves. This is what respect means when translated into clinical practice.

Christopher's story

Alan and Verity are close friends from my local church, All Souls, in the heart of London's West End. My wife Celia and I have known them for many years, and, as two couples, we have shared our lives. In the spring of 1996, as we enjoyed an evening together, Verity told us that she was expecting a baby. We discussed the news with anticipation and excitement. But only two weeks later the outlook had changed. A routine ultrasound scan at twenty weeks showed major abnormalities. The diagnosis was Edwards syndrome, a tragic and rare chromosomal disorder which causes multiple malformations, severe mental impairment and a uniformly fatal outcome. In this condition nearly all obstetricians will recommend abortion. What possible point can there be to continuing a pregnancy where there is no hope of long-term survival? Yet, after agonizing and heartfelt discussion, Alan and Verity decided not to have an abortion but to continue the pregnancy. What follows is the transcript of an interview in which Nick Page asked them to talk about their experience.

Nick: Why did you choose not to have an abortion?

Verity: I think by the time we'd reached twenty weeks, we'd already seen the child on the scan, seen his features, his limbs, known every condition that he suffered from. By then he'd already become a real person and it seemed terrible, the thought of ending a life that was already, in our opinion, so complete.

Nick: Looking back, what would you say was the legacy of Christopher for you two as a couple?

Verity: I think it was the chance to be a parent, one that we would have been denied completely if we'd have had an abortion. Each of us was able to be as normal a parent as we could be with a child with that condition, with all its joys, and with a lot of the normal things associated with parenthood.

Alan: You see, what would have happened if we had decided to have an abortion for this handicapped child, and then discovered we couldn't have any other children? We would have had absolutely nothing.

Verity: And the other thing is the way we were able to connect with him as a human being. I mean, we didn't know the extent of his handicap, to what extent he would recognize us, but we really connected with him. He communicated with us and we did with him. And that ability to create a relationship with another human being is . . . wonderful.

Nick: The impact Christopher had not just on yourselves but on everyone around you was very interesting. Why do you think that was?

Verity: He seemed to have the ability to draw love out of people in quite a unique way. People were able to hold him. He was a very peaceful baby but he seemed to melt the coldest heart and to really make people love him.

Nick: He had a particular effect on the local hospice, I gather.

Alan: Yes, that was quite remarkable. Verity sometimes used to visit the local hospice, St Christopher's Hospice in Sydenham, and take Christopher round the wards. Here there were people who were dying and yet they were able to hold a baby who was also dying and in need of terminal palliative care. And somehow that shared experience between a baby who was dying and an adult who was dying was quite remarkable.

Verity: One of the patients, Beatty, who was dying of leukaemia, was especially fond of Christopher and one day when I visited her, she said, 'Now, Christopher, I don't know who's going to die first, whether it's going to be you or me, but I'll be waiting for you in heaven with my arms open ready to welcome you when you arrive.'

Nick Page asked Richard Bewes, the Rector of All Souls Church, to talk about the effect that Christopher's life had on the congregation.

Richard: His life exercised a most extraordinary ministry. There he was, the smallest little shrimp within the congregation. Here was the weakest member among us, easily the weakest member, and yet he did exercise a strong, strange hold upon us. Indeed, in a real way we shared him among the congregation. He became, in the end, almost public property. His parents would be one side of the room, and he would be shared amongst people the other side of the room. People would take it in turns to cuddle him and then to learn from his own life and from the attitude of his parents, Alan and Verity. They themselves were quite obviously growing through that experience, in trust, in faith and, I think, in service too. So the three of them exercised a strong hold in those precious, very short, seven months that will live indelibly with us, all those of us who were members of the church at that time.

When Christopher was born he was the smallest member of the church, and when he died, seven months later, he was still virtually the same size. A friend summed up his influence: 'Although he was unable to grow, he helped others to grow.' Christopher died in the summer of 1997. Yet his influence still carries on. I do not want to imply that there was no sadness. There was and still is a deep sense of grief and loss at Christopher's disability and untimely death. Alan and Verity and their family and friends have known tears and heartache, and those feelings continue. But behind it all is the Christian conviction that even the weakest and most malformed human being has a life of unique value. Christopher in his way was a Godlike being, a masterpiece. His life was an example of Christian theology in practice, and it was a privilege to know him.

God's broken image

Here is a strange paradox. Sometimes we see the image of God most clearly not in the perfect specimens of humanity, not in the Olympic athlete or the Nobel Prize winner. We see Christ in the broken, the malformed, the imperfect. It is an example of the Easter mystery. God is revealed not in glorious majesty but in a broken body on a cross. This is the vision of the L'Arche communities founded by the French Catholic, Jean Vanier. Vanier developed a way of caring for the profoundly disabled individuals who are so often rejected and abandoned by society. He saw them as in some way representing the presence of Christ in our midst. 'The person perceived by society as a problem, useless, a burden, we see as a source of life, drawing us towards truth, towards Jesus and the Gospel . . . For me to follow Jesus is to be with those who have been cast aside and to meet him in and with them' (Vanier 1996: 16).

Is this just sentimentality, life-denying, sugar-sweet religiosity of the worst and most mystical kind? I can imagine the responses of the cynical clinician, the radical philosopher and the hard-bitten health economist. But no, it is not sentimentality. It is a vision of caring which fits with the Christian worldview and the biblical revelation. I am increasingly struck at how this vision of caring also makes sense to ordinary people in our society. It 'rings bells'; it fits with the deepest intuitions of our hearts.

Over the years, I and my professional colleagues, especially Anthea Blake, Senior Nurse on the neonatal unit at University College Hospital, have had the privilege of caring for many dying babies. We have found a way of caring for them and for their families that recognizes the unique value and dignity of even a dying baby. Under Anthea Blake's leadership and together with the hospital chaplaincy team, we have developed an interdenominational Christian service for parents who have lost babies at our hospital, as a result of neonatal death or stillbirth. Once a year we invite bereaved parents and their families to a simple service in a local church. The content of the service is chosen entirely by parents. Often they contribute poems, either of their own or gleaned from other sources. At the climax of the service, the children present, brothers and sisters of those who have died, bring to the front cards, each one bearing the name of a baby who died, in a simple act of dedication.

It is always a weepy and intensely moving experience. It may sound rather sentimental and maudlin. Yet we have been struck by the depth of commitment which many bereaved parents have shown to this service, many of whom would claim no Christian or other religious faith. Some parents and families come year after year to remember a baby who lived maybe for only a few hours. Many parents have written to tell us how helpful and healing the experience has been. Why do so many people come to this simple service? Why do they see this straightforward act of commemoration as so important? I suggest it is because the service represents a public recognition of the particular significance and worth of their dead baby. It says that their baby was not just a nonentity, but a unique person – valued, grieved and missed. It fits with the deepest intuitions of a parent's heart.

I have tried to summarize what I have learned over the years about the intuitions of the many parents for whose babies I have cared. 'My baby is a unique individual with a history, an identity and a name. My baby is a person, not a thing; a "she" [or a "he"], not an "it". My baby must be treated with gentleness and respect by those who are caring for her. My baby can never be replaced, although I may have other babies in the future. If my baby's outlook is hopeless, then it may be the most compassionate act to withdraw treatment and "keep her comfortable", knowing that she may die. Withdrawing treatment and allowing my baby to die is not the same as deliberately killing her. If my baby does die, I need to have permanent reminders and mementoes of her short existence, to honour her memory as a unique person, my beloved child.'

It is obvious from my clinical experience that the intuitions of most parents are light years away from the philosophy of Peter Singer. To nearly all of us, babies are not 'non-persons'. They are unique, vulnerable and precious members of the human community. I am continually struck by the fact that the deepest intuitions of ordinary people, parents and families, in our pluralistic and multifaith society, are so often similar to the convictions of orthodox Christian theology. When we put forward a Christian perspective about the disabled and dying baby, we are not just defending a sugary sentimentality. We are telling it like it is. The biblical Christian worldview works; it fits with reality.

In the next chapter we continue our progress from the beginning of life to its end, by addressing the controversial issues of euthanasia and assisted suicide.

9. A good death?
Euthanasia and assisted suicide

'Death, like the sun, should not be stared at.' So said the French philosopher quoted in the Introduction. Yet advances in medicine force us to do just that. Of course, all generations have discovered that they cannot evade the reality of death. But if we are going to develop an authentic Christian response to the issues of euthanasia and medically assisted suicide, we need to stare at death with renewed intensity. We need to stare at its mystery and awful finality, at the questions and fears that it raises, and at our own mortality. As with the other issues in this book, death and dying are not just 'out there' as abstract theoretical issues. Death is here in our midst. You, the reader, carry your future mortality with you as you read this book. To be a little over-dramatic, I am writing as a dying man to dying people.

According to the cynic, 'Life is a sexually transmitted degenerative condition with a mortality of 100%.' So we all have a direct and personal interest in this subject. As I prepared for the London Lectures and reflected again about death, I found it personally challenging, even disturbing. How would I like to die? What will happen, who will be there, who will care for me? How will I spend my last days, my last hours, my last moments? Will I die well, or in pain and distress?

'It's not that I'm afraid of death, it's just that I don't want to be there when it happens.' Those are the well-known words of Woody Allen, who has built much of his career on his quirky humour about death and dying. Why is Woody Allen funny? Because what he has to say rings true. On balance, we do not want to be there when it happens. The problem is that we have little choice in the matter. As we shall see, it is the drive for choice, for control, for personal autonomy, which is at the heart of the current moves towards the legalization of euthanasia which are taking place across the world.

The drive for euthanasia legalization

In the Introduction we looked at the tragic case of Lillian Boyes and her doctor Nigel Cox. Simply to read through the eye-witness accounts is painful. Here is a caring senior doctor confronted with the tragic spectacle of his patient of thirteen years who has reached the degrading final stages of rheumatoid arthritis. There are ulcers and abscesses on her skin, fractured vertebrae, deformed limbs, inflamed joints, gangrenous flesh. And worst of all there is the uncontrollable pain. This poor lady 'howled and screamed like a dog' whenever she was moved or touched. There was pain that did not respond to massive doses of diamorphine. Is it any wonder that Dr Cox felt a desperate necessity to end her life? Was this not the compassionate and caring act of a doctor who put his patient's interests first?

The arrest and subsequent trial of Dr Cox focused national and international attention on the question of the legalization of medical euthanasia, and the 'right to die'. Many philosophers and ethicists wrote publicly to argue in favour of a change in the law. The respected philosopher Janet Radcliffe Richards, for example, wrote in the *Guardian Weekly* of 27 September 1992:

> The problem with voluntary euthanasia has nothing to do with the dangers of letting doctors decide whether patients live or die. The real question is quite different. It is whether people who are trapped in bodies or institutions they cannot control should be allowed to make choices freely available to us. Most of us can choose to end our lives if they seem not worth living. But many people who are incapacitated by illness or accident, and who may have the most reason to want to die, simply cannot do so. At present the law allows them no escape. This is a pretty remarkable state of affairs. We are supposed to feel sympathy when people cannot make choices for themselves . . . But when people who want to kill themselves can't do so, we suddenly see things differently . . . Whether we like it or not, many people seriously want to die. Some have the power to kill themselves; others have not, and the law prevents anyone from helping them. This in itself seems appalling, and if we are not to change matters we need very good reasons indeed . . . Dr Cox has apparently done as any good doctor should; he used his technical skill to do what his patient would have liked to do for herself but could not. This is just what experts are for. The only good thing about the monstrous position in which he finds himself is that it may make the pressure for change overwhelming. Let us hope this happens before we ourselves are prisoners of pain and institutions, with an archaic law cutting off our only means of escape.

Richard Smith, the editor of the *British Medical Journal*, shortly after the trial verdict had been announced, wrote: 'Dr Cox's case may well prove to be a watershed. Euthanasia is rising up the agenda in many countries. [There is a] slow but steady change in public opinion [which is] reminiscent of what happened with abortion: in the past thirty years many countries have moved from extremely restrictive to liberal laws on abortion, and over the next thirty years euthanasia may move from being covert to being legal' (*BMJ* 1992: 305:728–729).

The Dutch experience has been repeatedly cited as the way forward. In July 1997 the *BMJ* carried a piece called 'A Very Special Day'. In it a Dutch doctor, Frederique Zwart, who was working in Britain, described the death by euthanasia of his grandmother in Holland.

My grandmother died recently. She made the decision and chose the date and the place. She came to a point when she thought life was not worth living and, as the doctors agreed, she was allowed to die quickly and painlessly . . . I have seen many people die, but none so peacefully as my Gran . . . Once the decision had been made, she relaxed and said her goodbyes . . . The doctor came, talked to her again and explained the procedure to us. Those who wished followed him to her room. The second-opinion doctor had seen her a few weeks earlier and all the paperwork . . . had been done . . . She decided at 8am and by 2pm the procedure had taken place . . . My Gran had carcinoma of the rectum with liver and lung metastases. She was troubled by severe fatigue but the loss of dignity was her prime concern. She was in no physical pain and she was alert up to the last second . . . All those who watched her suffer – the long nights, the fatigue, the hopelessness – were incredibly relieved. We had seen her become very depressed. I am very proud of my grandmother. In Holland it is only certain people who choose to die this way. Her consultant said afterwards that this was one of his reasons for being a doctor: to relieve suffering this way. Is there any reason why this is not part of my duties as an English doctor? Is this not the most dignified way to treat patients who openly ask you to relieve their suffering? (*BMJ* 1997: 315:260).

Definitions

Words are slippery things, and in this debate, phrases such as 'the right to die', 'a merciful death' and 'relief of suffering' are often used loosely, leading to confusion and misunderstanding. An old Chinese proverb states: 'The beginning of wisdom is to call things by their proper names.' The phrase 'the right to die' sounds so reasonable, and yet it can mean at least five different things to different people: (1) the right to refuse life-sustaining treatment which is burdensome or futile; (2) the right to refuse life-sustaining treatment for any reason; (3) the right to commit suicide for 'rational' reasons; (4) the right to obtain help in committing suicide; or (5) the right to be killed by a doctor at one's own request.

Of these, (1) is both legal and accepted as a basis of good medical care, and (2) and (3) are not illegal, whereas both (4) and (5) are illegal in virtually all legal systems in the world. When we enter into the debate about euthanasia we must challenge people to use words accurately and carefully. The term 'euthanasia' means literally 'a good death', but in practice the definition which I shall adopt is the following, which is identical or very similar to that which most doctors and ethicists have agreed on: 'Euthanasia is the intentional killing, by act or omission, of a person whose life is thought not to be worth living.'

First, this definition puts the emphasis on *intentional* killing, a deliberate and premeditated act to take life, to introduce death into a situation. Secondly, it implies that euthanasia may be performed either positively by deliberate act, or negatively by omission. It is the *intention to kill* which is central to the definition. In the past, the phrases 'active euthanasia' and 'passive euthanasia' were widely used, but most ethicists now agree that they are ambiguous and should be dropped.

Euthanasia can be divided into *voluntary* euthanasia, killing carried out at the patient's explicit request, and *involuntary* euthanasia, where no immediate or unambiguous request has been given, although a previous willingness may or may not have been expressed. (Some have added a third category, 'non-voluntary euthanasia', where the patient is not competent to express a wish.) In Holland, the word 'euthanasia' is nearly always taken to imply an explicit request, so Dutch doctors say that 'involuntary euthanasia' is a contradiction in terms. But elsewhere, most agree that this terminology is helpful.

Under what situations has involuntary euthanasia been suggested? Here are some possibilities, although, of course, the list is not exhaustive. First there is the malformed or brain-damaged infant, whose life is considered to be worthless, or so limited due to disability that death is preferable to continued existence. Then there is the child with a terminal disease who may have expressed a desire to die, although such patients are technically incapable of giving legally valid consent because of their age. Thirdly, there is the comatose or unresponsive patient, such as those in the persistent vegetative state. Fourthly, there is the confused or demented patient who may have previously expressed a wish to die but is now incapable of understanding his or her current situation. Finally, there is the person with a severe untreatable psychiatric disease or personality disorder who feels that his or her life is worthless but who is unable to give legally binding consent due to mental incompetence. In all such cases euthanasia has been advocated, and has indeed been practised on occasion by doctors, on the ground that it is a truly compassionate act.

It is important to distinguish euthanasia from two other clinical practices:

the withdrawal of life-sustaining medical treatment which is regarded as futile or burdensome, and the giving of symptom-relieving treatment in order to benefit the patient, which may have the unintended side-effect of shortening life. Both of these are an accepted part of normal medical practice. In the next chapter I shall argue that they are consistent with the Christian worldview, whereas euthanasia, intentional mercy killing, is not.

Physician-assisted suicide

If euthanasia is defined as intentional mercy killing, its close relative is physician-assisted suicide – the deliberate assistance by a physician in the suicide of a patient who intends to end his or her own life. It is intentional killing, but at one remove. The doctor provides the means – the drugs, the apparatus and the technical knowledge – explaining what to do and how to do it, but drawing back from the final act. The patient must take the tablets, put the bag over his or her head or throw the switch. As in the rest of medicine, we should not be too surprised that recently technology has got in the act. Now it is possible to perform physician-assisted suicide more cleanly.

Dr Philip Nitschke, an Australian physician, has designed a computer-linked machine which can be used to administer lethal drugs. The doctor inserts an intravenous line into the patient and connects the apparatus, which is capable of administering three drugs in a carefully controlled sequence. Phenobarbitone and thiopentone are administered to cause unconsciousness, followed at an interval of a few seconds by altracurium to paralyse the respiratory muscles, leading to rapid death from shortage of oxygen. Once hooked up, the patient has to answer three simple questions on the laptop computer. The final question is: 'In 15 seconds you will receive a lethal injection and die. Do you wish to proceed? Answer yes or no.'

Physician-assisted suicide, whether in its new technological guise or in the old-fashioned form of leaving a lethal mixture of tablets at the patient's bedside, clearly shares with euthanasia the same intention to kill. In November 1996, Dr Nitschke used his machine to kill Bob Dent, a patient with carcinoma of the prostate. Dr Nitschke intended that Mr Dent should die. That was the sole purpose of choosing and connecting up the three drugs. But he drew back from the final act. Although Dr Nitschke can claim that he is not technically a killer, and that he kept his hands clean, morally and ethically his action seems little different from voluntary euthanasia. Both euthanasia and physician-assisted suicide have been forbidden under almost every known code of legal practice. All accepted codes of medical ethics forbid them, although both have been known since ancient times.

The Hippocratic Oath, which originated several centuries before Christ, specifically rules out both euthanasia and physician-assisted suicide. 'I will use treatment to help the sick according to my ability and judgment, but I will never use it to injure or wrong them. I will not give poison to anyone though asked to do so, neither will I suggest such a plan . . .' (Temkin 1991: 21).

Despite more than two thousand years of medical tradition, there is now increasing international pressure to change both the law and the official codes of medical practice. Physician-assisted suicide seems to be more acceptable to the public than euthanasia, and is the focus of pioneering legislation in several countries. In May 1995 the Northern Territory of Australia passed the Rights of the Terminally Ill Act, which allowed physician-assisted suicide. Four people including Bob Dent died under the provision of the Act before it was narrowly overturned by the state authorities. In March 1998, an elderly woman in Oregon became the first reported person in the United States to die as a result of legally approved physician-assisted suicide. Unlike the cases in Australia, the method did not involve technology. A doctor had prescribed drugs which the woman, who had advanced breast cancer, swallowed with a glass of brandy (*The Guardian*, 27 March 1998). The death occurred under the jurisdiction of the recently ratified Oregon law that allows the terminally ill to kill themselves with a doctor's help, provided they are of sound mind and are expected to die within six months. According to *The Guardian*, the state authorities have published a ninety-one-page book laying out strict guidelines for the medical profession. The diagnosis must be confirmed by two doctors, and the fatal dose may be prescribed, but the doctor is not allowed to administer it or even hand it to the patient. In the United States the debate about the legality of physician-assisted suicide has gone to the Supreme Court. The case has turned on whether the US Constitution provides citizens with a 'liberty interest in choosing the time and manner of their deaths'.

In the UK, the Voluntary Euthanasia Society continues to campaign for the legalization of euthanasia, claiming that a large number of British doctors practise mercy killing covertly in patients' homes. The British Medical Association has repeatedly rejected calls for euthanasia legislation, but an increasing minority of doctors seem to be in favour. In 1994 a survey of NHS doctors found that 32% had acceded to patients' requests to hasten their death, and 46% would consider steps to bring about a patient's death if this were legal (*BMJ* 1994: 308:1332–1334). In another survey, published in the *BMA News Review* of March 1995, 34% of a group of British doctors agreed that the law should be changed to allow the physician-assisted suicide of terminally ill patients.

In July 1997 Michael Irwin, chairman of the Voluntary Euthanasia Society, told the *Sunday Times* that he had assisted around fifty patients to die during his career as a general practitioner. In his view it is pure hypocrisy to allow doctors to prescribe huge doses of morphine with the stated purpose of relieving suffering, but not to allow them to prescribe drugs which are clearly intended to kill. In a public debate, Irwin complained that opponents of euthanasia used the word 'killing'. 'The word "to kill" is an inappropriate word when someone is asking for release. What we are doing is relieving suffering. That's what the compassionate doctor is there for. We are providing a compassionate service for the community.'

A new 'improved' version of the Hippocratic Oath has been suggested by Dr Louis Weinstein, from the University of Arizona, for use by doctors in favour of euthanasia. It includes the words: 'I shall always have the highest respect for human life and remember that it is wrong to terminate life in certain circumstances, permissible in others and an act of supreme love in others' (letter to the *Journal of the American Medical Association* 1991: 265:2484).

Do-it-yourself death

The reluctance of most doctors to assist in the suicide of their patients has led to a rash of self-help books on the subject. In July 1991, Derek Humphry, the Executive Director of the Hemlock Society, a voluntary euthanasia society based in Oregon, wrote a book called *Final Exit: The Practicalities of Self-Deliverance and Assisted Suicide for the Dying*. The cover stated: '*Final Exit* is intended to be read by a mature adult who is suffering from a terminal illness and is considering the option of rational suicide, if and when suffering becomes unbearable. It also gives guidance to those who might be supportive of this action.' The book shot to the top of the *New York Times* bestseller list in the 'Advice, How-to and Miscellaneous' category, leaping over sex manuals and paperbacks on how to make money. Printed in large type, to make it easier for the elderly to read and follow its directions, the book contains a lethal drug dosage table, suggestions for obtaining and storing drugs and tips on ways to avoid criminal prosecution. In an interview with the London *Sunday Express*, Humphry was disarmingly candid: 'It tells you how, where and when to kill yourself or someone else. It breaks the last taboo. Follow my instructions for a perfect death, with no mess, and no post-mortem' (quoted by Marker 1994: 200).

The book sold hundreds of thousands of copies and remained on the bestseller lists for weeks. Humphry had warned people in a few sentences not to kill themselves if they were merely 'unhappy' or could not 'cope with life', but it was not long before accounts of suicides using Humphry's methods started to emerge. Many of those who died were not terminally ill, and some were in their twenties and thirties (Marker 1994: 204).

The Aids epidemic has contributed to heightened public interest in suicide. It has led to a new phenomenon, a substantial group of articulate, well-educated and independent young men who face a degenerative and terminal illness. Brian Smith, who is in charge of an Aids counselling programme in San Francisco, says that most Aids victims talk about taking their own lives. Many of them begin to squirrel away potentially lethal pills as soon as they are diagnosed (cited by Dworkin 1995: 183).

The heart of the debate

What then are the forces which lie behind the campaigning, the demonstrations, the vociferous propaganda for the legalization of euthanasia? I suggest that much of the debate is driven not by *compassion* but mainly by *fear*. Several years ago I had the opportunity to engage in public debate with a well-known and highly respected campaigner for legalizing euthanasia. I was struck by his words. 'Basically I'm afraid. It's not so much that I'm afraid of death, but I am afraid of the process of dying.' It seems to me that three fears lie at the heart of the debate.

Fear of pain

By 'fear of pain' I mean much more than merely physical pain. I am referring to what palliative-care specialists call *total pain*. It is a concept which includes physical pain but also emotional, relational and spiritual pain. Total pain is hard to define. It is distress which has many components. Take an elderly person dying from cancer. He is in physical distress because the disease has spread to the bones, causing a continual grinding discomfort. He is in psychological distress because he is frightened at what the future may hold. Will the pain get worse and worse until it is unbearable? Will he have to leave his home and be admitted to hospital? He is in relational distress because his family is putting on a brave face and refusing to acknowledge the reality of what is happening. He is in spiritual distress because he is confronting the ultimate reality of death without any sense of meaning or purpose. What has his life been for? What is there to hope for? This is total pain.

As a society we have lost the belief that suffering can have any positive value at all. Pain is useless, futile, destructive, incomprehensible, terrifying. For many, the purpose of existence is to maximize personal happiness, but if we cannot be happy at least we can try to anaesthetize the pain. When we think of Lillian Boyes in agony, we are deeply disturbed. The action of Nigel Cox seems profoundly compassionate; at least he stopped the pain.

Fear of indignity

Most people are not in great physical pain when they die. But to die with a tube in every orifice; to die with a rubber sheet on the bed in case we make a mess like a child; to require help even to have a shave or comb our hair, is not the way we want to live. It is undignified. When we look at the life of a person such as Tony Bland in the persistent vegetative state, we again feel disturbed and distressed. As far as we can tell, such a person is not in pain. He is not suffering in any identifiable meaning of the word. And yet we feel his life has lost dignity.

Ludovic Kennedy, a doughty pro-euthanasia campaigner, wrote at the time of the Nigel Cox case: 'For many people the fear of being snuffed out before our time has been superseded by a greater fear, that of suffering a painful and lingering death when all possibility of revival has gone, being kept alive but deteriorating all the time. It is not death that people fear most, but undignified dying' (*Evening Standard*, November 1992).

I was struck by the wording of an 'advance directive' form (sometimes known as a living will) which has been widely circulated by the Voluntary Euthanasia Society. '. . . I wish it to be understood that I fear degeneration and indignity far more than I fear death. I ask my medical attendants to bear this statement in mind when considering what my intentions would be in any uncertain situation.' This is a deep anxiety as modern people face ageing and infirmity: fear of 'degeneration and indignity'.

Finally, there is the deepest-rooted fear of all: we fear becoming dependent on others and on machines for our basic functions and needs.

Fear of dependence

These are the words of Friedrich Nietzsche, one of the most formative influences on postmodern society: 'In a certain state it is indecent to live longer. To go on vegetating in cowardly dependence on physicians and machinations, after the meaning of life, the right to life, has been lost, that ought to prompt a profound contempt in society . . . I want to die proudly when it is no longer possible to live proudly' (quoted by Dworkin 1995: 212).

Ronald Dworkin, the legal philosopher, argues that any individual's way of death should fit with how that person has lived. Otherwise a bad death might mar the whole story of a life, just as a bad ending can ruin a beautiful novel. If I have lived my life by choosing, taking responsibility for my own existence, telling my own story, then I must be free to end my life in my own way, in a way that fits. 'Death has dominion because it is not only the start of nothing but the end of everything, and how we think and talk about dying – the emphasis we put on dying with "dignity" – shows how important it is that life ends *appropriately*, that death keeps faith with the way we want to have lived' (Dworkin 1995: 199). He argues that we worry about dying in indignity because of the effect of life's last stage on the character of our life as a whole, 'as we might worry about the effect of a play's last scene or a poem's last stanza on the entire creative work'. 'People's views about how to live color their convictions about when to die . . . There is no doubt that most people treat the manner of their deaths as of special, symbolic importance: they want their deaths, if possible, to express and . . . confirm the values they believe most important to their lives . . . None of us wants to end our life out of character' (1995: 211–212).

People who have lived their lives as an expression of self-determination and self-reliance are horrified by the prospect that their death might express a completely contrary reality of dependence on others. Instead, they want to be free to die as they wish, even if that form of dying is not what others might wish.

'People who want an early, peaceful death for themselves or their relatives are not rejecting or denigrating the sanctity of life; on the contrary they believe that a quicker death shows more respect for life than a protracted one.' Dworkin argues that even if we feel that our own dignity is at stake if another person treats his or her own life as valueless, 'a true appreciation of dignity argues decisively in the opposite direction – for individual freedom, not coercion, for a regime of law and an attitude that encourages each of us to make mortal decisions for himself. Freedom is the cardinal, absolute requirement of self-respect: no-one treats his life as having any intrinsic objective importance unless he insists on leading that life himself, not being ushered along it by others' (1995: 239).

John Harris draws the same conclusion. 'The point of autonomy, the point of choosing and having freedom to choose between competing conceptions of how, and indeed why, to live, is simply that it is only thus that our lives become in any real sense our own. The value of our lives is the value that we give to our lives' (Harris 1995: 11).

This is a deeply rooted conviction for many people in our society, especially younger people who have grown up with postmodern concepts of radical individualism. 'I am master of my fate, captain of my boat. Others may not approve, but it doesn't matter. I do it my way.' The idea of writing one's own script is a powerful one. I believe it is no accident that one pro-euthanasia society chose the name Exit. It comes from the theatre. When the play is ended, when we reach the last page of the script, we will say, 'Thank you, friends, goodbye and goodnight.' *Exit stage right.*

The existentialist concept of self-authentication is, of course, constantly being challenged by the reality of the human condition and the world we live in. The arrogant claims to self-determination can seem a little hollow in the light of subsequent reality, as in this example of postmodern graffiti:

'God is dead: but considering the state the species Man is in, there will perhaps be caves, for ages yet, in which his shadow will be shown.'

Friedrich Nietzsche – 1882

'Nietzsche is dead.' *God – 1900*

How do modern people cope with deep-rooted fears about death and dying? They hope for a rapid and unexpected death. It is fascinating that whereas to many previous generations, sudden death was one of the worst ways to die, now it has become the best. To be catapulted into eternity without preparation, without a chance of repentance, unable to say goodbye, was viewed with horror by our forebears. Some saw sudden death as evidence of God's judgment on a godless life. But to modern people it has become the ideal. The catastrophic accident, the explosion, the sudden cardiac arrest: 'Well, at least he went quickly, never knew what hit him, lucky beggar. I hope I go like that.'

But if we do not go quickly, if we have to face the ultimate horror of a slow, protracted dying, then we want euthanasia. That way, we do not need to be afraid. We can relax. Provided that euthanasia or assisted suicide is there as an option for us, we can face death with equanimity. There will be someone there to help. Euthanasia is the answer to our deepest fears. So we think.

If fear is the main force driving the euthanasia debate, there are other more sinister forces, rarely acknowledged in public.

Social pressures in favour of euthanasia

First is the breakdown of traditional family structures coupled with steadily increasing life expectancy. This means that modern societies contain increasing numbers of elderly people, many of whom are isolated and unsupported by relatives or children. How can we cope with the desperate problems of social isolation and ostracism? Some social planners see a nightmarish vision of future society where large numbers of abandoned elderly people are kept alive by improvements in medical care, only to suffer a pointless and degrading existence. Would a liberal euthanasia and assisted-suicide policy not provide some kind of solution to this horror? Discussing those whose lives had been greatly prolonged by medical care, one doctor put it like this: 'Those who have enjoyed unnatural life must be prepared to accept unnatural death.'

Secondly, there is the increasing pressure on scarce health resources. Every developed nation is witnessing a spiral of healthcare costs which seems to be out of control. Every medical advance brings a new and more expensive treatment. How can health planners find a way to control their runaway budgets? The truth is that high-quality multidisciplinary care for the terminally ill and chronically disabled is very expensive, whereas euthanasia is remarkably cheap.

Thirdly, there is the growing epidemic of Alzheimer's disease in our society. A 1990 study from the Alzheimer's Disease Society concluded that about half a million people in the UK have the condition. The total is likely to rise to three quarters of a million by 2030. The percentage of affected sufferers rises from 16% between seventy-five and eighty-five years to as high as 47% over eighty-five years (Dworkin 1995: 219). Finding an appropriate way to care for Alzheimer's sufferers represents a major and largely unsolved challenge for the medical and caring professions. Perhaps euthanasia will offer a solution?

Fourthly, there is the desperate shortage of organs for transplant. As transplant surgery techniques have improved, they offer the prospect of success for an increasing range of severe medical conditions. But at the same time, to the intense frustration of medical specialists and patients alike, the supply of organs, mainly from accident victims, has steadily declined. Most natural deaths are prolonged and the organs are unsuitable for transplant. But death by lethal injection offers the prospect of an almost limitless supply of valuable organs. Think of how much good we could do for other people!

In 1997, a distinguished working party known as the International Forum for Transplant Ethics suggested that patients in the persistent vegetative state should be killed by lethal injection, so that their organs could be used for transplant into other patients. Although this proposal has been greeted with horror by several groups, *The Guardian* reported that Tony Bland's parents backed it. The grisly report has recently come from the USA that legal executioners are changing their method from electrocution to lethal injection. This is because the executed prisoners' organs can then be used for transplant surgery.

Gilbert Meilander comments: 'There are circumstances in which we can save life only by destroying the kind of world in which we all should want to live. Perhaps if our noble desire to prolong life leads to such ignoble means, we need to be sent away to shudder' (Meilander 1997: 101).

Euthanasia in the Netherlands

Holland is seen by many in the pro-euthanasia lobby as the promised land. It is the only place in the world where euthanasia, although technically illegal, is openly practised by trained physicians, under legally approved guidelines. Euthanasia receives wide support in Dutch society. A public advertisement disseminated by the Dutch Voluntary Euthanasia Society shows an elderly man in pyjamas sitting comfortably in an open coffin with the caption, 'Everyone should have the right to die like a gentleman.'

Within the Dutch legal framework, doctors can defend themselves against the charge of intentional killing if they can claim that euthanasia was *necessary*, because the doctor's duty to alleviate suffering overrides the duty not to kill. In order to mount a successful defence of 'necessity', the courts have laid down a number of conditions which should be fulfilled (Keown 1995: 264):

1. The request for euthanasia must come only from the patient and must be entirely free and voluntary.

2. The patient's request must be well-considered, durable, and persistent.

3. The patient must be experiencing intolerable (not necessarily physical) suffering, with no prospect of improvement.

4. Euthanasia must be a last resort. Other alternatives to alleviate the patient's situation must have been considered and found wanting.

5. Euthanasia must be performed by a physician.

6. The physician must consult with an independent medical colleague who has experience in this field.

7. A detailed record must be kept.

8. The cause of death must be accurately reported to the authorities.

In 1990, the Dutch Government formed an official commission to perform a nationwide study of euthanasia and medical decisions at the end of life. Their results, the Remmelink Report, have been published in several forms including a paper in the *Lancet* (1991: 338:669–674). Dr John Keown, of the Faculty of

Law at Cambridge University, has published a detailed analysis in his authoritative book *Euthanasia Examined* (Keown 1995: 266–289). In brief, the findings were as follows. In 1990, out of a total of 130,000 deaths in Holland, about 2,300 were due to voluntary euthanasia. In addition, some 1,000 deaths occurred where doctors gave drugs with the explicit purpose of hastening the end of life without an explicit request from the patient, 400 deaths occurred by physician-assisted suicide, and in a further 1,350 deaths doctors gave palliative drugs with the explicit purpose of shortening life at the patient's request. In summary, nearly 4% of all deaths, or one in twenty-five, occurred because doctors were explicitly aiming to end life, and many more deaths occurred where the primary intention of the doctor was unclear.

The finding that about a thousand deaths occurred without explicit request has caused controversy in Holland, as this is strictly illegal according to official guidelines. The official commission, however, defended these cases as 'care for the dying', and said that the justification for killing in these cases was the patient's unbearable suffering. In fact, the reasons given by doctors themselves for euthanasia were rather different: 60% cited absence of any prospect of improvement, 39% the futility of all medical therapy, 33% needless prolongation of life, 32% the relatives' inability to cope, and 31% low quality of life. Pain and suffering were mentioned in only 30% of cases. When the reasons that *patients* gave for requesting euthanasia were analysed, 57% spoke of 'loss of dignity', 46% 'not dying in a dignified way', 46% 'pain', 33% 'dependence' and 23% 'tiredness of life'.

The survey found that 'More than half of the physicians regularly caring for terminal patients had committed euthanasia; more than half of the doctors questioned said that they had killed without request or would be prepared to do so. Only 12% of doctors said that they would never perform euthanasia' (Keown 1995: 269).

The Remmelink Report defended the action of doctors who killed in the absence of a patient's request:

> The ultimate justification for the intervention is in both cases [*i.e.* voluntary and involuntary killing] the patient's unbearable suffering. So medically speaking, there is little difference between these situations and euthanasia, because in both cases patients are involved who suffer terribly. The absence of a special request for the termination of life stems partly from the circumstance that the party in question is not (any longer) able to express his will . . . and partly because the demand for an explicit request is not in order when the treatment of pain and symptoms is intensified. The degrading condition the patient is in, confronts the doctor with a case of *force majeure*. According to the commission, the intervention by the doctor can easily be regarded as an action that is justified by necessity, just like euthanasia (quoted in Keown 1995: 284).

Other controversial aspects of mercy killing have been reported in Holland. In December 1992 the American *Journal of Disease in Childhood* carried an article on paediatric euthanasia in Holland (Orlowski *et al.* 1992). Five of eight major neonatal centres which were surveyed actively terminated the lives of newborns with a predicted poor quality of life, and three of the eight centres in certain circumstances openly terminated the life of older infants with severe birth defects. One authority estimated that 300 handicapped newborn babies are intentionally allowed to die, and the lives of ten such babies are actively terminated, each year. In a random sample of thirty-five infants who died in the first week of life, two had received medication designed to end their lives, and four had received medication for pain with the intended purpose of shortening their life. An anonymous paediatric oncologist apparently acknowledged that he supplied drugs to an average of six children in his care each year, sometimes without their parents' knowledge, to enable them to commit suicide if they wished.

In 1995, a Dutch court held that a paediatrician charged with murder for killing a disabled newborn at the parents' request 'had made a choice which – given the special circumstances of the case – can reasonably be considered justifiable' (quoted by Keown 1995: 29). Another recent case concerned a fifty-year-old woman who was depressed following the death of her two sons. Following repeated requests to die, her psychiatrist assisted her to commit suicide. He was prosecuted but subsequently acquitted (*British Medical Journal* 1994: 309:492). An official committee of the Royal Dutch Medical Association and the Dutch Commission for the Acceptability of Life Terminating Action has recommended that active termination of life may be acceptable in severe dementia, but only if symptoms of a severe physical nature occur and an advance directive has been made and signed. The commission also called for public debate on whether the life of a patient suffering from severe dementia could be terminated when such a request is present in an advance directive (*British Medical Journal* 1993: 306:1364). The authors of another official report on euthanasia ask: 'Is it not true that once one accepts euthanasia and assisted suicide, the principle of universalizability forces one to accept termination of life without explicit request, at least in some circumstances? In our view the answer to this question must be affirmative' (quoted in Keown 1995: 287).

These examples illustrate a very important logical inconsistency in the arguments for voluntary euthanasia. On the one hand, if personal *autonomy* is a justification for killing people, then it is not logical to restrict mercy killing only to people who are about to die and in severe pain. If people choose to die, why should we be prepared to help them only if they are terminally ill or suffering greatly? On logical grounds we should be prepared to kill them at their request whether they have a terminal illness or not. On the other hand, if severe *suffering* is a justification for killing people, then it is not logical to restrict mercy killing only to people who can choose to die. We should be prepared to kill those who are suffering even if they are not capable of expressing a wish to die.

This is the basis of the 'slippery slope' argument. Once euthanasia is legalized, it seems both logically and practically impossible to prevent the gradual extension to voluntary euthanasia of those who wish to die even if they are not terminally ill, and involuntary euthanasia of those whose lives seem futile and pain-filled. To a number of observers of the Dutch scene, it seems that this progression down the slippery slope is slowly but inexorably taking place. It is surely not a coincidence that hospice care is virtually unknown in Holland, and that a report on palliative care in Holland concluded that a majority of cancer patients in pain suffered unnecessarily because of health professionals' lack of expertise (Keown 1995: 280).

What is the psychological effect on Dutch doctors of committing euthanasia? A film shown on Channel Four television contained an interview with a doctor about her first case of euthanasia. 'I was very nervous, shaking all over . . . I was sort of shocked. It all happened so quickly. You have to act as a doctor but as a human being you are very shocked yourself.' I have heard that some have recommended that doctors travelling to a patient's home in order to commit euthanasia should not drive themselves. Experience has shown that there is an increased rate of accidents because some doctors are preoccupied and distracted by their involvement in euthanasia.

In 1992 the British Government formed a distinguished Select Committee of the House of Lords to investigate whether there should be a change in the British law to allow euthanasia. Its members decided to visit Holland to see for themselves. It seems that they were not impressed with what they found. The chairman, Lord Walton, reported that 'Members of the committee returned from the visit feeling uncomfortable, especially in the light of the evidence indicating that non-voluntary euthanasia was commonly performed.' Another member of the committee, Lord Meston, also expressed his reservations: 'The evidence of the Dutch experience was not encouraging: in the Netherlands, which apparently lacks much in the way of a hospice movement, there seems to be a gap between the theory and practice of voluntary euthanasia. One cannot escape the fear that the same could happen here . . .' (quoted in Keown 1995: 288). Observers have suggested that the committee's experience in Holland was one of the most important factors in their eventual decision against a change in the law to allow voluntary euthanasia in the UK (Report of the Select Committee on Medical Ethics, 1994; London: HMSO).

Practical risks of euthanasia legalization

What are the practical dangers of a change in the law to allow euthanasia?

There is, first, the possibility of wrong diagnosis. Sadly, serious mistakes in diagnosis are not uncommon, even in specialist centres. The last decade has seen a number of public scares as major errors in diagnostic pathology laboratories have come to light. Most experienced clinicians can give individual examples of serious diagnostic errors. What if euthanasia is carried out in the mistaken belief that the patient was terminally ill, when in fact the disease was self-limiting?

Then there is the problem of predicting the future. Even when doctors make the right diagnosis, they are frequently wrong as they attempt to predict how long a patient will survive. Most medical prognostication in terminal illness is more akin to educated guesswork than to scientific calculation. Yet proposed euthanasia legislation assumes that the doctor can confidently predict that the patient is terminally ill and that death will occur within a period of weeks or months.

There is the possibility of abuse by doctors and other healthcare staff, who may be tempted to end the lives of patients for less than altruistic reasons, such as financial reward or to conceal evidence of medical negligence. We have already mentioned the low cost of euthanasia relative to care for the terminally and chronically ill; these financial pressures could lead to the possibility of abuse by health managers.

There is also the possibility of serious abuse by relatives who see euthanasia as an opportunity to relieve themselves of a burden of caring, and to prevent the dissipation of life savings on expensive nursing care. This is not to imply that most relatives harbour malevolent thoughts towards the terminally ill. But their own emotional distress can be a major source of pressure for health carers: 'I can't bear to watch her in this state. Why can't you give her something to end it all?' Similarly, elderly patients, seeing the financial burdens on their relatives, may feel that it is their 'duty' to request euthanasia. If euthanasia legislation is on the statute book, how long will it be before the 'right to die' becomes a 'duty to die'?

There is the very real possibility that euthanasia legislation would increase anxieties for elderly and disabled people admitted to hospital, and erode trust in the actions and motivation of health staff. The patient–carer relationship would be unavoidably altered. Instead of a climate of trust, intimacy and protection, vulnerable people in our healthcare system would experience suspicion, distancing and an exacerbation of their sense of defencelessness.

There would also be the psychological effect on doctors who have broken deep human intuitions and cultural taboos against the intentional taking of human life. Would doctors and other staff be brutalized by the experience? Would the doctor who has just committed euthanasia fight as hard as she might have done to save the life of her next patient? What are the psychological consequences for carers, when the overriding duty of care is transformed into a duty to kill?

Finally, there would be the effect on society of legalized killing, and the existence of a specialized group of people who are authorized to kill under certain circumstances. Would this cheapen respect for life in society as a whole?

Is this the way we as a society wish to go? The book *Deadly Compassion* by Rita Marker (1994) provides a disturbing insight into the euthanasia movement. It tells the story of Derek Humphry, the author of *Final Exit*, from the perspective of his second wife, Ann. Humphry had won great fame and admiration for his book *Jean's Way*, in which he described how, as an act of compassion, he helped his first wife Jean, who was suffering from cancer, to die. Subsequently, his second wife, Ann, who had been co-founder of the Hemlock Society with Humphry, also developed cancer. According to Ann, Humphry had abandoned her because she would not kill herself as he suggested, and he was not prepared to care for her. The bizarre story took a tragic twist when Ann committed suicide, and in her final note claimed that Humphry had in fact murdered Jean because he wanted to get rid of her.

The Nazi euthanasia programme

Before moving on, I want to refer briefly to the experience of the German medical profession under the Nazis. Understandably, the pro-euthanasia lobby is extremely sensitive to any comparison with the appalling crimes of the Nazi era. It is all too easy to use the Nazis to make cheap rhetorical points, and I do not wish to fall into this temptation. There is clearly no comparison between the act of Dr Cox, driven to kill in a compassionate attempt to relieve the suffering of his patient, and the hideous acts of the SS physicians and executioners.

Yet the whole terrible episode is of great importance for all doctors. It illustrates how a noble profession can become inexorably corrupted by intense social and political pressures. The story is recounted in several sources including the important book *Racial Hygiene: Medicine under the Nazis* by Robert Proctor (1988). Proctor and other historians point out that the awful crimes against humanity performed by respectable and high-ranking German doctors started out with small beginnings, long before the outbreak of war. In 1920 Alfred Hoche, a professor of medicine, and Rudolf Binding, a professor of law, had published their book *Release and Destruction of Lives Not Worth Living*. They argued that the principle of 'allowable killing' should be extended to the incurably sick. The right to live, they asserted, must be earned and justified, not dogmatically assumed. Those who are not capable of human feelings – those 'ballast lives' and 'empty human husks' that fill our psychiatric institutions – can have no sense of the value of life. Theirs is not a life worth living, and hence their destruction is not only tolerable but humane (Proctor 1988: 178).

By 1935, popular medical and racial-hygiene journals carried charts depicting the costs of maintaining the sick at the expense of the healthy. One poster shows a healthy man carrying two disabled individuals. The caption reads, 'You are Sharing the Load! A Genetically Ill Individual Costs Approximately 50,000 Reichsmarks by the Age of Sixty.' A 1935 school mathematics textbook included problems where the average cost to the state of providing care for inhabitants of homes for the epileptic and institutions for the mentally ill was to be calculated by students. These calculations formed the basis of the euthanasia programme which was established by many of the German medical profession. After the war, detailed calculations of the savings achieved for the German state by one euthanasia centre, Hartheim, were found in a safe. The 'disinfection' or extermination of 70,273 individuals in the course of the operation at Hartheim had saved the German economy a total of 245,955 Reichsmarks per day (Proctor 1988: 184).

In 1949 an American psychiatrist, Leo Alexander, who had attended the Nuremberg war trials, wrote an important paper entitled 'Medical Science under Dictatorship', published in the *New England Journal of Medicine* (1949: 241:39–47). In it he traced the historical roots of the Nazi euthanasia movement. How was it that respected doctors could have participated in such horrendous acts? 'It started with the acceptance by doctors of the idea, basic in the euthanasia movement, that there is such a thing as a life not worthy to be lived. This attitude in the beginning referred to the severely and chronically sick. Gradually the sphere of those to be included was enlarged to encompass the socially unproductive, the ideologically unwanted, the racially unwanted . . . But it is important to realize that the infinitely small lever from which this entire trend of mind received its impetus was the attitude towards the incurably sick.'

'The life not worth living.' It is a concept at the heart of the modern euthanasia movement too, and is promoted by ethicists, philosophers and health economists. For those with a sense of history, it is a phrase that has uneasy resonances.

The persistent vegetative state

As we saw in the tragic case of Tony Bland, the persistent vegetative state (or PVS) is an extreme case of severe brain injury, leading to loss of contact with the person. To many philosophers, such as Peter Singer, the PVS sufferer is a prime example of a life 'not worth living'. The absence of normal cortical activity means that the PVS sufferer is a 'non-person', on the basis of 'ethically relevant characteristics'. In fact, the patient is an 'it', rather than a he or a she; a being whose life has no personal value or significance, and who can demand no special duty of care or protection from the rest of us. The quality of such a being's life is so low that it is below zero; it is 'negative'. It is therefore better for someone in Tony Bland's condition, and for the rest of us, if his life comes to an end. Our only duty to him is to end his life painlessly and cleanly. It would be an insult to his memory, and a terrible waste of health resources, to allow his body to linger on. Here is the ideal case for involuntary euthanasia.

Singer does not explicitly state that all PVS sufferers should be killed, but leaves it as a veiled implication:

Our decisions about how to treat such patients should not depend on lofty rhetoric about the equal worth of all human life, but on the views of families and partners who deserve consideration at a time of tragic loss. If a patient in a persistent vegetative state has previously expressed wishes about what should happen to her or him in such circumstances, they should also be taken into account. (We may do this purely out of respect for the wishes of the dead, or we may do it in order to reassure others, still alive, that their wishes will not be ignored.) At the same time, in a public health-care system, we cannot ignore the limits set by the finite nature of our medical resources, nor the needs of others whose lives may be saved by an organ transplant (Singer 1995: 192).

Singer regards the decision of the House of Lords, that artificial feeding could be withdrawn from Tony Bland, as a landmark move away from the traditional view of British law regarding the sanctity of life. Nevertheless, he regards the action of intentionally starving and dehydrating patients, while drawing back from killing them with a lethal injection, as irrational and indefensible.

In determining our view of, and response to, those with very severe brain injury, we need to ask three important questions.

Is the diagnosis right?

PVS is an extreme example of a clinical illness in which we have lost contact with the person. It is important to stress that PVS is totally different, both clinically and conceptually, from brain-stem death. In brain-stem death, there is no brain activity at all. The brain has permanently ceased any integrated function. The biological functions of the body are maintained purely by artificial life-support machinery. Nearly all Christian thinkers have accepted that brain-stem death can be regarded as equivalent to the death of the individual, and that artificial life support can be discontinued in such cases.

In PVS, however, the brain is working. Electrical activity in the cortex can be measured. There are periods of sleep followed by waking. The connections of the brain circuitry are deranged, but doctors do not know in detail what the effects are, or if that derangement is permanent. There is something going on in there, but there seems to be no way to communicate, to access the experience of the individual.

Yet not all those who appear to be unresponsive are in fact so. On 8 December 1995, Jean-Dominique Bauby, the forty-two-year-old editor of *Elle* magazine in Paris, was on his way home when he suffered a massive stroke and slipped into a coma. When he regained consciousness three weeks later, he discovered that he was completely paralysed, speechless and able to move only one muscle: his left eyelid. Although this condition can be mistaken for PVS, the diagnosis was very different; it was the rare condition known as 'locked-in syndrome'. Fortunately, the medical team made the correct diagnosis.

Using a simple code, Bauby laboriously dictated his story, letter by letter. The book was published in France in 1997, and rapidly became a bestseller. *The Diving Bell and the Butterfly* is a moving account of the reality of an awake mind, an intact person, trapped in a paralysed body. He saw his inert body as a diving-bell in which was trapped the 'butterfly' of his soaring mind and imagination. An observer focusing solely on his motionless body might have viewed him as a perfect case for euthanasia. But Bauby was not asking to die; he was striving to live, to remember, to communicate, to reach out in love to his children and family.

At the heart of the diagnosis of PVS is the conclusion that the state of profound coma and unresponsivenes is *permanent* (Report of Royal College of Physicians Working Party, March 1996). But a number of neurological experts have emphasized the difficulty of establishing the correct diagnosis and predicting whether some degree of recovery may occur. The diagnosis of PVS is different from most other medical diagnoses. People recover from severe brain injury at different rates, depending on the nature and severity of the injury. If recovery of conscious activity occurs rapidly, the syndrome may be referred to as 'concussion'. If recovery takes weeks or months, the condition is called 'prolonged coma'. It is only if recovery has not occurred after an arbitrary period of twelve months that a diagnosis of persistent vegetative state is made. There are well-documented cases of recovery beyond this period, and virtually complete recovery has been seen as late as four years after the onset of the condition. As every month goes by, however, recovery becomes less likely. Dr Keith Andrews, a consultant at the Royal Hospital of Neurodisability in Putney, has probably more experience of caring for profoundly disabled adults than anyone else in the UK. He stresses the difficulties in the diagnosis of PVS which require considerable skill and prolonged assessment, sometimes continuing over months, and the variable severity of the condition. (Tony Bland's case was apparently one of the most severe examples of PVS.) According to Dr Andrews' report, published in the *British Medical Journal* (*BMJ* 1993: 306:1597–1600), 42% of those referred to his hospital by other specialists were misdiagnosed as being in PVS. Eleven out of forty-three patients diagnosed as being in PVS regained awareness, and ten of the eleven were able to communicate with their carers. Four patients were able to feed themselves and two became independent in daily activities. Dr Andrews argues that all patients with profound brain damage should be offered the opportunity of a specialist rehabilitation programme.

Is artificial feeding a form of medical treatment?

A further crucial issue in the care of PVS sufferers is the status of artificial feeding. PVS is quite different from many severe conditions, in that the sustenance of life is not dependent on major and invasive technology. PVS sufferers are able to breathe, metabolize food and excrete waste without medical assistance. They do not require life-support machinery, intravenous infusions or complex drug therapy. The only medical assistance they need is artificial feeding through a tube into the stomach.

Does this form of feeding represent a medical *treatment*, which can and should be withdrawn if its burdens outweigh the benefits? Or does it represent basic *nursing care*, which is part of the duty of care that we owe to all human beings, however damaged or disabled they may be? Some have argued that the artificial-feeding equipment is conceptually no different from the adapted feeding apparatus, such as specially designed forks and spoons, which some severely disabled people use. Others maintain that the requirement for professional medical input in the insertion and management of feeding-tubes demonstrates that this is a form of medical treatment. The debate continues with little sign of a consensus.

What is the significance of the life of the PVS sufferer?

Within the framework of Peter Singer's philosophy, the significance and contribution of the life of the PVS sufferer seem negligible. But within the Christian worldview, we must draw back from accepting this verdict. Ultimately, the value of an individual life can be known only to God. But if we take seriously the belief that the value of human beings is intrinsic, in the stuff of their creation, rather than in their functioning or attributes, then we must conclude that even PVS sufferers have a *prima facie* case to be considered as members of the human community, persons to whom, for all their tragic disability, we owe wonder, respect, empathy and protection.

Although the legality of withdrawing feeds in PVS was established in the UK in 1993, scarcely more than ten similar cases came to the courts in the following five years, although it is estimated that there are approximately a thousand PVS sufferers in the UK. Could it be that most carers have deep intuitions that the withdrawal of feeds is not the best way to express caring for these profoundly damaged individuals?

Dr Andrews' experience should also give us pause before we agree to stop artificial feeds. Are we sure that there is no aware individual in that body? If we really want to demonstrate care, perhaps we should be concentrating attention on research, such as on new drug treatments to limit damage to the brain, and attempts to find new ways to establish contact with brain-damaged individuals.

Dementia

Severe dementia, such as occurs in advanced Alzheimer's disease, is another tragic and debilitating condition in which communication with the person inside is lost. There are other causes for dementia, but the diagnosis of Alzheimer's disease is the best-known and will be taken as an example in this chapter. In these patients, the brain is active, but communication is disjointed and broken. Memories are distorted and fragmentary. The person expresses wishes and desires, but these change rapidly. One of the characteristics of dementia is that its severity may fluctuate, especially in the early stages of Alzheimer's disease. At times, people may have nearly normal memory and behaviour. At other times, they are profoundly confused and disorientated. This, of course, may add to the distress and feelings of terror involved in the condition, as sufferers may have periods of painfully accurate insight into their condition and what the future holds for them. Dementia is deeply troubling, above all, because it threatens our understanding of personal continuity and identity.

> Often Mary was afraid, a nameless, shapeless fear . . . People came, memories came, and then they slipped away. She could not tell what was reality and what was memory of things past . . . The tub was a mystery. From day to day she could not remember how to manage the water: sometimes it all ran away, sometimes it kept rising and rising so that she could not stop it . . . Mary was glad when her family came to visit. Sometimes she remembered their names, more often she did not . . . She liked it best when they just held her and loved her (Dworkin 1995: 220).

Andrew Firlik, a medical student, wrote an article in the *Journal of the American Medical Association* (1991: 201:265) following his meeting with a fifty-four-year-old Alzheimer's sufferer called Margo. He visited her daily in her apartment. Margo was always reading novels, but 'her place in the book jumps randomly from day to day . . . maybe she feels good just sitting and humming to herself, rocking back and forth slowly, nodding off liberally, occasionally turning to a fresh page.' And yet, as Firlik commented, 'despite her illness, or maybe somehow because of it, Margo is undeniably one of the happiest people I have ever known'. She took endless delight from eating peanut butter and jam sandwiches! But where is the individual, when memory and personality seem so disconnected? As Firlik asks: 'When a person can no longer accumulate new memories as the old rapidly fade, what remains? Where is Margo?'

To Ronald Dworkin, as for many others from a liberal perspective, dementia is a horrifying and degrading reality. If the essence of our human existence is to create a personality by a series of autonomous choices – to write our own script – there can be few prospects so appalling as the loss of an ability to choose.

Dworkin argues that the right of individual autonomy 'makes self-creation possible. It allows each of us to be responsible for shaping our own lives according to our own coherent or incoherent – but in any case, distinctive – personality' (Dworkin 1995: 224). But severe dementia strikes at the heart of this possibility of self-creation. If a demented person's 'choices and demands, no matter how firmly expressed, systematically or randomly contradict one another, reflecting no coherent sense of self and no discernable even short-term aims, then he has presumably lost the capacity that it is the point of autonomy to protect'.

Instead, Dworkin argues we must respect the *previous* autonomous wishes of the individual before he or she developed dementia. If, before she developed dementia, Margo had expressed a wish to die should this condition befall her, then the fact that Margo is now happy and enjoying her peanut butter and jam sandwiches is irrelevant. She no longer has any capacity for autonomy, and, if she is allowed to carry on her existence, this will irrevocably mar the story of her entire life. Margo's previous wishes take precedence over her current experiences even if the latter are enjoyable. To allow her to live on in a demented state against her previous wishes is to inflict a harm on her. We must allow her to die, or even, if it is legally permissible, arrange for her to be killed. 'We cannot say that we would be showing compassion for Margo if we refused to do what she wanted when she was competent, because that would not be compassionate toward the whole person, the person who tragically became demented' (Dworkin 1995: 232).

In response to Andrew Firlik's question 'Where is Margo?', Dworkin answers, in effect, 'The *real* Margo has gone.' But although she has gone, we must respect her wishes, much as we respect the wishes of the dead expressed in a will. We respect this being because of what she once was.

In the next chapter we look at Christian responses to these painful and complex questions concerning the end of life and the challenge of euthanasia. Is there an alternative to mercy killing? It is not enough to defend abstract moral principles. What practical answers can we provide to the terrible modern fears of pain, indignity and dependence?

10. A better way to die

In this chapter we shall attempt to respond to the challenge of euthanasia from the perspective of the Christian worldview. What insights can we gain from the biblical material we have already outlined? Can mercy killing be regarded as an act of compassion, a way to respect individual choices and personal integrity? Or is it a perversion of medicine and the start of a slippery slope which might lead even to the horrors of the Nazi era? We shall look briefly at the responses of Christian carers to these dilemmas, and at practical initiatives in the care of the dying, many of them pioneered by Christian people.

Christian thinking about life and death
Human life is sacrosanct because of the image of God

As we saw in chapter 2, the biblical worldview regards all human life as uniquely valuable because all human beings are made in God's image. In orthodox Christian thought, human beings, even in the agony of suffering like that of Lillian Boyes, or in the twilight state of Tony Bland, are Godlike beings. And any being made in God's image deserves a range of responses: wonder, respect, empathy, and above all *protection*: protection from abuse, from harm, and from manipulation.

But some will argue that mercy killing can be seen as a way of protecting vulnerable people from harm. Did not Nigel Cox protect Lillian Boyes by killing her? No. Biblical thought always draws a line between removing *suffering* and removing the *sufferer*. In biblical thought human life is sacrosanct.

We are not at liberty to destroy innocent human life, however noble may be the motive. Here again are the solemn words of the *lex talionis* as given by God to Noah:

> Whoever sheds the blood of man,
>   by man shall his blood be shed;
> for in the image of God
>   has God made man.

(Gn. 9:6)

As Dr Roy Clements has pointed out, this ancient text combines two biblical themes. First there is the ancient blood taboo, a reverence for blood because it represents a spilled life; and secondly there is the condemnation of murder, the intentional destruction of innocent human life. To destroy human life is uniquely scandalous because it desecrates God's image, God's masterpiece. Clements put it like this: 'A human life is not just a gift of God's grace – it is a reflection of his person' (1994: 2). The Christian view of life as a gift received from God is often caricatured by opponents in terms of ownership: God is the slave-owner and humans are his slaves, and therefore God 'owns' each life. We are not free to dispose of our own life as we wish because God 'owns' it. But this is a distortion of the biblical view. We are not merely slaves. Human beings are special because of how they are made – because they are a mysterious expression of God's character.

This is why orthodox Christian thought has always been opposed not only to homicide, the taking of another human life, but also to suicide. The deliberate destruction of one's own life also desecrates God's image. In many ancient cultures, suicide has been glorified as a noble way to die. The Norwegian warriors saw suicide as a path to heaven; in Buddhism, self-immolation is a prime example of the renunciation of desire; in traditional Hinduism, the suicide of bereaved widows is encouraged; in Japan, until recently, hara-kiri was a noble form of death; in ancient Greece, the Stoics encouraged the heroic suicide. But in all cultures influenced by the Judaeo-Christian revelation, suicide has been opposed. It is never glorified in the Bible. Samson is the only example of a heroic suicide whose act is in some sense approved. In the rest of the Bible, suicide is associated with godlessness, for example in the tragic ends of Saul and Judas Iscariot. Despite this, it is interesting that suicidal thoughts are not uncommon in God's people. Elijah wanted to die, but was sent on a sabbatical instead. Job wished he had never been born, but learns that God is in control of his life (Clements 1994: 2).

In biblical thought, God gives human beings a wonderful and terrifying freedom of action. We are free to act and choose as responsible moral agents who are accountable to one another and ultimately to God. But there are God-given limits to our freedom as moral agents. The limits are part of the hidden moral order of the creation, the moral warp and woof of reality. And one of those limits, which we must not transgress, is to choose to destroy our own life or the life of another. 'Within the story of my life I have the relative freedom of a creature, but it is not simply my life to do with it as I please . . . Suicide . . . expresses a desire to be free and not also finite – a desire to be more like the Creator than creature' (Meilander 1997: 59). Self-destruction is a harm to be avoided, not a right to be assisted.

Yet there is a paradoxical character to Christian thinking about laying down one's life. After all, Jesus is the supreme example of a life deliberately laid down for others. To sacrifice one's own life for the good of others, or in the face of persecution, is seen as the height of Christian love. So what is the difference? Sacrificing your life because there is something worth dying for is Christian martyrdom. Sacrificing your life because there is nothing worth living for is suicide. The Christian martyr does not aim at death but aims to be faithful to God, foreseeing that death may occur as a result. 'Forbidding suicide and honouring martyrs, the early Christians recognized life as a real but not ultimate good – a great good but not the highest good' (Meilander 1997: 70).

Christians, then, view human life as sacrosanct; both intentional killing and suicide are contrary to the Christian worldview. Even when tempted to kill out of compassion, we come up against the limits of our creatureliness. It is not only those with an explicit Christian faith who sense a deep resistance to the taking of human life. The unease and distress expressed by many doctors and healthcare workers who have participated in euthanasia or assisted suicide are evidence of profound intuitions about the sacrosanct nature of human life – intuitions which stem from our creation in God's image. When we assist in the killing of another human being, however compassionate and rational our motives might be, we damage our own humanity.

The human family

In Christian thought, not only is each individual human life special, but we are all part of the human family. We are created to be in community. Why do we try to prevent suicides in our society? Why are brave police officers expected to try to save the life of a man attempting to jump from a high-rise building, for example? Why on earth do they bother? If he wants to die, surely we should let him. Why risk the lives of valuable citizens attempting to save someone who does not value his own life? It is because our society, though penetrated by liberal individualism, is still deeply influenced by Christian thought. From a Christian perspective we are not autonomous individuals doing our own thing. We are locked together in community, bound together by duties of care, responsibility and compassion. Respect for life, and the prohibition of suicide, is part of the glue which binds society together. It is part of the moral order, the hidden moral grain which God has placed in the creation.

Imagine a society which quietly encouraged the depressed, the inadequate, the isolated or the disabled to take their own lives; where doctors made available lethal mixtures for their patients; where suicides were left to get on with it. What kind of society would that be? Would we wish to be members of it? Instead, here is a Christian view of society, expressed in the well-known words of John Donne: 'No man is an Island, entire of it self; every man is a piece of the Continent, a part of the main; if a clod be washed away by the sea, Europe is the less, as well as if a promontory were . . . any man's death diminishes me, because I am involved in Mankind; And therefore never send to know for whom the bell tolls; it tolls for thee' (*Devotions upon Emergent Occasions*, Meditation XVII, 1624).

Although the act of self-destruction is often born out of desperation and loneliness, suicide can have devastating effects on others. In fact, it can be one of the most selfish and destructive acts anyone can perform. Whether intentionally or not, the suicide hits out at all those in community with him, wounding and damaging them, often for life. To commit suicide is to strike at the heart of what it means to live in community. As we saw in chapter 2, we are designed to depend on one another. It is part of the creation order. We are all called to share the burdens of the physical life which God has given us.

Death: an outrage and a mercy

Death as a consequence of the fall is an evil and an outrage to be fought against. In the same way, the evils of ageing – the loss of function, infirmity, and the degenerative illnesses – are real evils. But old age itself is not an evil. It is part of the human narrative, a stage of life to be respected and honoured. And in God's providential care for fallen human beings, ageing and death may be, to use C. S. Lewis's phrase again, a 'severe mercy'. Human lifespan is limited, not just as a curse, but out of God's grace. In God's providence, death may be a merciful release from an existence trapped in a fallen and decaying body. So Christian attitudes to death must always reflect this strange ambiguity. Even though human death is fundamentally an evil to be fought against, and a reality which can never be sought intentionally, it may also at times be accepted, even welcomed, as a sign of God's mercy.

Human suffering: a mystery of human dependence

In a modern secular worldview, suffering seems to have no ultimate meaning. It is pointless and destructive, the ultimate threat to individual human autonomy and self-direction. Therefore suffering is an evil to be eliminated by whatever means are to hand. It is thus natural that the elimination of suffering becomes the prime goal of medicine, and it is an easy step to accept that, in the name of eliminating the suffering, we are forced to eliminate the sufferer.

Yet, as we saw in the book of Job, suffering can never be meaningless in a biblical worldview, even if it has that appearance. Suffering is a painful reality which we have to *accept* from the hand of a loving God. Dr Rob George, a consultant in palliative medicine in London, has pointed out that even the word 'to suffer' implies an element of passivity. It comes from the Latin *suffere*, meaning literally 'to bear under', and hence 'to permit or to allow'. The original meaning of the English word was 'to put up with', and hence the root meaning of suffering is the idea of submitting or being forced to submit to, or endure, some circumstance which is beyond our control. In the words of H. R. Niebuhr, 'Suffering is the exhibition of the presence of that which is not under our control' (quoted by Hauerwas 1986: 28). Suffering is a reality of our human condition which we can either accept or reject. Here is the fundamental reason why suffering is regarded by secular philosophers as an affront to liberal ideas of individual autonomy. It is not so much that suffering impairs our ability to choose, but that suffering threatens our belief that we are in ultimate control. Suffering challenges our tendency to be control freaks. It challenges the widespread fantasy that we can be autonomous, choosing individuals. It emphasizes our deep and inescapable creaturely dependence. The suffering person cannot escape the reality of his or her ontological dependence on others and ultimately on God.

As Stanley Hauerwas points out, for most of us, the initial reaction to witnessing suffering in another human being is to be repelled. It is to make the other a stranger. 'Suffering makes people's otherness stand out in strong relief.' Yet suffering in another human being is a call to the rest of us to stand in community. It is a call to *be there*. Suffering is not a question which demands an answer, it is not a problem which requires a solution, it is *a mystery which demands a presence*. 'It is the burden of those who care for the suffering to know how to teach the suffering that they are not thereby excluded from the human community. In this sense medicine's primary role is to bind the suffering and the nonsuffering into the same community' (Hauerwas 1986: 25–26). The sad reality is that, so often, modern medical and healthcare systems have precisely the opposite effect. They isolate and marginalize those who are suffering and those who are disabled from the rest of the human community.

The duty of care by which doctors and other professional carers are bound is a moral commitment to *be there* for those who are ill, those who are suffering, those who are dying. The role that the caring professions are called to play in society is a practical demonstration of the covenant bonds of community. It is to say, 'We are the community's representatives, and we promise to care for you whatever will happen, whatever it may cost.'

As Hauerwas argues, this does not mean that we ought to welcome or enjoy suffering. This is to pervert Christian thinking into a form of masochism, a view rightly regarded as pathological. Suffering is not to be sought, but it should, at least to some degree, be accepted. What medicine must attempt to do is to eliminate not all suffering and death, but *unnecessary* suffering and *untimely* death.

A dissenting voice

Since the end of the Second World War there has been a remarkable consensus in opposition to euthanasia among Christians of all traditions, Catholic and Protestant, orthodox and liberal. In 1995, however, the distinguished Roman Catholic theologian Professor Hans Küng of the University of Tübingen published *A Dignified Dying*, in which he and a fellow academic, Professor Walter Jens, argue passionately in favour of the legalization of voluntary euthanasia. 'There is no overlooking the fact that today there are more people than before who can no longer bear their already destroyed life, whose indescribable pain is not relieved even by the strongest sedatives of palliative therapy. They do not want to be made unconscious by means of psychotropic drugs and morphine and so be deprived of dialogue with family and friends. They want to say good-bye with a clear consciousness and die. And as they cannot die, they want effective help towards dying a dignified death' (Küng & Jens 1995: 19). Speaking out of the painful experience of the death of his own brother from cancer in the 1950s, Küng argues for a Christian acceptance of human responsibility at the end of life. If Christians use contraception, recognizing that God has given us responsibility in the creation of human life, then 'would it not be consistent to recognize that the same God now, more than before, has made the end of human life a human responsibility? This God does not want us to foist responsibility on him that we ourselves can and should bear. With freedom God has also given human beings the right to utter self-determination . . . How can anyone presume to decide whether another person shall live or die and seek to compel him or her to go on living and suffering?' (1995: 30–32).

Küng argues that medical technology has precipitated a new phenomenon. For many elderly people, life has become an intolerable burden. He argues against medical paternalism in favour of the individual's right to end his or her life responsibly before God. He proposes the development of medical guidelines on euthanasia and assisted suicide, and a change in the law, similar to that in Holland. 'Why shouldn't the elementary principle that human beings have a right to self-determination even in dying, be prescribed by the law?' (1995: 34).

As a Christian and a theologian I feel encouraged now to argue publicly for a middle way which is responsible in both theological and Christian terms: between an anti-religious libertarianism without responsibility ('unlimited right to voluntary death') and a reactionary rigorism without compassion ('even the intolerable is to be borne in submission to God as given by God'). And I do this because as a Christian and a theologian I am convinced that the all-merciful God, who has given men and women freedom and responsibility for their lives, has also left to dying people the responsibility for making a conscientious decision about the manner and time of their deaths. This is a responsibility which neither the state nor the church, neither a theologian nor a doctor, can take away (1995: 37–38).

Küng's argument is superficially persuasive, but ultimately it seems to me that he rides roughshod over orthodox biblical thinking. There is no simple symmetry between the act of creating human life and the act of destroying a life. In biblical thought, God has delegated to human beings a degree of responsibility in the creation of human life, while withholding to himself the right to destroy human life, except in the specific circumstance of capital punishment or, possibly, defence of the vulnerable. This is part of the moral order of creation which cannot be supplanted. It is surely naïve to argue that human beings have now reached such a state of maturity and wisdom that we are able to take responsibility before God for the ending of our own and other people's lives. I do not see how there can be a logically consistent 'middle way' between a secular libertarianism which allows individual autonomy to be pre-eminent at the end of life, and a Christian perspective which takes seriously God's loving and sovereign rule and the hidden moral order of creation. We are free to act as responsible moral agents, but only within the limits of the authority which God has delegated to us.

Practical responses in the medical care of the dying

If, then, euthanasia is not an option, how can we relate an orthodox Christian worldview to practical medical decisions about the care and treatment of the dying?

Good medicine knows its limits

One of the driving forces for euthanasia is a type of modern medicine that does not know when to stop; medicine driven by fear, by inexperience or by medical machismo. We saw an example in the case of Samuel Linares, and sadly this kind of medical madness seems all too common in our hospitals. I strongly believe that, as Christians, we should stand out against it. As we have seen, healthcare professionals are called to struggle against death while recognizing the ultimate futility of our struggle. We must try to discern when active life-sustaining treatment becomes inappropriate, and when the dying process becomes a severe mercy. The temptation for modern doctors is to attempt to use medical means as a technological fix for the ultimate realities of the human condition. Just as we are tempted to use technological fixes for the human realities of unwanted pregnancies, infertile couples and disabled children, so we are enticed to use technology to eliminate suffering and death. But doctors, above all, must recognize the limitations of their abilities and callings. 'Good physicians will know the limit of their art and they can help us to avoid the notion that there is any ultimate technological fix for the human problems of suffering and death.' This means that there are limits to what doctors can do to relieve suffering and death. 'A willingness to discern such limits as best we can – and, having discerned them, to act in accord with them – is deeply embedded in the Christian understanding of the moral life' (Meilander 1997: 67).

In fact, it can be argued that one of the primary roles of medical professionals in modern society is to teach modern people what are the limits that arise from our physical nature. 'Medicine can be viewed as an educational process for both doctor and patient, in which each is both teacher and learner. It is from patients that physicians learn the wisdom of the body. Both physicians and patients must learn that each of them are subject to a prior authority – the authority of the body . . . medicine represents a way of learning to live with finitude' (Hauerwas 1986: 48).

In other words, the essence of being a good doctor is to know when 'enough is enough'. But how do we know when we should withdraw treatment, or withhold it? It is when the burdens of any particular medical treatment outweigh its benefits. Doctors and patients together need to weigh up the burdens and the benefits. An obvious example is in advanced cancer. Is the burden of chemotherapy treatment, with all its unpleasantness, complications, risks, hospital visits, tests and expense, worth the benefit of, maybe, an extra three months of survival? The answer is, 'It all depends.' In different circumstances the balance between burdens and benefits will change. In some situations those extra three months might enable all kinds of 'unfinished business' to be completed: the reconciliation of long-standing broken relationships, the fulfilment of a long-cherished ambition, the chance to enjoy the presence of children or intimate friends. In other situations those three months may seem to bring little benefit compared with their burdens.

It seems clear that if the burdens of any particular treatment outweigh the benefits, then that treatment should be withdrawn. There is, however, a fundamental difference between making *treatment* decisions and making *value-of-life* decisions. Doctors are qualified to make treatment decisions: to decide which treatment is worthwhile and which is not. But doctors are no better qualified than anybody else to make value-of-life decisions: to decide which life is worthwhile and which is not. Doctors may determine whether a treatment is futile, but they can never determine whether a life is futile. When we withdraw or withhold treatment, we are expressing a belief that the treatment is valueless, not that the patient is valueless.

Good medicine recognizes the difference between intention and foresight

The pro-euthanasia lobby ridicules the traditional view that doctors may give a drug to relieve suffering that may incidentally shorten life, but may not deliberately give a poison to end life. This is regarded as pure hypocrisy, as an attempt by doctors to cloak their life-terminating activities in a charade of respectability. Closely related is the widely disseminated propaganda to the effect that morphine is a highly dangerous and lethal poison, and that when doctors give morphine they are intending to kill, but are covering their tracks to prevent prosecution. This is dangerous and misleading nonsense. Morphine and other opiates are highly effective painkillers, but they are not dangerous lethal drugs. We saw earlier that Nigel Cox gave an enormous dose of diamorphine to Lillian Boyes, with absolutely no effect. It would be quite hard to kill most patients with morphine. A few patients, particularly those with pre-existing respiratory pathology, have a high sensitivity to the depressant effects of morphine and other opiates, but this is not common. When doctors perform euthanasia, they do not use morphine. They use completely different drugs, those of the anaesthetist, which are capable of inducing instantaneous coma and muscle paralysis. The propaganda about morphine is dangerous because, as a result, ill patients may refuse to take adequate amounts of opiates for pain relief, fearing that the doctor is secretly trying to end their lives.

Nevertheless, good medicine recognizes the difference between intention and foresight. This is the so-called 'principle of double effect'. Some years ago, as a junior doctor, I spent some time treating patients with cancer. Every day I would inject highly toxic poisons into people's veins. I well knew about their effects: hair loss; weight loss; damage to the bone marrow, heart muscle and bowel lining; and increased vulnerability to infections. They carried a real risk of death. Does this mean that my actions were unethical? No, because the intention of administering these poisons was to heal, to treat various forms of cancer and leukaemia. I could foresee what the side-effects might be, but they were not my intended goal. I was acting according to the principle of double effect, a fundamental principle on which many therapeutic decisions are based.

In the same way, in the treatment of dying patients, my intention in withdrawing treatment such as intensive life support, or in giving opiates or sedation, is to relieve suffering, to bring benefit to these patients. I can foresee that my treatment decisions may shorten life, but that is not my intention. If it had been possible to use another drug to bring the same benefit to the patients without any shortening of life, then I would have used that. In fact, however, opiates such as morphine are, for most people, the most highly effective pain relievers known to medicine. In terminal cancer, their benefits outweigh their burdens.

The principle of double effect enshrines the difference between intention and foresight. It is, in fact, exactly the same principle which encompasses the Christian acceptance of martyrdom but not suicide. The Christian martyr does not aim at death, but aims to be faithful to God, foreseeing that death may occur as a result. Martyrdom becomes suicide when the intention deviates from faithfulness to God and becomes instead the achievement of death itself. Behind the principle of double effect lies a contrast between two ways of thinking about the actions of a moral agent.

To many secular philosophers, human beings are totally responsible for the consequences of their actions whether they are intended or not. Thus if I perform action *A*, and *B* results, I carry full responsibility for *B*, even if I intended *C*. If I give a therapy intended to heal, but my patient dies as a result, I am as responsible for that person's death as if I had intentionally committed murder. My intentions are irrelevant. It is the *consequences* which allow us to assess the morality of the act. It is as though the future is being constructed as a human artefact by the actions of each person. The future is a product of all our choices, good or bad.

But the orthodox Christian way of thinking views the stream of world history as ultimately under God's providential control, not as a product of human choices. My responsibility as a moral agent is to *act wisely*. It is as if I am called to toss into the continually flowing stream of history wise and moral actions which are intended to do good. The eventual consequences of my actions 'down stream' are outside my control and ultimately part of God's providential rule of the universe. Sometimes I try to do good things, and terrible consequences seem to result. Provided that my action at the time was wise, then the consequences are not ultimately my sole responsibility. They are under God's control. This does not, of course, absolve me from concern about the consequences of my actions. Part of acting wisely is to recognize the likely effects of my actions. But the ultimate consequences are not under my control. I must learn to live with the reality of my finitude.

Stuart's story

Stuart was a friend of mine who died well. I had known him for years as a fellow member of All Souls Church. We were both pianists (he was a professional musician), and we shared an interest in music and harmonization. Stuart was quiet and rather shy. He was absorbed in academic musicology, researching a rather obscure and technical aspect of church music in the Reformation. Then, out of the blue, he developed an unpleasant form of disseminated cancer, a lymphoma. He spent weeks in hospital, receiving the full gamut of intensive chemotherapy and radiotherapy. His hair fell out. He became emaciated. The cancer retreated, then came back in a more aggressive form. The oncologists were talking about 'one more push' with a new, experimental treatment. He was in pain, weak and distressed.

Stuart and I had several intense and painful conversations about his predicament, and about what the future held. It seemed to me that Stuart was much closer to death than he realized. We talked about the shift from curative medicine to symptom control, about recognizing that death was inevitable, about letting go from the desperate attempt to be cured. I suggested that perhaps he should think about refusing further aggressive cancer treatment and instead ask for referral to palliative-care specialists. I remember asking him, 'If I told you that you could have three months of pain-free, useful life followed by death, how would you want to spend those months?' His reply surprised me. He had been talking about completing his thesis, writing up his research. Now he changed. When death was staring him in the face, his priorities were different. 'I want to tell people about my faith. I want to talk to the students at All Souls. I want to write letters to my friends, to my family, to my old contacts in the musical world. I want to tell them what is happening to me and share my faith.'

Stuart was transferred to a local community-based palliative-care team in central London. He started receiving effective pain relief and appropriate symptom control. He knew he was going to die, but he was determined to make the most of the time he had left. After his death, Nick Page recorded an interview with Richard Bewes (the Rector of All Souls) and Diane Baird (the leader of its student work).

Nick: Richard, how did Stuart react when he knew he was going to die?

Richard: It had to be with a mixture of emotions. There was wistfulness, deep wistfulness of what might have been. I remember him talking about the career that he had in front of him, the prospects, the plans, the hopes, the dreams. And all that was going to come to an end. He was changing his scenario. But he did so with a very wonderful and Christian equanimity of spirit, so although there was wistfulness, I must say there was no trace, honestly, of terror.

Nick: But there must have been more than wistfulness, there must have been deep sadness, the awareness of loss, tears.

Richard: Oh, there were tears, of course there were. And naturally there was much prayer. So we would gather round him. Several of us did, for a short service of healing, when together we asked God as strongly and as unitedly as we could that God would touch him and make him well. Because we were quite sure that God had the ability to do that. Nevertheless, we also said that the ball was entirely placed in God's court. That was, to Stuart himself, a great relief.

Diane: Stuart had such a solid faith, it was breathtaking in a way. He was only thirty-nine years of age and yet he saw what many people don't see. He knew that beyond death there was something else, and he knew that when he died he was going to see Jesus. And that just gave him a steady calmness, I think, towards the end. And the confidence with which he faced death. It didn't hold fear for him.

Nick: So, those last few months weren't wasted?

Diane: Completely not. He touched more people in those last few months than I think he probably had done in the preceding fifteen years of his life. I mean, he said that. And certainly he affected my life and, I know, the lives of many, many students very deeply.

Nick: And, I think he wrote more letters in those last few months than most of the rest of his life.

Diane: He was constantly writing letters. He had a big list that he was working through. I think he wanted to share the confidence that he had in the face of death, with friends who didn't know Jesus and hadn't the same confidence – people he'd met over the years. He really was bursting to tell them about this hope that he had. He was always writing letters and he was always telling me who he had written to that day and who he needed to write to. And he hoped he wouldn't die before he'd got all these letters written. So there was always a bit of pressure there at the end of his life to get these letters in the post.

Nick: You said he affected the student group that you lead at All Souls. How was that?

Diane: Well, students are just starting off their lives. The time that he came down to speak to the students, you could have touched the atmosphere that night. Everybody was in tears, and they were, I think, just amazed at the bravery with which he was facing it. And just his strength and the assurance he had of where he was going. It really spoke to the students. Because we don't tend to think about our own death. But here was a young man who was absolutely struggling, I mean the sweat was rolling off his face that night as he spoke, and he could hardly get a breath. Yet the glory with which he spoke and the joy with which he spoke just filled the room. And people were absolutely kind of gob-smacked really with him.

Nick: And how did the church react to his impending death?

Richard: The whole church knew what was happening. He had visited the student group, he had met with the various groups in the church. And also, because he was one of our public musicians, a pianist, it meant that he was regularly on show. So it came to a head finally; the last service that I can recall him taking part in was a massive communion service at which there were at least a thousand of us present. I was presiding and Stuart was playing the piano. And at some point in the service, just before the breaking of the bread, and the pouring out of the cup, I was able to say, 'It's wonderful we are all here from our different backgrounds. It's wonderful that here is Stuart playing the piano for us on this very important night.' And that meant there was a fellowship, a deep fellowship of prayer, and of suffering and of the cross. The cross was there at the centre and we felt that we were all gathered together with Stuart at the cross. Everybody knew that he was dying, and I suppose most of us knew that this was perhaps the last time we would see him among us. But there was fellowship in that too, and a deep understanding.

Diane: I know he was often in a lot of pain, but the actual death itself, he was actually looking forward to it. 'The big sleep', he used to call it.

At his memorial service there were many people who had received a special letter from Stuart: a letter in which he had poured out his heart to them, in an unusually open and forthright way. And, sitting in that service, I suddenly realized that, in a strange sense, I was envious of Stuart. He had had an opportunity to write those letters that most of us never write, to say those things to his friends that most of us never say. The truth is that most people do not die like Stuart. They die unexpectedly over a few days or weeks, without warning; a sudden shock. They have little or no opportunity to experience the intensity of dying that Stuart did. Stuart died well. Those last three months were a wonderfully rich, profound experience for him, as well as for his many friends and contacts.

The opportunities of dying well

Here is a strange paradox. Dying is a terrible mystery, but it is an opportunity for growth. Stuart was an ordinary person, not some superhuman saint. But during those last few months he grew emotionally, internally. While his body was deteriorating his spirit was growing. Dying is an opportunity for personal growth.

Secondly, dying well is an opportunity for healing, from the inside; for the restoration and reconciliation of broken relationships, twisted by years of bitterness and hurt. It is a never-to-be repeated opportunity for forgiveness and starting again, and for the re-creation of family ties which have been severed.

Thirdly, dying well is an opportunity for letting go: for relinquishing tasks which will never be fulfilled; for accepting with grace that the myth of life as a self-directed and controlling individual must be abandoned; for recognizing the element of passivity which goes with a true understanding of suffering; for opening a hand which has been tightly grasped and self-centred.

Fourthly, dying well is an opportunity for re-ordering priorities, for expressing what is really important in life. I think Stuart was slightly surprised by his own reaction to his imminent death: when death was staring him in the face, music took a back seat in his life, and his desire to tell other people about his Christian faith came to the fore. He learnt about himself and about what was really important to him.

Finally, dying well is an opportunity to fulfil dreams. Many people have found that it is only when they are dying that their lifelong dreams can come to the fore, and be recognized, acknowledged and, to some extent, fulfilled.

Growth, internal healing, letting go, reordering priorities, fulfilling dreams: that is what dying well can offer. Stuart experienced all of these to some degree. Death does not have to be unrelieved gloom and doom; there can also be elements of adventure. The Christian hope transcends the grave. Clement of Alexandria expressed it beautifully: 'Christ has turned all our sunsets into dawns.'

Dealing with fear

What then are the answers to the three fears of the euthanasia debate: fear of pain, fear of indignity and fear of dependence? What prescriptions do we have to offer from the perspective of Christian medicine?

Palliative care

The answer to the fear of pain is good palliative care. Until the middle of the twentieth century, there was very little answer to the pain, especially in cancer. It was as though doctors were confronted with an impossible choice: to watch their patients die in agony or to kill them out of compassion.

How should Christians react when confronted by two totally unacceptable choices? Should we simply look for the lesser of the two evils? No. The answer is to invent a new alternative, a third way, which reflects Christian values, concerns and obligations. This is what a group of remarkable pioneer spirits did, especially Dr Cicely Saunders of St Christopher's Hospice, London, who founded the modern hospice movement and led to a quiet revolution in the care of the dying (see du Boulay 1984). I have become convinced that, as Christian carers, perhaps the single most important attribute we need is creativity. Often it seems that we do not lack compassion, expertise or resources. But we seem to lack the creativity, the originality, the ability to innovate, the perception to see a new way forward. Cicely Saunders provides a wonderful example of innovative Christian caring – caring that refuses to accept old defeatist attitudes.

Modern palliative care is a way of using specialized medical and nursing techniques, and a multidisciplinary team of carers, to treat the whole person in response to the 'total pain' of dying (see above, p. 176). It is a way of helping dying people to make the most of their lives. In the words of one of the slogans of the movement, 'Not only will we help you to die in dignity, but we will help you to live before you die.' It is a positive and practical alternative to euthanasia. It is not necessary to kill the patient in order to kill the pain.

A modern hospice is not a gloom-ridden place of death and shadows, but a place of hope and laughter as well as tears and pain. Hospices are places where people do indeed live before they die. Increasingly, palliative care is moving into homes, into mainstream hospitals, and into local health centres and surgeries. It is a concept, a way of caring, much more than an institution. Dr Robert Twycross, another pioneer of the movement, wrote: 'Palliative care developed as a reaction to the attitude, "There's nothing that can be done for you." This is never true. There's always something that can be done' (*Hospital Doctor*, 11 September 1997).

But can all pain be controlled? Specialists say that, with appropriate expertise, pain can be completely abolished or dramatically ameliorated in over 95% of cases. In fact, physical pain in terminal illness is rarely a major problem for doctors these days. The problem is spiritual pain, emotional pain, relational pain. There is deep-rooted agony in the hearts of many dying people in our society – the agony that goes along with loneliness, isolation and bitterness. Mother Theresa once said that the worst disease in the world is not leprosy or tuberculosis but the feeling of being unwanted, unloved and abandoned by everyone.

An experienced consultant in palliative care reflected with me on the Lillian

Boyes case. What was striking to him, reading the accounts of her death, was the rapid escalation in her terrible distress, which failed to respond to huge doses of diamorphine. This was not a characteristic of physical, organic pain. He commented that it seemed likely that there was a deep-rooted emotional or spiritual pain or fear. Perhaps that was why Mrs Boyes was crying out in agony despite massive doses of painkillers, and why Dr Cox felt moved to kill her.

How can we respond to the pain of dying, to the internal, spiritual suffering? It is by Christian caring, above all by *being there*.

The story is told of a little girl who is going to sleep in the bedroom upstairs while her mother is working in the kitchen.

'Mummy, Mummy, I'm scared. It's dark in here. I need someone to cuddle me.'

'I'm sorry, dear, both Mummy and Daddy are busy and can't come now. Just remember that God is with you. He will look after you.'

Long pause.

'But Mummy, I need someone with skin on!'

People who are dying need to feel God's love physically. They need human contact. They need to feel arms around them. They need the sound of a human voice. This is the way God made us. The Christian prescription for the fear of pain is God's love expressed in a human presence.

Compassion and respect

The answer to the fear of indignity is 'compassion mingled with respect'. The fact that many people feel that medical care leads to indignity is an indictment of our modern medical systems and attitudes, both of which tend to distance and demean our patients. We desperately need to recapture a sense of 'respect-love', which recognizes and honours the unique dignity of every human being made in God's image, every flawed masterpiece. The strange dignity which Mother Theresa and her sisters were able to perceive, even in dying leprosy victims with maggots in their wounds, is the dignity of humanness. It is the dignity derived from the image of Christ. This is the Christian prescription for the fear of indignity.

The Christian gospel

The fear of becoming dependent on others, arising from the desperate desire to remain in control, is, in my view, the hardest fear for modern people to conquer. In one sense the answer is the Christian worldview. We have to learn for ourselves, and teach one another, that dependence on others is part of the human story. This is where the educative role of the health professional is both most needed and most resisted. To learn dependence requires humility and maturity. It also requires trust, and, for many people in our society, trust in others has been steadily eroded and ultimately destroyed. But how can we die well if we cannot trust anybody?

The answer to this deep fear is the Christian gospel. It involves recognition of the painful and liberating truth that we cannot 'do it our way', trapped in what Malcolm Muggeridge once called the 'dark little dungeon of the ego'. If we are to grow and develop as human beings, we have to relinquish our desperate attempts at self-sufficiency. We have to learn about grace (God's unmerited favour), and that the most valuable things in life come as a free gift.

Standards of palliative care

There is, then, good news for those facing terminal illness. Modern palliative care is a wonderful development in caring, invented almost entirely by Christians, which has taken much of the force out of the euthanasia debate. We should be thankful that we live at a time when, thanks to the ongoing contributions of many dedicated carers, it is possible to die well.

Yet there is another side to the story. Decades after Cicely Saunders invented a better way of caring, people in Britain and around the world are still dying in agony. Thousands of terminally ill people die in pain, inappropriately cared for; with no treatment or the wrong treatment; with no support, or the wrong kind of support. In all the publicity about the Lillian Boyes case, there was one aspect which received little attention. Dr Cox was severely criticized by the General Medical Council and by experts in palliative care. Although he practised as a consultant in the NHS, he was apparently unaware of modern methods of pain relief. He was instructed to undergo a training course in palliative care, 'to become familiar with the full range of techniques', before he could return to his post as a consultant.

In 1994, the results of a study on the care of dying patients conducted in four large teaching hospitals were published in the *British Medical Journal*. 'More than half of all patients retained consciousness until shortly before death. Basic interventions to maintain patients' comfort were often not provided, oral hygiene was often poor, thirst remained unquenched, and little assistance was given to encourage eating. Contact between nurses and dying patients was minimal; distancing and isolation of patients by most medical and nursing staff were evident; this isolation increased as death approached. In summary, care of many of the dying patients observed in these hospitals was poor' (Mills *et al.*, *BMJ* 1994: 309:583–586).

This study was conducted in so-called 'centres of excellence', where the doctors and nurses of the future are being trained. When I hear these reports, and see the evidence with my own eyes, I feel distressed and, indeed, angry. The pain and distress of all those dying people seem so unnecessary. It is an outrage at the heart of medical services, not just in Britain, but across the world. Is it any wonder that people fear death and wish to have the option of euthanasia? Why are there such low standards of palliative care in many hospitals? It is possible to identify at least five reasons.

First, training in palliative care for medical students, doctors and nurses is inadequate. Palliative care forms only a very small part of the modern medical curriculum. Much more emphasis is placed on the scientific and technological basis of medical practice than on practical methods of pain and symptom relief.

Secondly, the staff who are caring for patients in hospital are often inadequately experienced. The care of the dying patient is a task which requires high levels of expertise, clinical experience and personal maturity, particularly for nursing staff. Ironically, the changes in nurse staffing which have taken place in NHS hospitals since the late 1980s have moved in precisely the opposite direction. On many wards, the senior, experienced nurses have been system- atically removed from direct patient care and replaced by junior, inexperienced nurses and untrained care assistants. Is it any wonder that the quality of nursing care for dying patients in general hospitals seems to have declined?

Thirdly, along with the lack of experience is the lack of adequate numbers of staff to provide suitable care. High-quality palliative care requires high staffing ratios and the expenditure of significant healthcare resources. But to health economists, the benefits of palliative care are largely invisible and impossible to quantify. The reduction of waiting-lists for minor medical conditions is politically sensitive, and this has recently become a major priority for health managers. By contrast, spending money to improve palliative care brings little political return.

Fourthly, many health staff are inadequately motivated to care for dying patients. The preoccupations of modern medicine are the high-technology, high-status treatments which save lives and make the headlines. There is little or no technology in the care of the dying patient. There are few academic or professional reputations to be made. What is the point of devoting time and energy to the care of patients whose imminent death is inevitable?

Finally, medical research into improved methods of pain relief and symptom control is very limited. Every year hundreds of millions of pounds and dollars are spent in research into potential new life-saving treatments for cancer and other diseases, many of them rare and exotic. And yet research to improve methods of symptom control for dying patients is seen as a low priority.

In the pecking order of the medical profession, palliative-care medicine comes somewhere near the bottom. And it is not just the health professionals who are to blame; we are all culpable. Members of the public support charities which pour vast sums into research into high-tech ways of prolonging life by a few months, and lap up documentaries about open-heart surgery and dramatic television soaps about modern medical life. Medical managers respond to public pressure, as happened recently when attention focused on breast cancer screening. Questions are asked in Parliament. Ministers jump to attention. Money is found. But people do not seem very interested in whether they will get proper pain relief when they are dying. Apparently it is not a matter of public concern. Yet only a few of us will require the wonders of extremely high-tech medicine, but every one of us is going to die.

Dementia and brain injury

In the previous chapter we looked at the deeply distressing problems caused by severe brain injury. If modern palliative medicine combined with Christian compassion can provide a better way than euthanasia in the care of the dying patient with cancer, what about the person with dementia or in the persistent vegetative state? Surely here is an argument for mercy killing. The tragic realities of dementia and PVS indicate how fragile our brains are. If human worth and significance are located entirely in our ability to think and to choose, in the functioning of a few millimetres of brain cortex, then our very humanity hangs by a thread. At any moment our brain functioning may become impaired, by disease or accident. Within the secular worldview of Ronald Dworkin or Peter Singer, the essence of our humanity, the ability to exercise autonomous choices, may be destroyed at any moment. This is why dementia is regarded with such horror by secular philosophers and by many ordinary people. To survive in this state is seen as ultimately degrading, dehumanizing and futile. Far better to have one's life ended than to linger on in this sub-human condition.

The reality of dementia threatens the self-worth of each of us. How can I be sure who I am, and how can I respect myself, when my own identity and worth are so evanescent and fragile? Of course, Christian believers too recognize the terrible degradation of dementia and PVS. This is not what human life was meant to be. But we cannot and must not respond to the brain-damaged individual with a sense of horror and revulsion. The Christian perspective enshrines a holistic view of human identity as a body-mind-spirit unity within community. It teaches us to value human beings in their complex totality, not just because of their brain function and rational abilities. Christianity teaches us to value human beings because of who they are, because of how they have been made and because they are known by God, rather than on the basis of what they can do.

The Christian view of human nature created in God's image provides a stability of human identity and significance throughout the whole of life, whatever events may befall. Even if my cortex is damaged, or my brain starts to malfunction, or I become confused and disorientated, I will still be me, a unique person, known and loved by others, and ultimately by God himself. No-one and nothing can take my human significance from me. I will always be worth what God thinks of me. Even if I become disabled, demented and despised by others, I can retain my own self-respect, and I can retain the right to be treated with respect by others.

Just as it is pointless to expect biology to reveal conclusively the point at which God's covenant involvement with a human individual commences, so it is pointless to use neurological examination to decide whether a human person is present within a body that is clearly living. As we saw earlier, Oliver

O'Donovan argues that we cannot demonstrate that a person exists by scientific testing for various attributes or capacities, such as rationality or responsivity. Instead, 'we discern persons only by love, by discovering through interaction and commitment that this human being is irreplaceable' (O'Donovan 1984: 59). In order to know one another as persons, we must engage not in objective scientific analysis, but in a covenant commitment of respect-love.

If respect and empathy are central to Christian caring, they must be reflected in our attitudes to those with Alzheimer's disease. One of the arts of caring for people with dementia is the ability to enter into the world of the other, to empathize, to enter into their experience. Alzheimer's disease frequently has a fluctuating course. In many cases there are periods of rationality and lucidity when communication can be established, human warmth and empathy can be communicated, and decisions can be rationally discussed. It is by attempting to understand that we can show respect and love. It is a fundamental Christian instinct. Treating the Alzheimer's sufferer in this way, with practical, respectful and compassionate caring, is not, of course, a soft option. It is emotionally and at times financially costly. It is a calling which is unglamorous and frequently disregarded by our society. It demands reserves of patience, fortitude, humour and compassion. A book for carers of people with Alzheimer's is entitled *The 36 Hour Day*, as testimony to the overwhelming demands that the disease can bring (Mace & Rabins 1981). It is easy for carers to feel isolated, ignored and demeaned.

Caring for people with respect does not mean that we are obliged to provide intensive and burdensome medical treatment to prolong life at all costs. As in all other clinical situations, the burdens of any proposed treatment must be weighed against its benefits. In severe and irreversible dementia, just as in terminal cancer, the benefits of medical treatment may be extremely small or non-existent. If infection or other life-threatening disease develops it may be right to withhold treatment, such as antibiotics or more intensive life-support measures, especially if they are unpleasant or invasive. But, as with the cancer patient, withdrawing or withholding medical treatment is not the same as intentional killing. We retain the basic attitudes of wonder, respect, empathy and protection. In the words of Joseph Pieper which we considered earlier, 'Love is a way of saying to another person, "It's good that you exist, it's good that you are in the world." '

In several centres across the UK and elsewhere, doctors and other professionals are trying to develop innovative ways to establish communication with severely demented sufferers. This is an example of a problem where we need more creativity and innovation, finding new ways of showing compassion mingled with respect, and finding ways of mobilizing the resources of lay Christians as a caring community for Alzheimer's sufferers. Is that not a better way than Ronald Dworkin's option of euthanasia by advance directive?

Sharon Fish, an experienced nurse from New York, has written a practical and helpful book entitled *Alzheimer's*. She speaks movingly from her own experience of caring for her mother as the disease slowly progressed, and of practical ways of establishing and maintaining communication. She writes of her own anger with God at the disruption to her personal life and the degradation to which her mother was subjected. 'My own struggles revolved as much around my own frustrated plans and desires as they did around my mother's disease and the devastating effects it had on her and my father' (Fish 1997: 192). Yet Sharon found spiritual healing and practical support in many areas, including a Christian community that was able to accept her and her mother. The spiritual care of Alzheimer's sufferers is an essential component of the holistic caring that reflects the Christian worldview. People with Alzheimer's often seem to retain some degree of spiritual insight and capacity long after the ability to think rationally has been lost.

Robert Davis, a Presbyterian minister, has written of the experience from the inside in *My Journey into Alzheimer's Disease*:

> In my rational moments I am still me. Alzheimer's disease is like a reverse ageing process. Having drunk from the fountain of youth, one is caught in the time tunnel . . . Cruelly it whips us back to the place of infancy. First the memories go, then perceptions, feelings, knowledge and in the last stage, our ability to talk and to take care of our most basic human needs . . . At this stage, while I still have some control of thoughts and feelings, I must learn to take on the role of the infant in order to make use of whatever gifts are left to me . . . Perhaps the journey that takes me away from reality into the blackness of that place of the blank, emotionless unmoving Alzheimer's stare is in reality a journey into the richest depths of God's love that few have experienced on earth. Who can know what goes on deep inside a person who is so withdrawn? At that time I will be unable to give you a clue, but perhaps we can talk about it later in the timeless joy of heaven. On second thought, all these heartaches won't really matter over there, will they? (quoted by Fish 1997: 211–212).

Robert Davis's moving words direct us towards the future hope to which all Christian caring points. In Richard Dworkin's view, we should treat Alzheimer's sufferers with respect solely because of what they *once were*. But Christians treat all human beings with respect not only because of what they were, but also because of what they are now, Godlike and wonderful beings, and *what they are to become*. It is a theme we shall return to in the next and final chapter.

I finish the present chapter with a sense of both optimism and frustration. There are practical and effective alternatives to euthanasia which reflect Christian values and priorities. There are ways of caring for dying and disabled people with respect and compassion, showing God's love in practical action.

These are messages which modern secular people (and modern philosophers) need to hear. But so often the Christian community does not seem to respond to the challenge. Where is the Christian voice in our society, arguing for better care of the dying and better education of professionals? Where are the professionals who will raise the status of palliative care, bringing new insights and fresh expertise to bear on the problems of the dying patient and the Alzheimer's sufferer? Where are the Christian believers who are prepared just to be there, to give practical care and emotional support for the vulnerable, the severely disabled and the dying?

In the final chapter we turn from the end of life to the future of medicine. What are the values which will guide health professionals as we move into the twenty-first century? Is it possible to defend the truth and relevance of Christianity in a secular society that has little time for religion as a source of ethical guidance? Can the Christian community provide new models of health relationships? How can we support and encourage the carers in our midst?

11. Old values for a new century: the Hippocratic tradition and modern medicine

Perhaps the most widely felt reaction to technological advances in biology and medicine is a sense of unease – not just among members of the general public who may feel they lack the expertise to evaluate them, but also among policy-makers and so-called opinion-formers. Increasing numbers in our society betray a mood of deep suspicion and hostility to biotechnological developments which, while offering the possibility of spectacular benefits, seem to change the fundamental givens of our humanity. It is a hostility which seems both emotional and irrational – the 'yuk factor'. To many scientists and philo-sophers, it is a purely negative, atavistic and retrograde phenomenon, a modern equivalent of the Luddites, who waged a futile campaign against the might of the Industrial Revolution. But from a Christian perspective, the 'yuk factor' can be seen as something more positive: an expression of profound moral intuitions about what it means to be a human being. These are still deeply rooted within our society, despite the corrosive acids of secularism.

In this final chapter we shall look at the debate about the fundamental values of medicine which is in progress within the profession, and ask what the history of medicine, and the strange alliance which was struck up between an ancient craft and the Christian church, can teach us. But first we examine a prominent feature of modern thinking about ethics: the distinction between facts and values.

Core values and the facts/values distinction

At the heart of the view of the world which derives from the Enlightenment is the distinction between facts and values. To most modern secular thinkers, it is self-evident that there is no connection between facts (what is the case), and values (what ought to happen). Facts are grounded in reality, but values are 'made up'. They are a product of human storytelling. They float free, detached from the physical stuff of reality.

From this perspective, our moral task, individually, as professional groups and as a society, is to *choose* the values by which we want to live. But where do we find those values if we cannot derive them from the facts, from the nature of reality which we perceive? Ultimately, values simply express personal preference, rather like choosing the flavour of ice-cream we prefer. Whether or not we personally are in favour of doctors committing euthanasia, or selecting the sex of future children, is a matter of personal inclination. These are not topics on which rational discussion and debate are helpful or even possible.

If we cannot argue for a particular set of values on a rational basis, where then can we find them? Where can a secular society and a secular profession find ethical principles which will both provide practical solutions to the agonizing dilemmas we face and fit with our deepest human intuitions? The question has been troubling the medical establishment for several years. In November 1994 many of the major players of the British medical profession called a conference entitled 'Core Values for the Medical Profession in the 21st Century'. The conference announcement stated: 'The values to which doctors have held fast over 2,000 years are being challenged by the evermore rapid advances in medical practice combined with changes in health systems. How relevant will these values be to the demands of today and tomorrow? We see the conference as the starting point of a crucial process of debate and consultation within the profession itself, with patients and society as a whole, with other professions, with health service managers and with the government.'

Following the conference, nine core values were identified and a detailed questionnaire was sent to more than 1,500 members of the British Medical Association, asking them to rank the values and express their opinions. The values, ranked in the order for which the members voted, were as follows: 'competence, caring, commitment, integrity, compassion, responsibility, confidentiality, spirit of enquiry, advocacy' (Core Values Survey Report, BMA, 1995).

But should we determine our values by means of a democratic process such as a referendum? And what are the central issues which need to be decided? I wish to suggest three crucial questions which health professionals will need to answer in the coming years.

1. *Humanity.* What does it mean to be a healthy human being? We need a renewed vision of humanity.

2. *Medicine.* What are we trying to achieve? We need a renewed sense of the goals and purpose of medicine.

3. *Caring.* How can we show compassionate involvement within ethical constraints? We need new models of caring.

How can we find a way forward in addressing these issues? To revisit the words of Archbishop William Temple, 'If you don't know where you are going, it is sometimes helpful to know where you have been.' In the confusion of a postmodern age, history has a crucial role in ethics, providing insights into how we got here in the first place. If we are to find a way forward together as a society, we need to understand how the ethical debates of today find their roots in the past. A discernible trend in moral philosophy is a renewed interest in different historical ethical traditions. In the same way, Christians who find themselves living in a postmodern age need to develop a renewed appreciation of our Christian history, especially, in my view, the history of the early church, and how it met the challenges of the pagan age in which it lived. So I make no apologies for a brief foray into the history of medical ethics, and the ancient craft of Hippocratic medicine.

Hippocratic medicine: an ancient tradition

The Graeco-Roman world into which Hippocratic medicine appeared had numerous healers. There were herbalists of various descriptions, including the practitioners of *pharmakeia*, referred to earlier – the professional abortionists and poisoners, whose dubious services could be obtained for a fat fee. In addition, various healers were attached to the mystery religions and cults, and there were philosopher-physicians, thinkers who dabbled in the healing arts. It was a common aphorism at the time that 'the doctor is physician of the body, the philosopher is physician of the soul'.

As we have seen, Graeco-Roman society at the time was often cruel and inhumane. But the Hippocratic physicians seemed to have had a different attitude to their fellow human beings. They were a professional sect, a craft, who traced their origins to the quasi-mystical figure of Hippocrates, an inhabitant of the Greek island of Cos around 400 BC. The Hippocratic band was a clique of skilled practitioners, passing on their mysterious and strange healing customs to carefully selected initiates, who were required to swear a solemn and pagan oath. 'I swear by Apollo Physician, by Asclepius, by Hygeia, by Panaceia and by all the gods and goddesses, that I will carry out, according to my ability and judgment, this oath . . .' (see full text in Cameron 1991: 24–25).

The oath summarizes the essential features of the Hippocratic tradition. First, it emphasized an arduous and prolonged apprenticeship in the art of medicine; the new doctor swore a binding and life-long allegiance to his teachers. Secondly, it stressed a duty of care to help the sick, and a specific abjuration of harm: 'I will use treatment to help the sick according to my ability and judgment, but I will never use it to injure or wrong them.' Thirdly, there was a refusal to abuse medical skill by taking human life by poisoning or abortion: 'I will not give poison to anyone though asked to do so, nor will I suggest such a plan. Similarly I will not give a pessary to a woman to cause abortion.' Fourthly, there was an emphasis on the protection of vulnerable patients from abuse and from sexual manipulation: 'In purity and holiness I will guard my life and my art . . . Into whatever house I enter, I will do so to help the sick, keeping myself free from all intentional wrong-doing and harm, especially from fornication with woman or man, bond or free.' Finally, there was a duty of confidentiality, to protect patients from the harm of scandal: 'Whatsoever in the course of practice I see or hear, that ought never to be published abroad, I will not divulge, but consider such things to be holy secrets.' The novel aspect of the Hippocratic tradition was the concept of a profession which married skilled technical abilities with a firm structure of ethical values.

How did this esoteric and pagan guild of physicians become so significant in the development of western civilization?

Trust

The genius of the Hippocratic band was that they recognized that *trust* was at the heart of the doctor–patient relationship. Historians have suggested that one of the reasons for the development of the oath was a widespread mistrust of physicians. The Romans, in particular, were intensely suspicious of those clever Greek physicians and their strange practices. They were known to have extensive knowledge of and access to lethal herbs and potions. They entered private bedrooms and performed intimate examinations and procedures behind closed doors. They were privy to the most extraordinary secrets and personal confidences. It is hardly surprising that physicians were regarded with some suspicion by their clients. 'There would be little point in solemnly forswearing murder, euthanasia, abortion, and fornication with patients, if doctors had never been known to participate in such deeds' (Temkin 1991: 21).

By formalizing and publicizing their professional code of conduct, the Hippocratic physicians managed to win the confidence of the public, and, just as importantly, they differentiated themselves from the numerous quacks, herbalists and witchdoctors of the time. Before patients put their life and welfare into the hands of a physician, they needed to know whether or not he was untrustworthy. Therefore, to the Hippocratic band, ethical conduct ranked even higher than technical skill. 'It is better to be a good man devoid of learning than to be a perfect practitioner of bad moral conduct and an untrustworthy man' (Temkin 1991: 21).

Philanthropy

They based their professional art on *philanthropy*, rather than on pure financial gain. What the ideal physician exhibited was a disinterested love and concern, not just for the élite of society, but for humanity as a whole. 'Like a saviour god, let the physician make himself the equal of slaves and paupers, of the rich and of rulers of men, and to all let him minister like a brother, for we are all children of the same blood' (Temkin 1991: 72). In the Hippocratic writings there is clear evidence of a humane professional tradition which treated all human beings as brothers and sisters. I find it fascinating that a pagan Greek craft should have been predicated on a view of humanity which was so similar to that of the coming Christian religion. 'If love of men (*philanthrōpiē*) is present, love of the art (*philotechniē*) is also present' (quoted in Temkin 1991: 30).

Medical historians continue to debate the philosophical roots which led to this philanthropic outlook. The historian Ludwig Edelstein suggested a link with the Pythagorean school of philosophy in the fourth century BC, which, unlike most schools of Greek philosophy at the time, was vehemently opposed to both suicide and abortion (Edelstein 1943: 15). The Pythagoreans represented a minority view, and, Edelstein suggests, for some reason the Hippocratic band adopted their unusual attitudes to human life. This meant that the Hippocratic group did not represent the general ethical stance of Greek physicians at the time. 'Far from being the expression of the common Greek attitude towards medicine or of the natural duties of the physician, the ethical code rather reflects opinions which were peculiarly those of a small and isolated group' (Edelstein, quoted by Cameron 1991: 39).

Separation of healing and harming

The Hippocratic tradition drew a clear distinction between healing and harming. Margaret Mead, the distinguished anthropologist, commented on the momentous significance of the Hippocratic tradition as follows: 'For the first time in the history of humankind there was a complete separation between killing and curing. Throughout the primitive world the doctor and the sorcerer tended to be the same person. He with the power to kill had the power to cure. He who had the power to cure would also be able to kill . . . With the Greeks, the distinction was made clear. One profession was to be dedicated completely to life under all circumstances, regardless of rank, age, or intellect – the life of a slave, the life of the Emperor, the life of the immigrant, the life of the defective child . . .' (quoted by Cameron 1991: 9). By a quirk of history which is still not fully explained, the ancient pagan craft of Hippocratic medicine had much in common with the radical Christian religion that was to spread throughout the Graeco-Roman world.

The Hippocratic-Christian consensus

As we saw in chapter 6, the early Christians, such as the writers of the *Didache* and the *Epistle of Barnabas*, attacked Graeco-Roman morality with its acceptance of the elimination of unwanted human life and its cruelty to the weak and despised. They found unlikely allies in the Hippocratic guild of doctors. The physician Luke became an important part of the early apostolic group, writing both a gospel and the history of the early church (Acts). Paul took him on his missionary journeys, probably to act in his professional role as personal physician to the members of the party. Like Luke, it seems that most of the physicians of the early church found that the Hippocratic oath fitted in with their own Christian perspectives (see Temkin 1991: 126–145). Jesus himself provided a model as a healer (albeit not in a professional sense). His ministry had emphasized the importance of physical healing, and in the gospel writings he had described himself as a physician to the morally diseased: 'It is not the healthy who need a doctor, but the sick' (Mt. 9:12).

Thus an unlikely alliance grew up between the pagan craft and the rapidly growing Christian religion. 'The pagan enterprise of medicine became suffused with the distinctives of the Judaeo-Christian revelation' (Cameron 1995: 4). In a remarkable way the Hippocratic medical art fitted both with Christian anthropology and with the ethical imperatives of the Christian church. As Osei Temkin, a distinguished Jewish historian of medicine, wrote: 'What was to distinguish the sincere Christian doctor from the pagan one, was a new relationship to his faith and his church, rather than a fundamental change in his professional ethics' (1991: 35).

Christian contributions to medical ideals

Christianity did not simply coexist with the old Hippocratic ideal; it brought an enhanced, radical vision of the medical task.

Christian thinking emphasized, first, the importance of the natural order. In the universe, God had created a physical order which extended to the physical structure of human beings. This is a theme which we addressed in chapter 2. By investigating how the body worked, Christian doctors were 'thinking God's thoughts after him', as Newton put it, many centuries later. Not only that, but God had created the hidden *moral* structure of the creation, and, by treating human life with reverence and respect, physicians were practising in accordance with the moral order of the cosmos.

Secondly, in the historical event of the incarnation, as we saw earlier, God affirmed the dignity and lasting significance of the human body. So Christian doctors treated the human body, for all its strange idiosyncrasies, with special wonder and respect because this was the form in which God chose to become flesh. When Christ was raised as a human being, God proclaimed his vote of confidence in humanity and the created order. Hence humanity was not demeaned as something which separated us from God. On the contrary, it was the means by which God was made known. Christianity provided for Hippocratic medicine a new anthropology, a way of thinking about human beings with wonder and respect as the bearers of the divine image, and as a universal family. It also provided an ethical framework in which personal integrity, truthfulness and covenant commitment were part of the moral order of the universe.

Thirdly, Christian thinking pointed to a deeper and richer reality beyond the physical. The material aspect of the universe is an important, but not the most important, part of reality. In Greek, the verb *sōzō* can mean both 'save' and 'heal', and it is hardly surprising that this word crops up more frequently in Dr Luke's gospel than in any of the other three. Perhaps Luke was fascinated by the ambiguity and the subtlety of *sōzō*. He recognized that in the ministry of Jesus, physical healing and spiritual salvation went hand in hand. They were two sides of the same coin. Jesus helped people not to *escape* from their humanity, but to become full human beings, human beings as we were intended to be. Christians thus affirmed the importance of physical healing, while recognizing that behind the physical body lay a deeper, a richer, an even more wonderful reality. The physical body was not the limit of reality; humans needed a deeper healing. Christianity affirmed and supported the importance and the dignity of the medical and caring professions, while at the same time relativizing their role.

Fourthly, Christianity provided a new definition of neighbourliness. The Old Testament law had taught about duties to the neighbour, and especially to the vulnerable and defenceless: orphans, widows, aliens, the poor. Yahweh, the mighty Lord, had proclaimed that he was their defender, and those who followed him should defend them too. Love for neighbour was part of the Jewish Torah: 'Do not seek revenge or bear a grudge against one of your people, but love your neighbour as yourself' (Lv. 19:18). The Rabbis had interpreted this instruction in a narrow, localized and parochial manner. My neighbour was the person next door, my friend, my compatriot, the one who was like me.

Jesus had combined the Old Testament commands to love God and to love our neighbour (Mk. 12:28–31). By doing so, he highlighted their inter-relationship; in loving and respecting our neighbour we are in fact honouring the God whose image he or she bears. But Jesus reinterpreted the command to neighbour-love in a startling, radical way, as recorded by Luke in his gospel (10:25–37).

The passage is so familiar to us that it has lost its original extraordinary impact. The expert in the Torah who had engaged Jesus in debate had started with a typically rhetorical debating point: 'What must I do to inherit eternal life?'

Jesus parried with the question: 'What is written in the Law? How do you read it?'

He answered: ' "Love the Lord your God with all your heart and with all your soul and with all your strength and with all your mind"; and, "Love your neighbour as yourself." '

'You have answered correctly,' Jesus replied. 'Do this and you will live' (verses 25–28).

But according to Luke, the rabbi 'wanted to justify himself', so he asked Jesus, 'And who is my neighbour?' In response Jesus told the story about the nameless traveller who was mugged on the way from Jerusalem to Jericho, the failure of the orthodox Jewish teachers to assist, and the practical, costly compassion of the hated and despised Samaritan, the half-Jew. Jesus comes to the punchline: 'Which of these three do you think was a neighbour to the man who fell into the hands of the robbers?' (verse 36).

As a number of commentators have pointed out, the question has subtly changed. The rabbi had asked, 'Who is my neighbour?' That is, 'Which of all my friends and contacts am I supposed to love? Who has a claim on me?' But Jesus turns the question around: 'Who out of these three in the story proved to be a neighbour? Who acted in a neighbourly way?' In other words, we discover who is our neighbour, to whom we owe a duty, when we act in a neighbourly way. The relation of neighbourhood between the Samaritan and the Jewish victim would never have become apparent if the Samaritan had not taken the initiative. Both the Samaritan and the Jew discovered that they were neighbours, because the Samaritan had first acted in a neighbourly way, by showing compassion towards an anonymous victim. We discover the humanity, the dignity and the worth of our neighbours when we have a prior moral commitment to them.

Turning the concept of the neighbour around and applying it to the agent rather than the object of the loving act, Jesus draws attention to the fact that neighbourhood is a *reciprocal* relation. 'Nobody can be a neighbour except to a neighbour,' commented Augustine. And by casting the story in the form of an adventure . . . Jesus emphasizes the *contingency* of the circumstances which can place us in an unlooked-for neighbourly relation with others. The Samaritan was discovered to be the Jew's neighbour, not by any judgment or evaluation on the Jew's part, but because he 'turned out to be' a neighbour in the event (O'Donovan 1994: 240).

The Christian concept of the neighbour is a commonplace to us in modern western societies, but we should try to recognize how strange and threatening it must have seemed at the time. The duty of love for others was not limited to my friend next door. Any stranger I happened to come across in the accidental events of life could make demands on me. My neighbours included the riff-raff, the slave, the tax-collector, the hated Roman collaborator, the leprosy victim, the prostitute, the unwanted baby, the pathetic, old, crippled widow, the weak, the vulnerable, the despised. Even the fetus was a neighbour to whom I owed a duty of compassion, respect and protection. Again, to the devout Jew it was obvious that God commanded us to act in a neighbourly way to those who deserved it, to the good and godly. But the radical nature of Christian love was also seen in Christ's command to 'Love your enemies and pray for those who persecute you, that you may be sons of your Father in heaven. He causes his sun to rise on the evil and the good, and sends rain on the righteous and the unrighteous' (Mt. 5:44–45).

As Michael Gorman put it, 'Jesus' new definition of neighbour yielded an ethical stance unique to the Ancient World. All distinctions between people – Gentile and Jew, man and woman, adult and child, slave and free, rich and poor, guilty and innocent – were obliterated' (Gorman 1982: 24). My fellow human being, in whatever form I find him or her, has a claim on my life simply by being human.

Of course, Jesus not only talked about the importance of the riff-raff; he lived it out as well. Luke, the Hippocratic physician, takes great delight in spelling out how Jesus was known for his practical compassion for society's outcasts. Luke records the lepers Jesus touched, the prostitute who kissed his feet, the unclean woman with a hidden haemorrhage who defiled everyone she touched, and those useless little children that, for some unaccountable reason, the Son of God wasted his time on.

Christian influence on the development of medicine

As Christianity spread through Graeco-Roman society, it was seen to be different from the mystery religions with which the empire was awash. And a central peculiarity of these Christians was that they *cared for the riff-raff*. Right from the start they set up distribution schemes to provide practical support for widows, orphans, the needy and the sick, referred to in several places in the New Testament (*e.g.* Acts 6:1–6; 2 Cor. 8 – 9; Jas. 1:27). They went round the rubbish bins, rescuing abandoned babies. Later they set up orphanages and hospitals for the dying. Practical care for the needy was the consistent teaching of the early church fathers, as exemplified by Clement of Alexandria: 'It behoves you to give honour to the image of God which is man, in this wise: food to the hungry, drink to the thirsty, clothing to the naked, care to the sick, shelter to the stranger, and visiting him who is in prison, to help him as you can.' Clement also exhorted the rich to abandon the Roman custom of buying one's own legions. Instead they were to form an 'army' of the poor and the weak by providing for their needs. 'Contrary to the rest of men, enlist for yourself an army without weapons, without war, without bloodshed, without wrath, without stain – pious old men, orphans dear to God, widows armed with gentleness, men adorned with love . . .' (quoted by Gorman 1982: 84).

The Emperor Julian, who attempted to resist the spread of Christianity, complained about these fanatics, the 'atheists' as he called them. 'It's their benevolence to strangers, their care of the graves of the dead and the pretended holiness of their lives that has done most to increase their atheism . . . the impious Galileans support not only their own poor, but ours as well!' (Julian, Epistle 22, cited by Ramachandra 1996b: 280). In the great plague which followed a period of persecution in 250–251, wealthy pagans were fleeing the city of Carthage. Bishop Cyprian preached to his congregation from the passage about love for enemies in Matthew 5:43–48, 'urging them not to save their own lives, not even to seek the survival of their Christian community, but to love their enemies who had recently been persecuting them. This was an opportunity to show the love of Jesus by staying in the city and nursing pagan and Christian alike' (Eusebius, cited by Ramachandra 1996b: 280).

Thus Christianity gave new life to the tradition of Hippocratic medicine – a new vision of the natural creation and of anthropology and moral order; a new sense of the significance of the physical body, while pointing towards a greater reality. Christianity redefined the obligations of neighbourliness enshrined in medical practice, and orientated it towards those on the lowest rungs of society's ladder. Primitive hospitals had existed before in several cultures. They had been set up in military establishments to keep troops healthy for battle. There were healing centres attached to temples of Saturn to which sufferers flocked. But when the Christian church and its physicians set up hospitals, they were different because they were based on the radical vision of the good Samaritan. They concentrated on treating strangers, travellers and outcasts, the abandoned and the destitute.

Here are the words of the eminent Jewish historian H. E. Sigerist:

The most important and decisive development in the special status assigned to the sick was introduced by Christianity. This new teaching, in contrast with the other religions which were for the healthy and the just, appealed to the sick, the weak and to the crippled. It spoke of spiritual healing, but it also spoke of bodily healing. The place of the sick in society was altered from its very foundation. Whereas disease in the entire history of medicine had sharply isolated the sufferer, in Christian times he was actually brought closer to his fellow men by the fact of his illness. To care for him was a Christian obligation. The birth-hour of large-scale organized care of the sick had come. The care of the ill is now the concern of the church. The Bishop is in charge, the deacons and the laity are his agents (cited in Aitken *et al.* 1984: 8).

The development of hospitals

It is not surprising that the early Christians built hospitals, including distinctly dangerous places such as specialist hospitals for plague victims and leprosy sufferers. Even the word has Christian roots. It comes from the Latin *hospes*, meaning 'a guest'. A hospital is a place where we practise hospitality, neighbour-love to strangers, a bizarre concept first introduced by one Jesus of Nazareth. Nearly all the Christian hospitals were built within monasteries run by the church authorities, like that of St Basil, who built a hospital of 300 beds for plague victims at Edessa. Not all Christians held a high view of the body, however, and the development of ascetic monastic communities in the third and fourth centuries encouraged a fanaticism which could be associated with a sense of loathing towards the physical body. Several of the church fathers opposed this tendency, emphasizing respect and a sense of awe towards the human body. Gregory of Nyssa wrote: 'Do not despise the wonder within you' (quoted by Temkin 1991: 34). It is an authentically Christian response to the body; a sense of awe and wonder at the mystery of humanness.

Many lay monks trained as Hippocratic physicians, and some of the religious sisters and brothers devoted themselves to the art of caring for the sick and dying, becoming specialized nursing sisters and nursing brothers (the male nurse is not a recent invention!). The rules of the Benedictine monastic order emphasized the importance of hospital duties to all its monks: 'Care for the sick stands before and over all. Accordingly one must help them as one would Christ.' As the classical world disintegrated, the so-called Dark Ages descended and most of the ancient learning was lost, it was the Christian monasteries that preserved the ideals of the old Hippocratic tradition. It was Christian monks who translated, taught and developed the ancient precepts of the Hippocratic ideal.

Many of the historic monastic hospitals still survive. In London, St Bartholomew's Hospital, St Mary's Spital, which later became the Bethlem Hospital for the Insane, and St Thomas's Hospital, were all founded adjacent to the thoroughfares and bridges of ancient London. Their positioning was deliberate. They provided practical medical help for travellers and pilgrims. They were the ancient casualty departments, enshrining the ethical commitments of the good Samaritan. The decimation of the English monasteries by Henry VIII had a disastrous effect on medical care, leading to the destruction of many monastic hospitals and the disbanding of the medical and nursing brotherhoods and sisterhoods which cared for the poor. The eighteenth century saw a rapid growth of hospitals for the poor which, most historians agree, was influenced, at least in part, by the Christian evangelical revival and by a renewed practical concern for philanthropy.

Although a small number of British hospitals were founded with secular roots (such as my own institution, University College Hospital, established on the utilitarian philosophy of Jeremy Bentham), they were the exception. Most of the major British hospitals had profoundly Christian roots, and it was not until the inception of the National Health Service in 1948 that these proud, independent institutions were absorbed into the UK welfare state, and became an arm of secular government. The development of the modern hospice movement, outlined in the last chapter, continues in the same Christian tradition of care for the needy.

International spread

Internationally, too, we find that medicine and nursing spread round the globe, driven largely by Christian ideals. This was especially true of the developing world of Africa and Asia. The great vision of missionary medicine came only relatively late on to the scene. It was not until around 1850 that the idea of Christian health professionals going from the West to care for the sick and dying in developing countries came to fruition. At that time it was estimated that there were only between twelve and fifteen Christian doctors working in Asia or Africa. But in the following century, more than 1,500 doctors went from Britain alone to work in developing countries, and thousands more missionary nurses and paramedicals went where there were no doctors. Wherever they went, they introduced the Hippocratic Christian ideal. I understand that, until the middle of the twentieth century, the only professional nurses in the whole of the Indian subcontinent were linked to Christian establishments.

An Asian Christian has written of the remarkable impact of Christian missionaries: 'Many of the finest medical institutions still standing on the Indian sub-continent were founded by Christians on their own initiative, often against the wishes of the European colonial powers. The missionary contribution to medical health in Asia and Africa has been nothing less than extraordinary; from the treatment of leprosy and pioneering discoveries in epidemiology, to the development of national health care systems, the training of primary health care workers, and the setting up of educational institutions for women doctors and nurses' (Ramachandra 1996a: 216). And yet Asia has been the site of several major world religions, especially Hinduism and Buddhism, stretching back thousands of years. Why was it that devout Hindu or Buddhist believers had never set up a system of practical medical and nursing care for the weak and disadvantaged, for the leprosy victims, the outcasts, and the untouchables? Why did the development of large-scale medical establishments in Asia depend on the influence of *Christian* doctors, nurses, and religious orders? Ultimately, all this can be traced back to the teaching and example of Jesus of Nazareth.

The historical dimension provides a different perspective on the current debates about the future of medicine. When we look backwards to see the historical roots of western medicine, we find Christianity at every turn. The improbable cross-fertilization between a pagan guild of physicians and a radical middle-eastern religion led to two thousand years of proud medical, nursing and healthcare history. Inevitably, the potted version I have provided oversimplifies the story. There have always been tensions and strains in this alliance. Western Hippocratic medicine has often lost contact with practical care for the disadvantaged, for example. In western society, physicians have frequently espoused a social position among the élite. The London Royal

College of Physicians was, and to some extent remains, a highly aristocratic institution. I suspect there was a distinct preference among its wealthy Fellows to hob-nob with Royalty and the aristocrats of Mayfair rather than frequent the Poor Hospitals in the East End of London, although there are outstanding examples of philanthropy among physicians to Royalty. For long periods of our history, the poor could not afford a properly trained Hippocratic physician. They had to make do with the apothecary, the herbalist or the quack doctor. Despite this, in most western countries the Hippocratic Christian consensus remained fundamentally intact until the 1960s. This Christian way of thinking was so much a part of the axioms of medical ethics that it was almost invisible and unquestionable. But, as we have seen, over recent decades the consensus has been steadily coming apart at the seams. Each of the five trends we explored in chapter 1 has been quietly eroding the partnership of two thousand years.

Erosion of the Hippocratic-Christian consensus
Motivation

Biological reductionism strikes at the heart of Hippocratic-Christian anthropology. If I am caring for a being made in God's image, I might have a motivation for philanthropy, for enshrining the values of respect and compassion. But if I am caring for a survival machine, for 'robot vehicles blindly programmed to preserve the selfish molecules known as genes', then, logically, why bother? After all, if the mechanisms of this particular survival machine are grossly abnormal, and it lacks the right DNA for the future of our species, why should we not help it on its way to the rubbish heap? There are many better-equipped survival machines which could benefit from medical help.

Values and aims

Technology changes the values and the aims of the medical enterprise. We do not have to accept our bodies as they have been given to us, we can improve their structure. Of course, in the days of the old Hippocratic-Christian consensus, this was hardly an issue. Most of the therapies the medical profession had to offer were of little use. The lover of the human (*philanthrōpiē*) could also be a lover of the art (*philotechniē*). But this was partly because the biological potential of the art was extremely limited. Today we have effective biological technology. We can really change the design. The concerns of the medical technologist thus becomes the concerns of the Lego constructor: does the new construction work? Is it safe? The original focus of Hippocratic medicine was on healing, and the ban on abortion and euthanasia prohibited many of the manipulative possibilities of the medical art. With the development of technology, seen most clearly in the field of reproductive technology, the original purpose of healing is being supplanted by a vast range of manipulative possibilities (Cameron 1995: 10).

The doctor–patient relationship

Consumerism changes the relationship between doctor and patient. In the past, Hippocratic medicine was a collaborative enterprise between the doctor and the patient. The relationship was frequently paternalistic and unbalanced, a parent–child relationship. Despite this, the doctor entered into a covenant with the patient to act solely in the patient's interests, within the ethical constraints laid down by the tradition of medicine. In a paternalistic relationship it was inevitably the doctor's values which were dominant. Now, in many cases, the relationship has been turned on its head. In a consumerist culture it is the consumer who is king. The enterprise becomes a client–technician relationship, and it is the client's values which become overriding. As we saw previously, the aims of prenatal screening have been officially described as allowing 'the widest range of informed choice to women and their partners'. This is a remarkable mission statement for modern healthcare. It represents the values of a modern service industry, offering the widest range of choices. 'Got to keep the customer satisfied', as Simon and Garfunkel sang. It is a slogan that market traders have been chanting since the dawn of time, but now it is becoming official policy in the medical world. The NHS 'internal market' model – forced on to the NHS in the teeth of strong opposition from most of the professionals within it – has further eroded the traditional ethics of medicine and nursing. The hospital staff are no longer carers or healers, but 'healthcare providers'. Instead of patients we have 'healthcare consumers'. Our role is to employ healthcare resources to satisfy the demand with both 'effectiveness' and 'efficiency' (vital elements of the jargon of modern medicine).

The modern concept of non-directive counselling also has affinities with the values of the service industry. Philosophically, it is another example of the facts/values distinction. The professional's job is simply to give the client the facts: cold, neutral, objective. What the client decides to make of the facts is up to him or her as a consumer. But genuinely non-directive counselling is a myth. We are all coming from somewhere. Whether atheist, Christian, agnostic or Buddhist, all health professionals have some core beliefs, a worldview which influences their perspective and colours the advice they give.

The healing ideal

Resource limitations have eroded the Hippocratic ideal of healing without harming. In a society in which economics becomes increasingly the most influential measure of all human activity, the terrible truth of what I earlier dubbed the 'first law of health economics' cannot be resisted. Antenatal screening and abortion will always be cheaper than medical and social care for the disabled. Euthanasia will always be cheaper than multidisciplinary support for the dying. If we as a society allow the monetary cost of caring to dominate our thinking, we will turn away from Christian ideals. Yet Christian caring must always be practical and realistic. We cannot ignore the ever-spiralling economic costs of healthcare. How can we enshrine Christian principles in the rationing and allocation of healthcare resources? We will return briefly to this complex issue below.

Ethics

As we have seen, some modern bioethicists are directly challenging the old Hippocratic-Christian consensus. Nigel Cameron has suggested that the very word, created in the USA in the 1970s, symbolized a wholly fresh approach to the values of medicine. 'What appeared at first to be an opening of medicine to scrutiny from outside . . . has rapidly been transformed into a field of reflection in which medicine itself can claim only a tangential place' (Cameron 1995: 3). It is certainly remarkable to see how the bioethical enterprise has increasingly been taken over by philosophers, ethicists and lawyers. Clinicians are generally regarded as having little to contribute to the development of the discipline! By cutting loose the discussion of ethical values from the constraints of the professional Hippocratic tradition, which is caricatured as obsolete and culturally bound, bioethicists are free to develop their radical theories unchallenged.

We should not be surprised if ethicists from non-Judaeo-Christian religious traditions have rather different concepts of the significance of the body and therefore of medical ethics. According to a news report in 1997 (*GenEthics* 17:9), the President of the International Association of Bioethics, Hyakudai Sakamoto of Nihon University, stated his support for genetic enhancement of human beings. Sakamoto said that in Asia, there is no fixed distinction between the natural and the artificial, and that in Buddhist thought, everything is constantly changing. Therefore genetic engineering should be used for what Sakamoto called the 'artificial evolution' of humankind.

Peter Singer has no illusions about the magnitude of the ethical change that is going on in our midst. 'After ruling our thoughts and decisions about life and death for nearly 2,000 years, the traditional western ethic has collapsed. To mark the precise moment when the old ethic gave way, a future historian might choose 4 February 1993, when Britain's highest court ruled that the doctors attending Tony Bland could lawfully act to end the life of their patient' (Singer 1995: 1). After describing several other landmark events, such as the approval of euthanasia guidelines by the Dutch Parliament, Singer continues in apocalyptic tone:

> These are the surface tremors resulting from major shifts deep in the bedrock of Western ethics. We are going through a period of transition in our attitude to the sanctity of human life. The traditional ethic is still defended by bishops and conservative bioethicists who speak in reverent tones about the intrinsic value of all human life, but once challenged, the traditional

ethic crumples. Weakened by a decline in religious authority and the rise of a better understanding of the origins and nature of our species, that ethic is now being undone by changes in medical technology with which its inflexible structures simply cannot cope (Singer 1995: 4).

How can we communicate and defend the Christian perspective in a pluralistic society which has little time for religion as a source of ethical norms?

Defending a Christian worldview

In essence, there are three fundamental answers to the question, 'Why should we as a modern secular society adopt a Christian worldview?' They are:

1. *Because it is true.* The Christian worldview fits with reality, with the way the world is made.

2. *Because it works.* Adopting the Christian worldview leads to beneficial consequences for individuals and for the community as a whole.

3. *Because it feels right.* The Christian worldview accords with the deepest intuitions of the human heart.

In developing a public apologetic, biblical Christians have concentrated to a very large extent on the first answer. They have engaged in arguments to demonstrate the truth of the Christian worldview on rational grounds. Arguments based on practical, social consequences of Christianity, or on the nature of human intuitions, have often been regarded as substandard or even 'dangerous'. Of course, rational arguments about the truth of the Christian worldview remain of vital importance. Yet in the all-pervasive mood of postmodernity, rational debate about absolute truth seems to founder, all too often, in a morass of relativism. In addition to maintaining and developing arguments for the truth of Christianity, we urgently need to develop a public apologetic which enshrines both the consequentialist argument (the practical effects of Christian beliefs) and the appeal to human intuitions.

In response to the challenge laid down by Peter Singer, it seems to me there are at least seven lines of argument which may be developed in the public arena, in defence of a Christian understanding of the sanctity of human life. In outline, these arguments are as follows:

1. The Christian perspective enshrines a holistic perspective of human identity as a body-mind-spirit unity within community, as sketched in chapter 2. It teaches us to value human beings in their complex totality, whereas the secular alternative tends towards a reductionist and purely biological view. In place of 'speciesism', the new bioethics offers a new form of discrimination which might be called 'corticalism'; human value is reduced to the efficient functioning of a layer of cerebral tissue.

2. The Christian view of human nature in God's image provides a stability of human identity and significance throughout the whole of life, whatever events may befall. As we saw earlier, even if my cortex is damaged, or my brain starts

to malfunction, or I become confused and disorientated, I will still be me, a unique person, known and loved by others, and ultimately by God himself. No-one and nothing can take my human significance from me. By contrast, within the new bioethical framework, my identity depends on whatever happens to me, on contingent factors. It is desperately precarious, vulnerable, and unstable. How can I be sure who I am, and how can I respect myself, when my own identity and worth are so evanescent and fragile?

3. The Christian worldview promotes social cohesion and mutual respect; we are a society of equals, because we are equal before God. A shared belief in the sanctity of human life provides protection for the weakest and most vulnerable within society. Respect for human life is part of the glue which binds society together. By contrast, the new bioethics creates a society where we are ranked according to our functional abilities. It creates an arbitrary distinction between persons and non-persons, and places a range of human beings – malformed babies, Alzheimer's sufferers and other 'riff-raff' – outside the human community. Is this the kind of society of which we wish to be part?

4. The Christian concept of the sanctity of human life provides the basis for a consistent legal framework in which the life of all human beings is protected from destruction. The attempt to create a just and stable legislative framework in which medical euthanasia may be safely allowed has posed insuperable problems for legislators around the world. If the concept of mercy killing becomes legally acceptable, the entire legal framework designed to protect human life becomes weakened. Ancient Hippocratic medicine drew an absolute distinction between curing and killing. For two thousand years the distinction has remained a foundation of our ethical and legal systems. The new bioethics wants to blur the distinction again.

5. The Christian perspective of human life fits with very widespread intuitions about the nature of human relationships, especially those within families. In Singer's book *Rethinking Life and Death*, he describes his meeting with several mothers who had given birth to infants with anencephaly, a rare and fatal abnormality in which the cerebral hemispheres fail to develop normally. Singer uses the anencephalic infant as an extreme example of a being who, although of human origin, has no rational ability and hence less intrinsic value than most sentient animals. Yet Singer movingly describes how one mother, Judy Silver, had lovingly cuddled and bathed her anencephalic baby, who died peacefully in her arms. ' "It was nice," Judy Silver said; and if that sounds banal when written down, no-one who heard her say it thought so at the time. For this mother, an anencephalic baby was still her baby, and some kind of person, whatever the doctors or philosophers might say about its lack of capacity for consciousness' (Singer 1995: 44). In my clinical work, I have been repeatedly struck at the way a Christian perspective on the sanctity and value of human life 'rings bells' with ordinary people – in fact, with nearly everybody in our society except philosophers!

6. The Christian view of human life provides motivation for sacrificial and empathic caring by professionals and lay carers alike. Authentic Christian caring is not a vague sentimentalism; it is motivated by a tough-minded and practical respect for the image-bearers of God, for God's creation. By contrast, the reductionism of the new bioethics tends to lead inevitably to contempt for anyone whose body is no longer functioning properly. It leads to the cynicism of the junior doctor who describes the elderly person under his care as 'just a bit of old crumble'. Most of us, when an elderly relative is admitted to hospital, confused, incontinent and bedridden, would prefer the staff to be motivated by different ethical principles.

7. Finally, the Christian worldview provides a safeguard against the abusive and manipulative possibilities of medical techniques in a period of unparalleled biotechnological advance. If the technological manipulation of human fetuses could provide a limitless supply of organs and tissues for medical use, this would have enormous advantage from a medical viewpoint. If we were to follow Singer's 'new commandments', it would be hard to find a logical reason to oppose such a development. On this basis, an artificially engineered fetus clearly has little intrinsic value, and, provided that any possibility of suffering was excluded, its exploitation seems entirely desirable if it will provide a benefit for adults, who possess a far greater significance. Can the new commandments of bioethics proposed by Peter Singer resist the mind-boggling potential which modern medical technology offers for the manipulation of vulnerable human beings in order to benefit others?

These are merely the outlines of a Christian response to the challenges of modern bioethics, and others are better equipped than I to develop and extend these concepts. It is possible to defend the traditional concepts of the sanctity of human life in our secular society, but only if we speak from a living community of faith which not only argues for these convictions but lives them out in practice. Historian Gary Ferngren asserts that 'The idea of the sanctity of human life will only maintain its influence in a pluralistic age so long as the Judaeo-Christian tradition that gave it birth continues to be a living force that is capable of relating its belief in the transcendent value of all human life to contemporary issues in biomedical ethics' (Ferngren 1987a: 42).

If it is possible to defend Christian concepts of the value of human life, entailing the provision of care which may be very costly, what do we have to say about the intractable problems of the allocation of health resources?

Christian responses to resource limitations

It is a commonplace observation that the real costs of healthcare are rising inexorably, year on year, in every developed nation worldwide. It is absolutely clear that no nation can afford all the possible treatments which might be provided for its citizens. At the same time, the shameful gulf in resources between the developed and less-developed worlds increases. Rationing of scarce health resources is inevitable in every society in the world. But how should resources be allocated in a way which fits with Christian convictions?

In the UK, the traditional solution within the NHS has been that of covert rationing by doctors and managers. In ways which are frequently concealed from the patient and the general public, doctors and managers have restricted the availability of treatment to those whom they believe can most benefit, or to those who seem most worthy of treatment. Traditionally, priority has often been given to those with the greatest medical need who were most likely to benefit from treatment. This has meant that those with serious acute illness and those with most dependants have often been given preference over people with learning disabilities, mental illness, the diseases of old age, or chronic disability. In response to public pressure and a desire by managers to reform the process of allocation, managers and health planners have started to experiment with alternative models which make allocation decisions more open and transparent.

The problems of resource allocation in modern societies are complex and divisive. They raise unavoidable political issues. I am reminded of the words of the murdered Salvadorean priest Oscar Romero: 'When I give bread to the children they call me a saint. When I ask why the children have no bread they call me a communist.' Christian thinking on these matters is underdeveloped, and there is an urgent need for fresh, innovative and practical solutions. Along with many other clinicians, I am conscious of my own limitations and lack of expertise in this area. All I can offer are some basic principles from within a Christian worldview.

1. The allocation of resources should be open and transparent rather than covert. Decisions need to be open to public debate and democratic challenge. We need to institute checks and balances which prevent abuse and manipulation by powerful interest groups. The UK spends less on health as a proportion of our national income than the vast majority of other developed countries. Is this because the UK public have decided that health is a lower priority than in other countries? Is it because our need for healthcare is less than that of other countries? No. Although our system of healthcare is almost certainly more economically efficient than that of many other countries, the health budget in the UK at least in part reflects covert rationing by politicians and civil servants. The question of the magnitude of health spending for the country as a whole has rarely been open to public debate and challenge. Over the history of the NHS, the democratic process has failed to provide a genuine debate. Similarly, we spend less on health aid to developing countries as a proportion of our national income compared with many other nations. Is this because the UK public is more selfish and less generous than people from other nations? Again, it seems to be a failure of the democratic process. Here is a challenge for innovative Christian political thinking and action.

2. We need to demonstrate a practical concern for the weak and vulnerable

in society. We need to defend the modern equivalent of the widows, orphans and aliens of the Old Testament law – the dying, the chronically disabled, the genetically stigmatized, the elderly, the immigrant, the abused child, the chronic psychiatric patient, and the malformed fetus. We need a system of healthcare allocation which does not allow the powerful, those with an influential voice or economic muscle, to silence the needs of the vulnerable. One of the major threats of the new biotechnology industries is the commercial power which distorts health priorities away from unfashionable low-tech caring towards exciting and profitable high-tech interventions. We need structures which will resist the growing power of commercial interests in the healthcare world.

3. We should strive for equality and fairness across social, racial and geographical divides. If we are all made as one family, locked together in bonds of mutual responsibility, mutual burdensomeness, then we need to care for one another with equality and fairness. Gross inequalities in health provision are destructive of social welfare and cohesion. Of course the most painful and inescapable inequalities lie in the gulf in health resources between rich and poor nations. It is an inequality which represents a scandalous affront to the dignity of the entire human family. As in the past, Christians should be in the forefront of international efforts to reduce gross inequalities in health resources.

4. We need to resist the reductionist economism which measures the costs and benefits of caring in purely financial terms. As an alternative, we need to develop a holistic approach to health economics which, while sensitive to the financial controls and efficiency which are part of good stewardship, appropriately values the human, social and spiritual aspects of caring relationships.

5. We need to allocate limited resources based on need and effectiveness, irrespective of fault. Although this raises complex issues of personal responsibility, Jesus stressed that Christian compassion should be impartial, bestowed alike on the deserving and the undeserving. We have already noted his words in the Sermon on the Mount: 'I tell you: Love your enemies and pray for those who persecute you, that you may be sons of your Father in heaven. He causes his sun to rise on the evil and the good, and sends rain on the righteous and the unrighteous' (Mt. 5:43–45). We need to find innovative ways of combining the distinctive biblical virtues of justice and mercy.

6. Finally, we need to encourage the community as a whole to develop realistic expectations of the benefits that healthcare treatments can bring, and foster responsible recognition of the limits imposed by finite medical knowledge and expertise, limited resources and the fundamental nature of our humanity. Christians can take a lead in opposing the idolatrous tendencies of modern medicine to seek technological solutions to all the problems of the human condition.

These are some of the principles which should guide the development of a Christian response. But I am painfully aware that it is not enough to enunciate theoretical approaches unless they lead to practical action within our community. We urgently need the assistance of those who have the ability and the experience to translate these principles into practical initiatives at a local, national and international level.

Christian answers to the quest for core values

Christianity can provide answers to the three crucial questions I raised earlier. First, what does it mean to be a healthy human being? In place of the Lego-kit model of humanity, we must defend a biblical anthropology, illustrated in the analogy of the flawed masterpiece. In this way healthcare professionals can recapture a sense of wonder at the mystery and dignity of each individual human life, dependent, made from the dust, fallen, yet a masterpiece of God's creative art, the form in which Christ became flesh.

Secondly, what is medicine for? What are we professionals trying to achieve? Are we scientists, are we technicians, are we secular priests, or are we social engineers? No, we are trying to be art restorers. We are aiming to protect flawed masterpieces from harm and restore them where possible. Our goal is to use our technological skills while respecting the creation order, the original artist's intentions. This means that we must also recognize the limitations of medicine. We have limited knowledge, limited resources. Our goals are limited. We cannot solve all the problems of the world. We cannot give everybody a perfect baby or a perfect body. We cannot abolish suffering or make everybody feel happy and fulfilled. We cannot help everybody to live to 120. We have limited goals. Together with the rest of society, doctors need to relearn that there are no technological fixes to the ultimate mysteries of the human condition. Human ingenuity can provide no solution to the terminal consequences of that ancient curse – pain, futility, suffering, death. Instead, medicine can provide a physical presence to help human beings face the mystery of suffering, and to 'bind the suffering and the nonsuffering into the same community' (Hauerwas 1986: 26).

Thirdly, Christianity provides new models of caring for patients.

The expert–expert relationship

As we saw earlier, the traditional form of medical interaction with the patient was paternalistic, a parent–child relationship. Modern consumerism and the emphasis on patient autonomy have tended to change it into a technician–client relationship. But both of these models are inadequate and inappropriate; we need a new model of health-professional relationships. There is an alternative paradigm which fits with Christian convictions: the expert–expert relationship. It is a collaborative relationship between patient and professional based on mutual respect and trust. Yes, the professional is the expert in the area of treatment options and possibilities, on medico-legal frameworks and ethical constraints. But the patient is an equally valid expert, with specialist knowledge in his or her own personal concerns, history, family roots, philosophy and way of life. Expert–expert relationships can flourish only in an atmosphere of mutual respect. The professional must respect the areas of expertise of the patient just as the patient must respect the professional's concerns and ethical codes. Instead of the manipulative possibilities of both paternalistic and autonomy-based approaches, expert–expert relationships should be a quest for consensus within a covenant of ethical commitment.

The expert–expert relationship emphasizes the centrality of respect. It seems to me that there are fundamentally two kinds of love: 'demeaning-love', and the 'respect-love' of which we have already spoken. Demeaning-love may be very caring, very professional, and very active. But as it cares, it humiliates. It is based more on pity than on respect. It is well described by Mother Theresa: 'I've found that practical help can actually put people down unless it is done with respect-love. No-one wants to have things done for them, or to be done to. The greatest injustice done to the poor is that we fail to trust them, to respect them. How often we just push and pull' (1985: 60). There is the authentic note of Christlike caring, of respect-love. It is love that treats each person as an individual. In Mother Theresa's words again: 'I never take care of crowds, only a person. If I stopped to look at the crowds, I would never begin' (1982: 37).

The example of Christ

But the Christian vision gives us not only a theoretical concept of respect. In Christ we see a new way to practical action, the way of self-giving and empathy. Jesus entered into the human experience of pain, suffering, loneliness and emptiness, as recorded in some detail by the gospel-writers. Here is an example written by Luke:

> Soon afterwards, Jesus went to a town called Nain, and his disciples and a large crowd went along with him. As he approached the town gate, a dead person was being carried out – the only son of his mother, and she was a widow. And a large crowd from the town was with her. When the Lord saw her, his heart went out to her and he said, 'Don't cry.'
>
> Then he went up and touched the coffin, and those carrying it stood still. He said, 'Young man, I say to you, get up!' The dead man sat up and began to talk, and Jesus gave him back to his mother.
>
> They were all filled with awe and praised God (Lk. 7:11–16).

Jesus and the disciples had been confronted by a sad little procession, one that was all too common in an era of high mortality. A young man, an adolescent, had been struck down at the very outset of adult life. Yet this little cameo was even more poignant than usual. This was the only son, the inexpressible treasure of his mother's heart. She had already lost her husband; now her child had been cruelly snatched away. Not only that, but in a society without any pensions or social welfare, the widow's son was her only hope of future financial security. Without him she might well face a destitute future.

Tragic as the circumstances were, this human story was hardly unusual. Mortality was high, widows were common, life was hard. But Luke records a remarkable observation. Jesus was strangely moved by this chance meeting. Dr Luke chose a technical word, *splanchnizomai*. In our reading it was translated 'his heart went out to her', in deference to modern sensibilities. Its literal meaning is much more visceral. It has the same derivation as our anatomical term 'splanchnic', meaning 'of the bowels, guts'. In current slang it is an emotion that gets you by the guts. It is not the sort of word a physician would use lightly, especially when referring to the Son of God. It sounds inappropriate, almost blasphemous, to our ears. Perhaps if we were writing an account of Jesus' reactions we would have been inclined to sanitize the language. Yet Luke chose this powerful, earthy word to describe the way that Jesus was moved by a chance encounter with suffering. It was this strong, visceral reaction that moved him to respond with tenderness, compassion and action.

Time and again, Luke and the other gospel-writers emphasize that Jesus was not a cool, disinterested observer of suffering and pain. He was deeply and emotionally involved. In this respect he was rather different from the old model of the Hippocratic physician. Jesus cared, even about the tragedy of an anonymous stranger. According to the Greek concept, God was unable to suffer. Suffering was part of an inferior human existence, but God was beyond this, remote and passionless. The gospel-writers, however, stress the theological profundity of the incarnation. God, through Jesus, has entered fully into the human experience, and is totally and emotionally involved in the joys and the agonies of his creation.

Caring in the Christian community

As we have explored Christian responses to the challenges of modern medicine, the importance of practical caring has been a recurrent theme. Christian caring needs always to be practical, down to earth, unsentimental, realistic, incarnational. It is a model of caring which the Christian community is uniquely equipped to provide. Christine Pohl, in an essay about abortion, expresses it well:

> The Christian community is called to model a hospitable welcome to the most vulnerable human beings even if it cannot require that welcome throughout society. In its life together, such a community can demonstrate that suffering and sacrifice have meaning, can offer welcome to unexpected strangers, and can provide networks of love and support that sustain women and families through difficult pregnancies and difficult child-rearing. In so doing, Christians offer a vision of a transformed community in which the

most vulnerable have a safe place. In such a community, the reality of God's sacrificial welcome is lived as it is proclaimed (Pohl 1995: 222).

At the heart of Christian caring is Christ. We are called to *see* Christ in those for whom we care. We are called to *be* Christ to those for whom we care.

Empathy and the cost of caring

The key emotion of the incarnation, the visceral emotion that Jesus displayed, was *empathy*. Empathy breaks down the divide between the professional and the patient. Paternalism says, 'I am the doctor, you are the patient.' 'I am the professional, you are the client.' But empathy says, 'We are the same, you and I. We are both human beings. I want to stand alongside you. I want to be there with you.' Christian love is self-giving love, and this concept derives ultimately from the doctrine of the Trinity. Within the mystery of the Trinity, God gives himself. In some mysterious sense, God's ultimate being is found not in glory, not in power, not in authority, but in self-giving. So this is how we express our created nature; how we find ourselves, as beings made in God's image – not in getting, but in giving. And if I may put it boldly, this is why the Christian carer is close to the heart of God himself.

The key emotion of the cross is empathy. Christ entered into the agony of judgment which human disobedience deserved. In his book *The Cross of Christ*, John Stott movingly reflects on the experience of Christ:

> I have entered many Buddhist temples in different Asian countries and stood respectfully before the statue of the Buddha, his legs crossed, arms folded, eyes closed, the ghost of a smile playing round his mouth, a remote look on his face, detached from the agonies of the world. But each time after a while I had to turn away. And in imagination I have turned instead to that lonely, twisted, tortured figure on the cross, nails through the hands and feet, back lacerated, limbs wrenched, plunged in God-forsaken darkness. That is the God for me! (Stott 1986: 335–336).

Jesus demonstrated a new shape of caring. Authentic Christian caring is *cruciform*. If we want to care for people as Jesus cared for people, we have to give ourselves, we have to pay a price. We have to enter into the pain of the other, and ultimately we must experience a kind of death – death to self, in order to give ourselves in love for others. That is the cost of being a carer. This is why we must respect and support the carers in our community, both professional and lay. Many health professionals, nurses, therapists and managers, as well as doctors, are facing burnout, depression, disillusionment. The British Medical Association has recently created an emergency helpline for doctors because of the unparalleled levels of stress and depression which they documented in a survey.

There are particular tensions for Christian professionals in certain areas of medicine, particularly obstetrics, infertility medicine and genetics. They are confronted on a daily basis with many of the complex ethical issues which we have addressed earlier. How do they reconcile their professional responsibilities to provide a specialist medical service within the state system, with their personal Christian beliefs and perspectives? Is their Christian integrity compromised by exploring a range of treatment options with their patients, recognizing that some patients will choose to act in ways that may not be consistent with Christian values?

These are perplexing questions, and it is all too easy for those on the outside to criticize Christian professionals who struggle with these dilemmas on the 'coal face'. A sense of ostracism and misunderstanding from other Christians can only add to the stress of their position. Understandably, there has been a tendency for Christian believers to avoid entering areas of medicine where the ethical tensions are greatest. But if this trend continues, and certain specialties become no-go areas for biblical Christians, the effectiveness of Christian influence in the profession will be seriously diminished.

Instead, as a Christian community we must encourage mature believers to enter these complex professional areas and provide the theological, practical and pastoral resources to support them in their role. At the same time, Christian professionals need to recognize that they cannot address these problems by themselves. They must put aside a tendency to professional isolationism, and instead be prepared to learn humbly from the perspectives and insights of other members of the Christian community.

If health professionals are to retain their Christian integrity, they must attempt to recognize the point at which their involvement in ethically questionable procedures (such as abortion, fetal screening or surrogate pregnancy, for instance) compromises their witness to Christian principles. It may be that different individuals will discern this crucial point of compromise at different places. For instance, some may conclude that it is wrong for them to have any involvement in counselling patients where abortion is one of the options. Others will conclude that giving accurate information in a balanced way, and allowing each patient to take responsibility for her own decision, is an appropriate Christian response. The Abortion Act legislation enshrines the right of doctors to refuse to participate in abortion on the grounds of conscience, although in practice an appeal to the 'conscience clause' may raise considerable practical difficulties. As ethically problematic tests and treatments enter increasingly into clinical medicine in the coming years, it may become necessary for Christian clinicians to appeal to a right of refusal to participate on the grounds of conscience in other areas as well.

The Christian community must find new ways of caring for and supporting the carers in its midst. For not only are the patients made out of dust; so also are the carers, health professionals and dedicated lay people. In my view, this should make us more gentle with each other, more supportive, encouraging one another like our heavenly Father:

> As a father has compassion on his children,
>   so the LORD has compassion on those who fear him;
> for he knows how we are formed,
>   he remembers that we are dust.

(Ps. 103:13–14)

The hope of caring

When the Bible describes human beings as created 'in God's image', this is not only a statement of present reality; it is a pointer to what, in God's grace, human beings can become. This is why Christian caring can never stop at the agony of the cross. It is shot through with hope, with expectation and with longing for the future.

In Christian thought, love is joined with the other virtues of faith and hope, as in 1 Corinthians 13: 'And now these three remain: faith, hope and love. But the greatest of these is love' (verse 13). They are virtues which all point to the future. To use theological jargon, they are eschatological virtues, pointing towards the end times. When we love someone in the present, showing practical, empathic, respectful, sacrificial caring, we are also pointing him or her to the future, to the hope of the resurrection. We are treating this person now *in the light of what he or she is going to be.* We saw an example of this in the previous chapter, when we reflected on the moving words of dementia sufferer Robert Davis: 'Perhaps the journey that takes me away from reality into the blackness of that place of the blank, emotionless unmoving Alzheimer's stare is in reality a journey into the richest depths of God's love that few have experienced on earth . . . At that time I will be unable to give you a clue, but perhaps we can talk about it later in the timeless joy of heaven.' This is why we can still respect and treat with dignity even the most tragically damaged of human beings. The anencephalic baby, the person in the persistent vegetative state, the profoundly demented individual, is a being who may, in God's grace, be transformed to become a new creation. So practical Christian caring for those with a degenerative condition such as dementia is not a sentimental nostalgic reaction, treating them with respect just because of what they once were. We treat them with respect because of the Godlike image which, in God's grace, they will display in the future. In fact, Christian love can be intelligible only in the light of the Christian hope.

In Christ's resurrection, God has said a final 'yes' to the Mark I model human being. 'As in Adam all have died, so in Christ all will be made alive' (1 Cor. 15:22). The Christian hope is that, one day, we will be 'conformed to the likeness of his Son' (Rom. 8:29). If we over-spiritualize the doctrine of the bodily resurrection, in an unconscious attempt to make it more acceptable to modern sensibilities, we lose the force of the biblical teaching. The redemptive work of Christ can come to fulfilment only in the 'redemption of our bodies' (Rom. 8:23). This passage in Romans is of great significance for a Christian understanding of medical ethics:

> I consider that our present sufferings are not worth comparing with the glory that will be revealed in us. The creation waits in eager expectation for the sons of God to be revealed. For the creation was subjected to frustration, not by its own choice, but by the will of the one who subjected it, in hope that the creation itself will be liberated from its bondage to decay and brought into the glorious freedom of the children of God.
>
> We know that the whole creation has been groaning as in the pains of childbirth right up to the present time. Not only so, but we ourselves, who have the firstfruits of the Spirit, groan inwardly as we wait eagerly for our adoption as sons, the redemption of our bodies. For in this hope we were saved (Rom. 8:18–24).

Only by the redemption of our physical bodies can the physical creation, of which they are part, be ultimately liberated. Christian medicine, in its concern and respect for the physical stuff of our bodies, provides a vital corrective to the over-spiritualizing tendency which has repeatedly crept into the thinking of the church. In its work of healing, and the continual fight to hold back death for a period, medicine anticipates the future resurrection. And in showing an unbreakable commitment and respect-love for human beings, terribly malformed as a result of the fall, or suffering as physical degeneration and death approach, medicine again bears witness to the Christian hope.

In chapter 2 we looked at Paul's analogy of the seed and the flower. 'The body that is sown is perishable, it is raised imperishable; it is sown in dishonour, it is raised in glory; it is sown in weakness, it is raised in power' (1 Cor. 15:42–43). The dramatic image is encapsulated in the strange paradox of the seed packet. The contrast between the tiny brown specks on the inside and the multicoloured splendour pictured on the outside of the packet is startling. Yet in those tiny and pathetic fragments of tissue is packed all the DNA that is required to create the glorious blossom. Add water and stand back! The two entities, which in appearance are so dissimilar, share a common hidden structure. And so it is for human beings, too.

> Then the new earth and sky, the same yet not the same as these, will rise in us as we have risen in Christ. And once again, after who knows what aeons of the silence and the dark, the birds will sing out and the waters flow, and lights and shadows move across the hills and the faces of our friends laugh upon us with amazed recognition. Guesses of course, only guesses. If they are not true, something better will be. For we know that we shall be made like him, for we shall see him as he is (Lewis 1964: 158).

This is the wonderful reality which awaits us. This is what Christian caring is pointing to. This is the destiny God plans for us, what he created us for and what he intends us to be.

References

Adams, S., Wiggins, S., Whyte, P., *et al.* (1993). Five-year study of prenatal testing for Huntington's disease. *Journal of Medical Genetics* 30:549–556.

Airedale Trust *v.* Bland (1993). *Weekly Law Reports*, 19 February.

Aitken, J. T., Fuller, H. W. C. & Johnson, D. (1984). *The Influence of Christians in Medicine*. London: Christian Medical Fellowship.

Alexander, L. (1949). Medical science under dictatorship. *New England Journal of Medicine* 241:39–47.

Amundsen, D. W. (1987). Medicine and the birth of defective children: approaches of the ancient world. In McMillan, R. C., Engelhardt, H. T. & Spicker, S. F. (eds.), *Euthanasia and the Newborn*: 3–22. Dordrecht: D. Reidel.

Andrews, K. (1993). Recovery of patients after four months or more in the persistent vegetative state. *British Medical Journal* 306: 1597–1600.

Ashley-Smith, J. (1994). The ethics of conservation. In Knell, F. (ed.), *Care of Collections*: 11–20. London: Routledge.

Barnicoat, A. (1997). Screening for fragile X syndrome: a model for genetic disorders? *British Medical Journal* 315:208.

Bauby, J.-D. (1997). *The Diving-Bell and the Butterfly*. London: Fourth Estate.

Beauchamp, T. L., & Childress, J. F. (1994). *Principles of Biomedical Ethics* (4th edition). Oxford: Oxford University Press.

Becker, W. M., Reece, J. B. & Poenie, M. F., (1996). *The World of the Cell*. California: Benjamin/Cummings Publishing Company.

Berry, R. J. (1996). *God and the Biologist*. Leicester: Apollos.

Blocher, H. (1984). *In the Beginning*. Leicester: Inter-Varsity Press.

Boulay, S. du (1984). *Cicely Saunders*. London: Hodder & Stoughton.

Cameron,N. M. de S. (1991). *The New Medicine*. London: Hodder & Stoughton.

————— (1995). The Christian stake in bioethics. In Kilner, J. F. *et al.* (eds.), *Bioethics and the Future of Medicine*: 3–13. Carlisle: Paternoster Press.

Carson, D. A. (1996). *The Gagging of God*. Leicester: Apollos.

Charlesworth, M. (1993). *Bioethics in a Liberal Society*. Cambridge: Cambridge University Press.

Chervenack, F. A., McCullough, L. B. & Cambell, S. (1995). Is third trimester abortion justified? *British Journal of Obstetrics & Gynaecology* 102:434–435.

Clements, R. (1994). Whose life is it anyway? *Cambridge Papers* 3(1), 1–4.

Dawkins R. (1976). *The Selfish Gene*. Oxford: Oxford University Press.

————— (1988). *The Blind Watchmaker*. London: Penguin.

Dennett, D. C. (1995). *Darwin's Dangerous Idea*. London: Penguin.

Dunstan, G. R. (1984). The moral status of the embryo: a tradition recalled. *Journal of Medical Ethics* 1:38–44.

Dworkin, R. (1995). *Life's Dominion* (paperback edition). London: Harper-Collins.

Edelstein, L. (1943). *The Hippocratic Oath: Text, Translation and Interpretation*. Baltimore: Johns Hopkins University Press.

Ferngren, G. F. (1987a). The Imago Dei and the sanctity of life. In McMillan, R. C., Engelhardt, H. T. & Spicker, S. F. (eds.), *Euthanasia and the Newborn*: 23–45. Dordrecht: D. Reidel.

————— (1987b). The status of defective newborns from late antiquity to the Reformation. In McMillan, R. C., Engelhardt, H. T. & Spicker, S. F. (eds.), *Euthanasia and the Newborn*: 47–64. Dordrecht: D. Reidel.

Firlik, A. D. (1991). Margo's logo. *Journal of the American Medical Association* 201, 265.

Fish, S. (1997). *Alzheimer's*. Oxford: Lion.

Glass, B. (1971). Science: endless horizons or golden age? *Science* 171:23–29.

Gorman, M. J. (1982). *Abortion and the Early Church*. Downers Grove, USA: InterVarsity Press.

Green, J. M. (1995). Obstetricians' views on prenatal diagnosis and termination of pregnancy: 1980 compared with 1993. *British Journal of Obstetrics & Gynaecology* 102:228–232.

Green, J. M., & Statham, H. (1996). Psychosocial aspects of prenatal screening and diagnosis. In Marteau, T., & Richards, M. (eds.), *The Troubled Helix*. Cambridge: Cambridge University Press.

Griffin, J. (1993). *Born Too Early*. London: Office of Health Economics.

Harris, J. (1985). *The Value of Life*. London: Routledge & Kegan Paul.

————— (1995). Euthanasia and the value of life. In Keown, J. (ed.), *Euthanasia Examined*. Cambridge: Cambridge University Press.

Hauerwas, S. (1986). *Suffering Presence*. Edinburgh: T. & T. Clark.

————— (1996). How Christian ethics became medical ethics. Verhey, A. (ed.), *Religion and Medical Ethics*: 61–80, Grand Rapids: Eerdmans.

Higginson, R. (1987). Life, death and the handicapped newborn: a review of the ethical issues. *Ethics & Medicine* 3:45–48.

House of Lords (1994). *Report of the Select Committee on Medical Ethics*. London: HMSO.

Humphry, D. (1991). *Final Exit*. Hemlock Society, Oregon, USA.

Huxley, A. (1932). *Brave New World*. London: Chatto & Windus.

Keown, J. (1995). Euthanasia in the Netherlands: sliding down the slippery slope? In Keown, J. (ed.), *Euthanasia Examined*. Cambridge: Cambridge University Press.

Kohn, I., & Moffitt, P. L. (1994). *Pregnancy Loss, A Silent Sorrow*. London: Hodder & Stoughton.

Kuhse, H., & Singer, P. (1985). *Should the Baby Live?* Oxford: Oxford University Press.

Küng, H., & Jens, W. (1995). *A Dignified Dying*. London: SCM Press.

Johnson, P. E. (1993). *Darwin on Trial*. Downers Grove, USA: InterVarsity Press.

Jones, D. G. (1984). *Brave New People*. Leicester: Inter-Varsity Press.

Jones, S. (1993). *The Language of the Genes*. London: HarperCollins.

Lewis, C. S. (1961). *Reflections on the Psalms*. Glasgow: Collins.

————— (1962). *Prince Caspian*. Harmondsworth: Puffin.

————— (1964). *Letters to Malcolm*. London: Geoffrey Bles.

————— (1978). *The Abolition of Man*. Glasgow: Collins Fount.

McCarthy, B. (1997). *Fertility and Faith*. Leicester: Inter-Varsity Press.

McGee, G. (1997). *The Perfect Baby*. Lanham, Maryland: Rowman & Littlefield.

MacKay, D. M. (1974). *The Clockwork Image*. Leicester: Inter-Varsity Press.

Mace, N. L., & Rabins, P. V. (1981). *The 36 Hour Day: A Family Guide to Caring for Persons with Alzheimer's Disease, Related Dementing Illness, and Memory Loss in Later Life*. Baltimore: Johns Hopkins University Press.

Marker, R. (1994). *Deadly Compassion*. London: HarperCollins.

Marteau, T., Johnston, M., Plenicar, M., Shaw, R. W. & Slack, J. (1988). Development of a self-administered questionnaire to measure women's knowledge of prenatal screening and diagnostic tests. *Journal of Psychosomatic Research* 32:403–408.

Marteau, T., & Anionwu, E. (1996). Testing adults. In Marteau, T., & Richards, M. (eds.), *The Troubled Helix*. Cambridge: Cambridge University Press.

Marteau, T., Plenicar, M. & Kidd, J. (1993). Obstetricians presenting amniocentesis to pregnant women: practice observed. *Journal of Reproductive and Infant Psychology* 11:75–82.

Meilander, G. (1997). *Bioethics: A Primer for Christians*. Carlisle: Paternoster Press.

Millard, A., & Bordreuil, P. (1982). A statue from Syria with Assyrian and

Aramaic inscriptions. *Biblical Archaeologist* 45 (Summer): 135–141.

Mills, M., Davies, H. T. O. & Macrae, W. M. (1994). Care of dying patients in hospital. *British Medical Journal* 309:583–586.

Minnis, S. (1996). Crisis pregnancy centres. *Nucleus* (January), Christian Medical Fellowship.

Monod, J. (1971). *Chance and Necessity.* London: Collins.

Moore, P. (1996). *Trying for a Baby.* Oxford: Lion.

————— (1997). *Pregnancy: A Testing Time.* Oxford: Lion.

Mother Theresa (1975). *A Gift for God.* London: Fount.

————— (1982). *The Love of Christ.* London: Fount.

————— (1985). *Contemplative at the Heart of the World.* London: Fount.

Nolan, C. (1987). *Under the Eye of the Clock.* London: Pan.

O'Donovan, O. (1984). *Begotten or Made?* Oxford: Oxford University Press.

————— (1994) *Resurrection and Moral Order* (2nd edition). Leicester: Apollos.

Orlowski, J. P., Smith, S. T. D. & Zwienen, J. V., (1992). Paediatric euthanasia. *American Journal of Diseases of Childhood* 146:1440–1446.

Pembrey, M. (1996). The new genetics: a user's guide. In Marteau, T., & Richards, M. (eds.), *The Troubled Helix.* Cambridge: Cambridge University Press.

Pohl, C. D. (1995). Abortion: responsibility and moral betrayal. In Kilner, J. F., *et al.* (eds.), *Bioethics and the Future of Medicine:* 212–226. Carlisle: Paternoster Press.

Poole, M. (1994). A critique of aspects of the philosophy and theology of Richard Dawkins. *Science and Christian Belief* 6:41–59.

Proctor, R. N. (1988). *Racial Hygiene: Medicine under the Nazis.* Cambridge, Massachusetts: Harvard University Press.

Ramachandra, V. (1996a). *Gods that Fail.* Carlisle: Paternoster Press.

————— (1996b). *The Recovery of Mission.* Carlisle: Paternoster Press.

Rawlinson, Lord (1994). *The Physical and Psycho-Social Effects of Abortion on Women.* London: Christian Action Research and Education.

Rothman, B. K. (1986). *The Tentative Pregnancy: Prenatal Diagnosis and the Future of Motherhood.* New York: Viking.

Royal College of Obstetricians and Gynaecologists (1996). *Termination of Pregnancy for Fetal Abnormality.* London: RCOG.

Royal College of Physicians Working Group (1996). The persistent vegetative state. *Journal of the Royal College of Physicians of London* 30:119–121.

Shakespeare, T. (1997). Choice and rights: eugenics, genetics and disability equality. Unpublished paper.

Shiloh, S. (1996). Decision-making in the context of genetic risk. In Marteau, T., & Richards, M. (eds.), *The Troubled Helix.* Cambridge: Cambridge University Press.

Silver, L. (1997). *Remaking Eden.* New York: Avon Books.

Singer, P. (1995). *Rethinking Life and Death.* Oxford: Oxford University Press.

Stacey, M. (1996). The new genetics: a feminist view. In Marteau, T., & Richards, M. (eds.), *The Troubled Helix.* Cambridge: Cambridge University Press.

Storkey, E. (1993). *Mary's Story, Mary's Song.* London: Fount.

Stott, J. R. W. (1986). *The Cross of Christ.* Leicester: Inter-Varsity Press.

———— (1990). *Issues Facing Christians Today.* London: Marshall Pickering.

———— (1992). *The Contemporary Christian.* Leicester: Inter-Varsity Press.

———— (1994). *The Message of Romans.* Leicester: Inter-Varsity Press.

Temkin, O. (1991). *Hippocrates in a World of Pagans and Christians.* Baltimore: Johns Hopkins University Press.

Thielicke, H. (1966). *Theological Ethics* 1. Philadelphia: Fortress Press.

Toffler, A. (1970). *Future Shock.* New York: Random House.

Vanier, J. (1996). *A Door of Hope.* London: Hodder & Stoughton.

Van der Maas, P. J., van Delden, J. J. M., Pijnenborg, L. & Looman, C. W. N. (1991). Euthanasia and other medical decisions concerning the end of life. *Lancet* 338:669–674.

Wald, N. J., Kennard, A., Densem, J. W., *et al.* (1992). Antenatal maternal screening for Down's syndrome: results of a demonstration project. *British Medical Journal* 305:391–394.

Wilmut, I., Schnieke, A. E., McWhir, J., Kind, A. J. & Campbell, K. H. S. (1997). Sheep cloned by nuclear transfer from a cultured cell line. *Nature* 385:810–813.

Wolf, N. (1997). *Promiscuities.* London: Chatto & Windus.

Wyatt, J. S. (1996). Ethical issues in the application of medical technology to paediatric intensive care: two views of the newborn. *Science and Christian Belief* 8:3–20.

Wyatt, J. S., & Spencer, A. (1992). *Survival of the Weakest.* London: Christian Medical Fellowship.

Useful addresses

There are many organizations which can provide information, useful publications and practical support, and this is an abbreviated list of those based in the UK. Organizations vary in their aims, and inclusion on this list does not necessarily imply unqualified endorsement by the author or publisher.

ACET (Aids Care Education and Training), PO Box 3693, London SW15 2BQ. *Tel:* 0181 780 0400. *Fax:* 0181 780 0450.

Age Concern England, Astral House, 1268 London Road, London SW16 4ER. *Tel:* 0181 679 8000. *Fax:* 0181 679 6069.
E-mail: ace@ace.org.uk

Age Concern Scotland, 113 Rose Street, Edinburgh EH2 3DT.
Tel: 0131 220 3345. *Fax:* 0131 220 2779. *E-mail:* acs@acs.org.uk

Alzheimer's Disease Society, Gordon House, Greencoat Place, London SW1P 1PH. *Tel:* 0171 306 0606. *Fax:* 0171 306 0808. *E-mail:*
101762.422@compuserve.com

ARC (Antenatal Results and Choices, formerly SAFTA), 73–76 Charlotte Street, London W1P 1LB. *Tel/fax:* 0171 631 0280. *Helpline:* 0171 631 0285.

CARE (Christian Action Research and Education), 53 Romney Street, London SW1P 3RE. *Tel:* 0171 233 0455. *Fax:* 0171 233 0983.
E-mail: mail@care.org.uk

Carers National Association, 20–25 Glasshouse Yard, London EC1A 4JT. *Tel:* 0171 490 8818. *Fax:* 0171 490 8824. *E-mail:* internet@ukcarers.org.uk

Centre for Bioethics and Public Policy, 58 Hanover Gardens, London SE11 5TN. *Tel/fax:* 0171 587 0595. *E-mail:* 100524.1567@compuserve.com

Child Bereavement Trust, Harleyford Estate, Henley Road, Marlow, Buckinghamshire SL7 2DX. *Tel/fax:* 01628 488101.

Christian Medical Fellowship, 157 Waterloo Road, London SE1 8XN. *Tel:* 0171 928 4694. *Fax:* 0171 620 2453. *E-mail:* 106173.332@compuserve.com

Christians in Caring Professions, Kings House, 175 Wokingham Road, Reading RG6 1LT. *Tel:* 0118 966 0515. *Fax:* 0118 926 3663.

Christians in Science: Mr Bennet McInnes (Secretary), 5 Knockard Place, Pitlochry, Perthshire PH16 5JF. *Tel:* 01796 472615.

Contact-a-Family (advice for families with a child with special needs), 170 Tottenham Court Road, London W1P 0HA. *Tel:* 0171 383 3555. *Fax:* 0171 383 0259. *E-mail:* info@cafamily.org.uk

Counsel & Care (advice for the elderly and their carers), Twyman House, 16 Bonny Street, London NW1 9PG. *Tel:* 0171 485 1550. *Advice line:* 0845 300 7585. *Fax:* 0171 267 6877.

Foundation for the Study of Infant Deaths, 14 Halkin Street, London SW1X 7DP. *Tel:* 0171 235 0965. *24-hr helpline:* 0171 235 1721. *Fax:* 0171 823 1986. *E-mail:* fsid@sids.org.uk

Help the Aged, St James Walk, Clerkenwell Green, London EC1R 0BE. *Tel:* 0171 253 0253. *Helpline:* 0800 650065. *Fax:* 0171 250 4474.

Help the Hospices, 34–44 Britannia Street, London WC1X 9JG. *Tel:* 0171 278 5668. *Fax:* 0171 278 1021.

Institute for Contemporary Christianity, St Peters Church, Vere Street, London W1M 9HP. *Tel:* 0171 629 3615. *Fax:* 0171 629 1284. *E-mail:* contemporary/christianity/edu.@msn.com

Jubilee Centre (The Relationships Foundation), Jubilee House, 3 Hooper Street, Cambridge CB1 2NZ. *Tel:* 01223 566319. *Fax:* 01223 566359. *E-mail:* r.f@clara.net

L'Arche Community, 10 Briggate, Silsden, Keighley, West Yorks, BD20 9JT. *Tel:* 01535 656186. *Fax:* 01535 656426. *E-mail:* larche@ukonline.co.uk

Medical Missionary Association, 157 Waterloo Road, London SE1 8XN. *Tel:* 0171 928 4694. *Fax:* 0171 620 2453. *E-mail:* 106333.673@compuserve.com

MIND (National Association for Mental Health), Granta House, 15–19 Broadway, Stratford, London E15 4BQ. *Tel:* 0181 519 2122. *Fax:* 0181 522 1725. *E-mail:* contact@mind.org.uk

National Council for Hospice & Specialist Palliative Care Services, 7th Floor, 1 Great Cumberland Place, London W1H 7AL. *Tel:* 0171 723 1639. *Fax:* 0171 723 5380.

Prospects (formerly Christian Concern for the Mentally Handicapped), PO Box 351, Reading RG1 7AL. *Tel:* 0118 950 8781. *Fax:* 0118 393 1683.

RADAR (Royal Association for Disability & Rehabilitation), 25 Mortimer Street, London W1N 8AB. *Tel:* 0171 250 3222.

SANDS (Stillbirth and Neonatal Death Society), 28 Portland Place, London W1N 4DE. *Helpline:* 0171 436 5881.

SCOPE (for people with cerebral palsy and their families), 6 Market Road, London N7 9PW. *Tel:* 0171 619 7100. *Fax:* 0171 619 7399. *E-mail:* information@scope.org.uk

Shaftesbury Society, 16–20 Kingston Road, London SW19 1JZ. *Tel:* 0181 239 5555. *Fax:* 0181 239 5580. *E-mail:* reception@shaftesburysoc.org.uk

Universities and Colleges Christian Fellowship, Professional Groups Administrator, 38 De Montfort Street, Leicester LE1 7GP. *Tel:* 0116 255 1700. *Fax:* 0116 255 5672. *E-mail:* email@uccf.org.uk

Whitefield Institute (centre for study in theology and ethics), Frewin Court, Oxford OX1 3HZ. *Tel:* 01865 202838. *Fax:* 01865 247198. *E-mail:* whitefieldinst@cix.compulink.co.uk

WorkNet Partnership, 56 Baldry Gardens, London SW16 3DJ. *Tel/fax:* 0181 679 0457. *E-mail:* worknetps@aol.com

Index

abortion, 14, 37f., 43, 46, 75, 81f.,
    94ff., 99ff., 109, 111, 119ff.,
    141ff., 165, 171, 225f., 237
  in ancient world, 119ff., 124f., 216f.
  in Judaeo-Christian world, 123f.
  psychological effects, 100f., 129ff.,
    156f.
  statistics, 128
Abortion Act (1967), 127ff., 133, 237
achondroplasia, 104f., 133
Adam (and Eve), 51, 54f., 58, 60ff.,
    71, 144, 151f., 238f.
adoption, 89, 91, 93, 125, 132
advance directive, 177
Aids/HIV, 30, 117, 175
Alexander, Leo, 186
Allen, Woody, 111, 169
Allwood, Mandy, 13, 20f., 32
Alzheimer's disease, 14, 24, 34, 43f.,
    55, 69, 179, 189f., 210f., 229,
    238
amniocentesis, 96, 109

Anderson, French, 114
Andrews, Keith, 188
anencephaly, 135, 229, 238
animals, 45, 52, 58, 65, 80
anthropology, 60, 140, 217f., 222
  biblical, 52, 55, 87, 142
Apostles' Creed, 146
Aquinas, see Thomas Aquinas
Aristotle, 147
art restoration, 87f., 91f., 117
Arthur, Leonard, 139
artificial insemination, 76
Ashley-Smith, Jonathan, 87
Augustine, 147
autonomy, 27, 35, 37ff., 46, 53, 57,
    63, 66, 68, 93, 110, 127, 133f.,
    137ff., 141, 170, 182, 195f.,
    198, 233f.

Babel, Tower of, 67f.
babies, infants, 32ff., 69, 89, 94, 98,
    132ff.

dead, dying, 72f., 159ff.
handicapped, 44ff., 74f., 133, 155, 172, 182, 229
longing for, 75ff.
premature, 34, 133, 159ff.
status, 46, 120f., 160, 168
unwanted, 44, 75, 125, 139
Baird, Diane, 202f.
Barnicoat, Angela, 103
Bauby, Jean-Dominique, 187f.
Beauchamp, Tom, 37, 41
beneficience, 37f.
Bernard of Clairvaux, 53
Berry, R. J., 146
Bewes, Richard, 166, 202f.
Bible, 15, 48ff., 141, 149, 151
Binding, Rudolf, 185
bioethics, 36ff., 43, 47, 228ff.
biology, human, 22ff., 26, 52, 149, 213
biotechnology, 29ff., 52, 108
Black, Tim, 131
Blake, Anthea, 167
Bland, Tony, 16ff., 21, 32, 36, 43, 164, 176, 180, 186ff., 192, 227
Blocher, Henri, 49f., 52
body, human, 24, 25f., 29, 31, 58, 62, 69ff., 85f., 88, 116, 199, 218f., 222f., 227, 239
Bourne, Aleck, 126
Bowen, Jaymee, 34f.
Boyes, Lillian, 15ff., 21, 43, 170, 176, 192, 200, 206f.
brain, 16, 25ff., 43, 209
damage, 16, 36, 44, 163f., 187ff., 209ff.
See also cerebral cortex
Brinsden, Peter, 114
British Medical Association, 174, 214, 236
Brown, Louise, 19, 76

Cameron, Nigel, 227

cancer, 14, 23, 30, 97, 112f., 176, 183, 200f., 205, 208ff.
care, 56, 93, 118, 150, 155, 157f., 162, 184, 186, 192, 206, 210ff., 215, 230f., 233ff.
neonatal, 159ff.
See also intensive care; palliative care
CARE for Life, 157
cerebral cortex, 16, 45, 163, 209, 228
chance, 27, 29, 109
Charlesworth, Max, 39ff.
children, 14, 30, 33, 55, 79f., 88ff., 108ff., 117, 120, 124, 134ff.
handicapped, 17, 38, 69, 100ff., 120, 127, 135, 157
Childress, James, 37, 41
chorionic villus sampling, 96
Christian thought/worldview, 14f., 48ff., 86, 108, 139f., 141ff., 167f., 189, 192ff., 206f., 209f., 228ff.
'Christopher's story', 165ff.
church, *see* community, Christian
early, 124f., 213, 215, 218
Clement of Alexandria, 124, 204, 221
Clements, Roy, 193
clone, cloning, 46, 11f., 116
coma, 16, 19, 188
community, 54, 150, 162, 194ff.
Christian, 75, 89, 93, 118, 158, 211f., 230, 235ff.
compassion, 57, 126, 161, 176, 192, 194, 205f., 210, 220f., 232
conception, 92f.
Constantine, 125
consumerism in healthcare, 32f., 47, 226, 233
consummation (of history), 49, 71ff.
conscience, 39, 237
continuity (of individual), 144f., 149
contraception, 80, 90, 197
cost of healthcare, 34ff., 103, 159, 179, 184, 226

counselling, 79, 97, 100, 102f., 131, 157f., 226
covenant, 68, 144f., 149, 151, 209, 219
Cox, Nigel, 15f., 170f., 176, 185, 192, 200, 206f.
Craft, Ian, 84
creation, 49ff., 144f.
  mandates, 61
  order/design, 50, 61ff., 72, 88, 93, 141, 194, 198, 218
Cyprian, 222
cystic fibrosis, 14, 30, 105, 110

Davis, Mary Sue and Junior Lewis, 20f.
Davis, Robert, 211, 238
Dawkins, Richard, 24f., 28f., 89
death, dying, 14, 34, 46, 63ff., 72f., 169ff.; *see also* babies, dead, dying
dementia, 172, 182, 189ff., 209ff., 238; *see also* Alzheimer's disease
Dent, Bob, 173f.
dependence, 52f., 177f., 181, 195f., 206
determinism, genetic, 116, 144
diabetes, 23, 30
diamorphine, morphine, 16, 170, 200, 206
dignity, 38, 52, 55, 58, 141f., 163f., 206
  loss of, 176f., 181
disability, 17, 32f., 38, 44, 56f., 59, 69, 94, 100ff., 104ff., 120ff., 139, 154ff., 163, 167; *see also* babies, handicapped; children, handicapped
discrimination, 41, 45, 105f.
disease, 23f., 80, 96, 102, 109f., 112ff.
  terminal, *see* death, dying; euthanasia
DNA, 23, 25, 58, 60, 89, 111, 113, 117, 151f., 225

doctors, 74, 87f., 101ff., 133ff., 156, 162, 173f., 180ff., 185ff., 194ff., 198ff., 210, 214ff., 237; *see also* health professionals
doctor–patient relationship, 216, 226
Dolly the sheep, 111f., 116
Domitian, 121
Donne, John, 195
donor insemination, 79, 83, 91
double effect, principle of, 200f.
'double listening', 14
Down's syndrome, 36ff., 95f., 103, 105f., 133, 135, 139f., 156
dualism, 16, 148, 151f.
Dunstan, Gordon, 146f.
Dworkin, Ronald, 38ff., 52, 55, 135ff., 177, 190f., 210f.

Ecclesiastes, 65f.
Edelstein, Ludwig, 217
Edwards, Robert, 76f., 82, 84
Edwards syndrome, 101, 165
egg donation, 77, 79ff., 110
  fetal, 81f.
elderly people, 34, 59, 179, 184, 197, 230
embryo, human, 76ff., 91f., 95ff., 110ff., 146ff.
  adoption, 77, 83
  donation, 77ff., 84, 91
  frozen, 19f., 31, 78, 82f.
  research, 19, 49, 77, 80f., 91, 108, 148, 152
  rights, 44
  selection, 110f.
  spare, 78, 80, 91
  status, 44, 46, 147ff.
  testing, 77, 80
  See also screening/testing, antenatal
empathy, 21, 57, 71, 118, 126, 162, 189, 210, 234, 236
Enlightenment, 14, 39, 42, 80, 85, 214

ethics, 213ff., 227ff.
  biblical/Christian, 55, 57, 62, 87,
    142
  medical, 13, 21, 36ff., 47ff., 87,
    134, 173
eugenics, 104ff., 160
euthanasia, 44, 46, 169ff., 192ff., 214,
    216, 225f.
  Christian response, 192ff.
  definitions, 171f.
  in Holland, 171f., 180ff., 197, 227
  legalization, 16, 170f., 183f.
  Nazi, 185f.
  social pressures, 179f.
evolution, 24, 27, 50f., 60f.
expert–expert relationship, 233f.

facts/values distinction, 62, 85, 102,
    213, 226
fall, 49, 63ff., 87, 195
family, 75, 84, 91f., 98, 152, 179
  Christian, 59
  Graeco-Roman, 120f.
  human, 59f., 139, 218, 232
fear, 31f., 64, 176ff., 204ff.
feeding, artificial, 17, 164, 187, 189
Ferngren, Gary, 230
fertilization, human, 19, 147f., 152
  in vitro, 20, 32, 76ff., 91, 96, 113f.
feticide, 109, 133ff.
fetus, 32f., 38, 55, 69, 74, 109, 134f.,
    142ff., 220
  formed and unformed, 146ff.
  research, 46
  rights, 44, 127
  screening, 94ff., 155f.
  status, 43f., 46, 82, 147ff.
  value, 44, 122f., 126, 137f.
Firlik, Andrew, 190f.
Fish, Sharon, 210f.
'flawed masterpiece', 55, 86f., 117f.,
    141, 144, 206
fragile X syndrome, 103

freedom, *see* liberty

gene therapy, 80, 96, 113, 115f.
genes, 14, 24, 28f., 89, 97, 110, 116,
    225
genetic engineering, 30
genetic enhancement, 29f., 33, 49,
    108, 117, 227
genetic screening, 94ff.
genetics, 23, 89, 102, 108ff., 149,
    151f.
George, Rob, 196
Glass, Bentley, 33
God, 49ff., 86f., 89, 116, 123, 142ff.,
    149ff., 195, 197f; 200.; *see also*
    image of God
good Samaritan, parable of, 219ff.,
    222f.
Gorman, Michael, 221
grace, 152f., 195, 207
Greek thought, 28, 52, 147f., 235
Greory of Nyssa, 50, 223

haemophilia, 81, 105
Harkin, Tom, 112
Harris, John, 46f., 58, 108ff., 178
Hauerwas, Stanley, 31, 196
health professionals, 56, 65, 97ff.,
    101ff., 133ff., 156, 162ff., 184,
    194, 196, 198ff., 207f., 211,
    214ff., 233, 236f.
Hippocratic Oath, 122, 173, 175, 215f.
Hippocratic tradition, 215ff.
Hitler, Adolf, 42, 106
HIV, *see* Aids/HIV
Hoche, Alfred, 185
hospice, 183, 205, 223
hospitals, 125, 207f., 222f.
House of Lords, 17, 43, 183, 187
human beings, humanity, 24, 44,
    48ff., 86, 92, 116ff., 123, 142ff.,
    150ff., 193, 209, 213f., 217,
    228, 233, 238f.

Human Fertilization and Embryology Act/Authority, 76, 78ff., 109, 113f., 133
Human Genome Project, 15, 23, 33
Humphry, Derek, 175, 185
Huntington's disease, 23, 28, 105
Hurley, Sandra, 103
Huxley, A., 111f.

ICSI, 82
image of God, 51ff., 60, 63, 71, 123, 141, 152f., 166, 192ff., 209, 219, 225
individualism, 38f., 53
Infant Life (Preservation) Act (1929), 126
infanticide, 44, 109, 119ff.
 in ancient world, 119ff.
infertility, 14, 20, 48, 74ff., 89, 100
intensive care (unit), 15, 18f., 34, 133f., 159f., 164
intuitions, 153f., 167f., 194, 213, 228
Irwin, Michael, 174
IVF, *see* fertilization, *in vitro*

James, Jacqueline, 18, 21, 32, 134
Jesus Christ, 55f., 69ff., 86, 118, 124, 126, 145f., 151, 153, 161, 166f., 194, 202f., 218ff., 232, 234f.
Job, 66f.
Jones, D. Gareth, 29, 147f.
Jones, Steve, 60
Julian (emperor), 221
justice, 37f., 56, 118, 145, 232

Kennedy, Ludovic, 177
Keown, John, 181
Kohn, Ingrid, 153f.
Küng, Hans, 197f.

law(s), OT, 68f., 123, 146
Lawson, Dominic, 106
'Lego kit', 31, 55, 85f., 118, 225

Levin, Ira, 111f.
Lewis, C. S., 59, 63f., 195, 239
lex talionis, 57, 193
leukaemia, 34f., 112f.
liberalism, 41f., 108, 136ff.
liberty, freedom, 38ff., 59, 62, 83, 110, 193, 197f.
life, human:
 'not worth living', 43f., 106, 185f.
 sanctity, 16f., 19, 39, 43, 46, 106, 135ff., 157, 178, 187, 192ff., 229
 value, 43f., 52, 55, 122f., 126, 136, 139, 178, 185f., 199
life support, 19, 164, 187, 200, 210
Linares, Samuel, 18f., 21, 32, 43, 162
living will, 177
love, 52ff., 56ff., 71, 88f., 91ff., 124, 126, 149, 154, 210f., 220, 236, 238
Luke, 145f., 218f., 221

McCarthy, Brendan, 90, 92, 149
McCormick, Richard, 163
McGee, Glen, 33, 101
MacKay, Donald, 24, 147
MacKinnon, Catharine, 130
managers, 35f., 162, 184, 208, 231
Marker, Rita, 185
marriage, 61f., 90
martyrdom, 194, 200
Mary (mother of Jesus), 145f., 154, 161
Mattes, Jane, 84
Mead, Margaret, 217
medicine, 55, 196ff., 213ff.
 Christian influence, 221ff.
 future, 24
 history, 215ff.
 limitations, 66, 162, 198f., 233
 missionary, 224
 values, 213ff., 225f.
Meilander, Gilbert, 59, 70, 117, 155, 180

mercy killing, *see* euthanasia
Mill, John Stuart, 39f.
miscarriage, 80, 96, 147, 157
Moffit, Perry-Lynn, 153
monasteries, 222f.
Monod, Jacques, 27
Moore, Peter, 75
morality, 37ff., 201
morphine, *see* diamorphine
Mother Theresa, 57, 161, 205f., 234
Muggeridge, Malcolm, 207
multiculturalism, 41f.
murder, 16, 58, 124f., 139, 201, 216
muscular dystrophy, 108

Nain, widow of, 234f.
National Childbirth Trust, 99
National Health Service, 34, 159, 208, 223, 231
Nazis, 106, 185f.
neighbour, 56, 124, 126, 219ff.
Newton, Isaac, 218
Niebuhr, H. R., 196
Nietzsche, Friedrich, 177f.
Nitschke, Philip, 173
Nolan, Christy, 105, 139, 154
nonmaleficence, 37f.
'nothing buttery', 24
nuclear transfer, 111ff.
nurses, 207f., 223f,; *see also* health professionals

O'Donovan, Oliver, 30f., 83, 93, 149, 209
Offences Against the Person Act (1861), 126
O'Sullivan, Christina, 17, 21, 33
O'Sullivan, Reece, 17f., 32f., 103

Page, Nick, 165ff., 202f.
pain, 14, 21, 71, 75, 89, 100, 118, 176, 181, 200, 204ff.
total, 176, 205

Paley, William, 27f.
palliative care, 164, 183, 197, 201f., 205, 207f., 212; *see also* symptom control
parents, parenthood, 31, 55f., 77, 79f., 84, 88ff., 91ff., 94, 98, 101ff., 108ff., 117, 134, 139, 149, 155, 165
Pascal, Blaise, 63
paternalism, 35, 40f., 102, 226, 233f.
Pearson, John and Molly, 139
Pembrey, M., 101
persistent vegetative state, 16, 49, 58, 172, 176, 186ff., 209ff., 238
'persons', 'non-persons', 43ff., 56ff., 139, 141, 148f., 153, 186, 229
pharmakeia, 124, 215
philanthrophy, 216f., 223, 225
Philo, 123
Pieper, Joseph, 154
Plato, 120f.
pluralism, 37, 40
Pohl, Christine, 235
Polybius, 120
pregnancy, 84, 97, 103, 127ff., 154ff.
experience of, 94, 98f.
multiple, 20, 77f.
surrogate, *see* surrogacy
pregnancy crisis centres, 157f.
preimplantation genetic analysis, 110f.
privacy, right of, 39, 137f.
Proctor, Robert, 185
protection (of vulnerable), 57f., 118, 147f., 150, 155, 160, 162, 186, 189, 192, 210
Psalm 139, 142ff.
psychiatric illness, 30, 126, 131, 172
Pythagoreans, 217

race, 41, 45, 110
Rainsbury, Paul, 109
Ramachandra, Vinoth, 52, 67f.
Rawlinson, Lord, 130

redemption, 49, 68ff.
reductionism, 22ff., 47, 151, 225
relationships, capacity for, 163
Remmelink Report, 180f.
reproduction, human, 48, 74ff.
reproductive technology, 29, 31f., 46,
    74ff., 114, 118, 225f.
  Christian perspectives, 85ff., 118
resource limitations, 34ff., 47, 103f.,
    179, 226f., 230ff.
respect, 'respect-love', 57, 117f., 161f.,
    164, 168, 189, 206, 209ff., 218,
    234
Richards, Janet Radcliffe, 170
right to life, 43ff.
Romero, Oscar, 231
Rothman, B. K., 98, 155
Royal College of Obstetricians and
    Gynaecologists, 134
Royal College of Physicians, 224f.

sacraments, 151f.
Sakamoto, Hyakudai, 227
sanctity of life, *see* life, sanctity
Saunders, Cicely, 205, 207
scan, *see* ultrasound
screening/testing, antenatal, 28, 36,
    94ff., 155f., 226, 237
sex, sexual intercourse, 89f., 92
sex selection, 33, 96, 108ff., 117, 214
Shakespeare, Tom, 104f., 139, 154
sickle-cell anaemia, 30, 105, 110
Sigerist, H. E., 222
Silver, Lee, 29f., 82, 110, 114
Singer, Peter, 43ff., 47, 55f., 139f.,
    160f., 168, 186, 189, 227ff.
Smith, Brian, 175
Smith, Richard, 171
society, 37ff., 41f., 44, 56, 58, 126,
    134ff., 184f., 194f., 214, 228f.
  Graeco-Roman, 120f., 215
Soranus, 121f.
speciesism, 45

sperm donation, 77f., 80, 84, 91f., 110
spina bifida, 17, 97, 103, 105, 135
Stacey, Meg, 107
Steel, David, 127
Steptoe, Patrick, 76, 82
Storkey, Elaine, 154
Stott, John, 14, 49, 71, 144, 152f.
'Stuart's story', 201ff.
suffering, 66f., 71, 157, 175, 180ff.,
    192, 195f., 199f., 204ff., 233,
    235; *see also* pain
suicide, 44, 75, 193ff., 200
  physician-assisted, 169, 173ff., 179,
    181f., 194, 197
surrogacy, 77, 80, 85, 91ff., 237
symptom control, 173, 201f., 208; *see
    also* palliative care

Tacitus, 123f.
technology, 29, 32, 46f., 66, 70, 87f.,
    131, 155, 197ff., 213, 225, 230
  corruption of, 67f.
  See also reproductive technology
Temkin, Osei, 218
Temple, William, 119, 215
Tertullian, 152
testing, *see* screening/testing, antenatal
'test-tube baby', 19, 76, 114
Thielicke, Helmut, 26
Thomas Aquinas, 147f.
toleration, religious, 38f.
transplant, 46, 113, 179
treatment, 17, 74, 189, 210, 232
  fertility, 75ff., 109, 114
  withdrawal, 19, 150, 162ff., 173,
    187, 199f.
Triple Test, 96
twins, 77, 79, 116, 147
Twycross, Robert, 205

ultrasound, 17f., 20, 98, 109, 144,
    156, 163, 165
utilitarianism, 46, 106, 161f.

value of life, *see* life, value
values, 213ff.
   core, 37, 41, 214, 233
   See also facts/values distinction
Vanier, Jean, 167
Voluntary Euthanasia Society, 174,
   177

Warnock, Mary, 79f.
Weatherall, David, 102

Weinstein, Louis, 175
Winston, Robert, 111
Wolf, Naomi, 131f.
wonder, 56, 87, 118, 162, 189, 210,
   218
Worthington, Christa, 84
'wrongful life', 17, 32, 103

Zwart, Frederique, 171